Research and Evaluation Methods in Special Education

Research and Evaluation Methods in Special Education

Donna M. Mertens   John A. McLaughlin

A Joint Publication

CORWIN PRESS, INC.
A Sage Publications Company
Thousand Oaks, California

For information:

Corwin Press, Inc.
A Sage Publications Company
2455 Teller Road
Thousand Oaks, California 91320
www.corwinpress.com

Sage Publications Ltd.
6 Bonhill Street
London EC2A 4PU
United Kingdom

Sage Publications India Pvt. Ltd.
B-42, Panchsheel Enclave
Post Box 4109
New Delhi 110 017 India

Printed in the United States of America

Library of Congress Cataloging-in-Publication Data

Mertens, Donna M.
Research and evaluation methods in special education /
by Donna M. Mertens, John A. McLaughlin.
    p. cm.
Includes bibliographical references (p.) and index.
ISBN 0-7619-4652-7 (cloth) — ISBN 0-7619-4653-5 (paper)
    1. Special education—Research—United States—Methodology. 2. Children with disabilities—Education—Research—United States—Methodology. 3. Educational evaluation—United States. I. McLaughlin, John A. (John Adams), 1943- II. Title.
LC4031.M46 2004
371.9´07´2—dc21

                              2003012010

This book is printed on acid-free paper.

04   05   06   07   7   6   5   4   3   2   1

Acquisitions Editor:	Robert D. Clouse
Editorial Assistant:	Jingle Vea
Production Editor:	Julia Parnell
Typesetter/Designer:	C&M Digitals (P) Ltd.
Indexer:	Jeanne Busemeyer
Cover Designer:	Michael Dubowe
Production Artist:	Lisa Miller

Contents

Appendices

Preface

Research with people with disabilities has always presented its own set of challenges. The first book that we wrote to address those challenges was *Research Methods in Special Education*, published by Sage in 1995. As we planned a revision of that text at the request of Corwin Press, we knew that many more challenges had been introduced for the researcher in this context. At the same time, we were aware of the additional resources and perspectives that had developed in the research community that could aid people doing such research.

We wrote the initial volume for persons who intend to conduct or critically analyze research conducted with special education populations. That purpose has been extended, and consequently the content of the book has been expanded as well. *Research Methods in Special Education* was intended to be used only as a supplementary text along with more comprehensive research methods texts. In this new text, the audience continues to be those who intend to conduct or critically analyze research with special education populations; however, it has been broadened to focus on addressing the need for empirically-based data for decision making in a variety of settings including federal, state, and local governments as well as the private and not-for-profit sectors. The book includes a discussion of the implications of the No Child Left Behind Legislation, program evaluation, and methods of providing information for decision making for those who set policy, implement and administer programs, teach students, and advocate for people with disabilities. While the reader may still find supplementary texts on specific topics such as psychometrics or statistics useful, this book is written in a more applied way, providing step-by-step guidance in the planning of research and evaluation. It is also redesigned to include resources available through the World Wide Web and in electronic formats.

Additional developments in the research world have provided us with guidance, especially writings related to resilience theory, positive psychology, the transformative paradigm, and empowerment. The shift in paradigm from a medical model to a cultural model for individuals with disabilities is more fully recognized as an important factor in the research process in this volume. The approaches to research are presented with the intention of: (1) changing people's views of people with disabilities to understand that the problem is not located in the individual, but rather in the societal response to the disability and (2) examining the ways that research can contribute to understanding how people with disabilities can better learn the skills and knowledge they need to have successful lives and how those who work with them can support this process through the application of research-based practice.

Acknowledgments

We both have deep roots in the special education community and in program evaluation. Thus, we must acknowledge the inspiration provided by our professional colleagues and students. Many people contributed to broadening our understanding of effective research and evaluation. Yvonna Lincoln and Egon Guba emphasized the importance of philosophical assumptions and paradigms in guiding research and evaluation practice. Patty Lather contributed concepts related to the emancipatory paradigm and the potential contribution of feminist thinking in evaluation. Carole Truman, John Stanfield, Ricardo Millett, Rodney Hopson, and Carol Gill illuminated the intersections of race/ethnicity, gender, disability, and sexual orientation. Michael Patton's emphasis on utilization of evaluation and the personal factor has influenced our thinking as well.

Elizabeth Whitmore and Amy Wilson provided an international perspective, and Amy Szarkowski and Carolyn Williamson, two of Mertens' doctoral students at Gallaudet University, brought the optimistic perspective to her theory of a transformative paradigm in the form of the positive psychology and resilience theory that they used as the theoretical bases for their dissertations. Ni Ya Costley, another graduate student from Gallaudet University, also deserves recognition for her contributions of searching literature and excellent skills in the use of technology. The research students at Gallaudet University also offered many helpful insights in the preparation of this book through their critiques of portions of the manuscript.

We would also both like to thank C. Deborah Laughton of Sage Publications and Robb Clause of Corwin Press for their helpful guidance in the publishing of this volume. For their careful reviews and many helpful suggestions, we thank Paige C. Pullen, Gerald Tindal, Diane Browder, James E. Ysseldyke, Frederick Brigham, and Dawson R. Hancock.

Finally, we would like to thank our families for their understanding and support during the long process of writing this book.

Corwin Press gratefully acknowledges the contributions of the following reviewers:

Paige C. Pullen, Ph.D.
Curry School of Education
Department of Curriculum, Instruction & Special Education
University of Virginia
Charlottesville, VA

Gerald Tindal
Area Head, Educational Leadership
Area of Educational Leadership
University of Oregon
Eugene, OR

Diane Browder, Professor
Department of Counseling, Special Education & Child Development
The University of North Carolina at Charlotte
Charlotte, NC

James E. Ysseldyke, Ph.D.
Associate Dean for Research
College of Education and Human Development
University of Minnesota
Minneapolis, MN

Frederick Brigham, Ph.D.
Curry School of Education
Department of Curriculum, Instruction & Special Education
University of Virginia
Charlottesville, VA

Dawson R. Hancock, Ph.D.
Department of Educational Leadership
The University of North Carolina at Charlotte
Charlotte, NC

About the Authors

**Donna M. Mertens** is a Professor in the Department of Educational Foundations and Research at Gallaudet University in Washington, DC. Her theoretical contribution to evaluation has centered on bringing the implications of the transformative paradigm to the evaluation community and the development of the inclusive approach to evaluation. Mertens has served as a member of the American Evaluation Association's Board as President-Elect (1997), President (1998), Past-President (1999), and as a Board member (2000-2002). She has authored or edited several books including *Parents and Their Deaf Children: The Early Years* with coauthors Kay Meadow Orlans and Marilyn Sass Lehrer (Gallaudet Press, 2003), *Research and Inequality* with coeditors Carole Truman and Beth Humphries (Taylor & Francis, 2000), *Research Methods in Education and Psychology: Integrating Diversity* (Sage, 1998), and *Research Methods in Special Education* with coauthor John C. McLaughlin (Sage, 1995), as well as journal articles published in the *American Journal of Evaluation, American Annals of the Deaf,* and *Educational Evaluation and Policy Analysis.*

She has conducted many different evaluations, ranging from a national evaluation of court accessibility for deaf and hard of hearing people, to the transformation of the nation's teacher preparation programs for teachers of the deaf through the integration of instructional technology, to the effects of international development efforts for people who are deaf, blind, and mentally retarded in Egypt, Costa Rica, and Mexico.

John A. McLaughlin has been actively engaged for the past 30 years in the design, delivery, and evaluation of programs in a variety of settings including federal, state, and local governments, as well as public and not-for-profit organizations. Over the past ten years, McLaughlin has been responsible for facilitating the strategic planning processes in a variety of settings including public and private schools, as well as state and local governments.

McLaughlin has been responsible for designing and implementing training and technical assistance opportunities for managers of federal, state, and local organizations as they migrated to a performance-based organization. He has been a member of several research teams whose work focused on the adoption and dissemination of an outcome-based management approach in a variety of public agencies, including education.

McLaughlin is a recognized leader in the use of interagency collaboration as a vehicle for enhancing service delivery to persons with special needs. He has trained local and state interagency teams and has conducted evaluations of interagency collaboratives in a number of states and localities. McLaughlin has designed and implemented training for local teams of stakeholders to evaluate the effectiveness of local special education programs in numerous states.

After serving nearly thirty years in higher education, McLaughlin is currently an independent consultant in strategic planning and performance measurement. He is an active member of the American Evaluation Association.

1

Introduction

Teachers of children with mild disabilities frequently encounter challenges in teaching these students to write different types of texts (e.g., fantasy vs. scientific). The Early Literacy Project used a variety of approaches, including an apprenticeship model of guided instruction. The teachers used think alouds and interactive conversations with students about reading and writing texts. For example, teachers might think aloud about how to read or write a particular text genre. Early Literacy Project students were significantly superior to the control students in reading achievement and writing fluency (Englert, Mariage, Garmon, & Tarrant, 1998).

In a study of parents' experiences with their young deaf or hard-of-hearing children, parents were asked to describe their child, including reasons they were proud of him or her. One parent commented, "His name is David. He is eight years old and he has cerebral palsy on his left side and he is hearing impaired. It is profound in his right ear and moderate to profound in his left. So, he wears two hearing aids and he does sign and he reads lips and he's learning how to read. And that's about it. Ya know, he's a sweet little boy. He has asthma and he's on medication for seizures. Other than that he's just like a normal little kid and you would never be able to tell he has all these problems" (Meadow-Orlans, Mertens, & Sass-Lehrer, 2003).

The preceding cases illustrate the type of research that was conducted with an emphasis on positive factors and accommodations that support people with disabilities in their quest for a full life. Previously, much of special education research derived from a deficit perspective that located the problem in an individual and focused on his or her disability as the reason that he or she could not perform certain functions or activities.

1

More recently, special education researchers have shifted to a sociocultural perspective that focuses on the dynamic interaction between the individual and environment over the lifespan (Seelman, 2000). This focus on strengths and modifications of contextual factors has emerged under a variety of names such as positive psychology (Seligman & Csikszentmihalyi, 2000) and resilience theory (Brown, D'Emidio-Caston, & Benard, 2001; Cooper, 2000).

In This Chapter

- The purposes and intended audiences for this book are introduced, along with reasons that research is important in special education.
- Trends and issues in special education are explored in terms of their implications for research methodology and the need for additional research.
- A discussion of philosophical orientations in research provides an organizing framework for the depiction of the steps typically followed in conducting research.

People with disabilities have been viewed through various lenses throughout history. Gill (1999) described the moral model and the medical model of disability. The moral model suggests that the disability is a punishment for a sin or a means of inspiring or redeeming others. The medical model sees the disability as a problem or a measurable defect located in the individual that needs a cure or alleviation that can be provided by medical experts.

Shifting Paradigms: Deficit to Transformative

- Swadner and Lubeck (1995) state that the deficit model emphasizes "getting the child ready for school, rather than getting the school ready to serve increasingly diverse children" (p. 18).
- Based on the belief that factors outside of the child place the child at risk, Boykin (2000) suggests eliminating the negative stigma attached to the term "children at risk" to "children placed at risk."
- Transformative research based on resilience theory focuses on the strengths of the individual and ways to modify the environment to remove barriers and increase the probability of success.

In the disability community, Seelman (2000) described a new paradigm that shifts the location of the problem from within the individual to the environmental response to the disability. This paradigm that evolved from the efforts of scholars, activists with disabilities, and their nondisabled allies departs from the former models in terms of its definition of disability problems, the scope of potential solutions, and the values underlying both the definition of the problems and solutions (Gill, 1999). The new paradigm frames disability from the perspective of a social, cultural minority group such that disability is defined as a dimension of human difference and not a defect (Gill, 1999; Mertens, 1998, 2000b). Within this paradigm, the category of disability is recognized as being socially constructed such that its meaning is derived from society's response to individuals who deviate from cultural standards. Furthermore, disability is viewed as one dimension of human difference. According to Gill (1999), the goal for people with disabilities is not to eradicate their sickness, but to celebrate their distinctness, pursue their equal place in American society, and acknowledge that their differentness is not defective but valuable.

A transformative paradigm for research has emerged in parallel with the emergence of the sociocultural view of disability. A paradigm is a way of looking at the world. It is composed of certain philosophical assumptions that guide and direct thinking and action. It is significant that the community of people with disabilities and their advocates, as well as the research community, are experiencing what might be termed a paradigm shift as they reexamine the underlying assumptions that guide their theory and practice. The potential of merging paradigms between these two communities at this juncture in time provides many possibilities. For those of you who drive the highways of the world, you know that the merge lane can be a means of accessing new frontiers or it can also be a danger zone that must be approached carefully. The authors think this is a very apt metaphor for the state of merging paradigms in the research and disability communities.

Philosophical Orientation of the Book

Educational researchers are engaged in examination of the merits of various paradigms for defining approaches to research. A paradigm is a worldview that includes certain philosophical assumptions about the nature of knowledge (i.e., epistemology). Historically, the postpositivist paradigm defined approaches to research in special education. Epistemologically, positivism is represented by the rationalistic paradigm, which typically employs a quantitative research design. The interpretive/constructivist paradigm is typically associated with qualitative research designs and is described as contextual, experiential, involved, socially relevant, multimethodological, and inclusive of emotions and events as experienced. The transformative paradigm holds that knowledge is not neutral but is influenced by human interests, all knowledge reflects the power and social relationships within society, and an important purpose of knowledge construction is to help people improve society (Banks, 1995). It is beyond the scope of the present text to explore the underlying axioms of each paradigm (see Denzin & Lincoln, 2000; Mertens, 1998; Nielsen, 1990); however, researchers should be familiar with the paradigm debate, read and reflect on this topic, and establish their own worldview as it affects their research activities.

In terms of philosophical orientation, researchers must not only identify their epistemological worldview, but also their ideological perspectives, that is, the researcher's position as to the use of research for political purposes. Langenbach, Vaughn, and Aagaard (1994) identified two ideological views prevalent in the research community as status quo and reform. Researchers who are not overtly political in their interpretation of their data are oriented toward the status quo. Researchers who explore political explanations of their data move into the realm of reform. These two positions, status quo and reform, actually represent two end points on a continuum, with many researchers falling in the middle. This overlay of ideology can be used within the positivist or the interpretive/constructivist orientation to research; however, it is central to the transformative paradigm.

Feminist researchers serve as one example of scholars who have written extensively about the reform ideology in research, and their perspectives have particular importance for researchers in special education for two reasons. First, "women with disabilities traditionally have been ignored not only by those concerned about disability but also by those examining women's experiences" (Asch & Fine, 1992, p. 141). Almost all research on men and women with disabilities seems to simply assume the irrelevance of gender, race, ethnicity, sexual orientation, or class. Second, Fine and Asch (1988) made the point that people with disabilities comprise a minority group, and most of their problems can and must be understood in a minority group framework. As a minority group, persons with disabilities have differential power and receive differential and pejorative treatment. As the authors of this text, we are sensitive to issues related to bias based on ethnicity, gender, class, and disability, and we include implications of the reform ideology in our exploration of working with special education populations throughout the research process.

The transformative paradigm places central focus on the lives and experiences of marginalized groups, such as women, ethnic/racial minorities, people with disabilities, and those who are poor. In this process, the researcher links the results of the inquiry to wider questions of social inequity and social justice. While acknowledging issues of advocacy and objectivity, transformative research has the potential to contribute to the enhanced ability to assert rigor in the sense that ignored or misrepresented views are included. One of its major contributions is exploration of the myth of homogeneity, that is, that all members of a minority group share the same characteristics. Diversity within the disabled population encompasses not only race/ethnicity, gender, language, economic level, severity and type of disability, but also functional limitations, limitations in performance of activities and instrumental activities of daily living, use of assistive devices, and receipt of specific benefits associated with disability.

EXAMPLE OF THE ROLE OF RESEARCH IN CHANGING PRACTICE

- Practices without evidence as to their effectiveness and unsupported myths have sadly affected the lives of children with disabilities (Gallagher, 1979; Van Cleve & Crouch, 1989). One such myth was that deaf children should not be taught sign language because it would inhibit their desire to learn to speak. In the 1960s, for example, research was conducted that suggested deaf children of deaf parents had higher scores than deaf children of hearing parents on reading, arithmetic, social adjustment, and writing and were no different in terms of use of speech and lip reading (Meadow, 1967). Within a short time after the appearance of that research, a revolution occurred in deaf education such that between 1968 and 1978, the majority of deaf programs changed from oral communication to total communication (Moores, 1987).

- Research can guide teachers in how to revise their own practice, as well as make contributions toward fundamental changes in educational practice. This is not to say that research by itself will be responsible for changes in practice, such as the dramatic changes in deaf education. Societal change is dependent in part on the use that is made of such information by politically-oriented advocacy groups, such as the National Association of the Deaf. Nor does it suggest that the issue is closed regarding the most effective communication system for deaf people. Debate rages on as to which sign communication system is best, and this continues to be the type of empirical issue on which research can shed light.

Purpose of This Book

Teachers and other educational personnel find themselves face-to-face with children who need an appropriate education for which there is either an inadequate research base or they are unaware of the research that exists. Thus, not only is there a need for more research in special education, but there is also a need for more critical analysis of existing research and improvement of the quality of research in special education. Those who conduct research in special education must be aware of the implications of the unique context and special populations for their work. No specific research methods are unique to special education; however, there are many contextual factors that are unique to special education that influence the way research is conducted (Gaylord-Ross, 1990-1992; Switzky & Heal, 1990). Special education adopted its research methods from such other disciplines as psychology, sociology, ethnography, and anthropology.

The purpose of this book is to enable the reader to use tools to design, conduct, and report research in a way that transforms, when appropriate, the delivery of special education. This book explores ways to adapt those research methods to the special education context by providing the reader with a framework for developing research questions and methods, as well as critically analyzing and conducting research focusing on the specific special education context. Unique contextual factors and populations in special education have implications for research conceptualization, design, implementation, interpretation, and reporting. For example:

- The definition of who constitutes the special education population is not clear cut. What are the implications of labeling someone "at risk" or disabled?
- How can appropriate identifications be made for such populations as developmentally delayed or learning disabled?
- What are the implications of conducting or critiquing research that addresses different types of functional impairments (e.g., mental retardation vs. paralysis, blindness vs. epilepsy)?

These are the types of contextual issues specific to special education research that are addressed in this book.

The approaches to research are presented with the intention of: (1) changing people's views of people with disabilities to understand that the problem is not located in the individual, but rather in the societal response to the disability and (2) examining the ways that research can contribute to understanding how people with disabilities can better learn the skills and knowledge they need to have successful lives, and how those who work with them can support this process through the application of research-based practice.

The audience for this book includes people who need information to support their decision making (note: this is program evaluation, which is discussed in Chapter 2). This includes those who set policy, administer and implement programs, teach the students, and advocate for people with disabilities. For all these people, this book provides guidance in the conduct or critical analysis of research with special education populations. The populations included are primarily those that are eligible for funds under the federal government's classification system of special education students in the Individuals with Disabilities Education Act (IDEA) of 1997, that is, mental retardation, hearing impairments, speech or language impairments, visual impairments, serious emotional disturbance, orthopedic impairments, other health impairments, specific learning disabilities, multiple disabilities, deafness/blindness, autism, and traumatic brain injury. (Readers interested in research with gifted students are referred to Buchanan & Feldhusen, 1991; Friedman & Shore, 2000; and Howe, 1999.) Additionally, the text includes discussion of infants and toddlers with disabilities and persons with developmental delays and those at risk.

Examples of Potential Users of This Book

- Stephanie is a fourth grade teacher who has spent the summer redesigning the reading program that she will use to teach reading to students with learning disabilities assigned to her class in the coming year. As part of her design process, she asks the question, "How will I know if my new program improves the reading performance of my students?"

• Pat, a state director of special education, has been responsible for designing and implementing a new state policy that requires local special education directors to prepare and carry out local improvement plans. Now she needs evidence to take to the State Board of Education regarding the impact of the new policy on the local school divisions and the students they serve.

• The local parent advocacy group has changed its approach from openly challenging the school division to viewing their relationship as a strategic alliance with the schools with a shared goal of quality educational experiences for all children. The group is pleased with the results of the shift in policy and wants to share their success with other parent advocacy groups.

• Bill, a faculty member at the local university, has observed that for the past several years, students with disabilities in his local school division who take the state's Standards of Learning assessments have performed poorly in comparison to their peers in other school divisions. He has devised a new system for teaching test-taking skills to students with disabilities and wants to gather evidence about what aspects of the program work and which might need improvement to enhance performance of students with disabilities on the assessments.

This text does not purport to replace research methodology texts (see, e.g., Bogdan & Biklen, 1998; Creswell, 2003; Denzin & Lincoln, 2000; Gall, Gall, & Borg, 2003; Harding, 1987; Mertens, 1998; Patton, 2002; Tashakkori & Teddlie, 2002) or educational assessment texts (see, e.g., Pellegrino, Chudowsky, & Glaser, 2001; Sternberg & Grigorenko, 2002). Rather it explores the adaptation of research methods to the special education context by providing the researcher with a framework for critically analyzing and conducting research within the special education context.

Trends and Issues Influencing Special Education Research

Special education research is affected by political, legislative, programmatic, social, and contextual factors that are unique to its functioning. These factors have implications for methodology at every stage of the research process.

Political and Legislative Changes

Beginning in the 1990s and extending into the twenty-first century, several key policy decisions at the federal level and their accompanying legislative mandates have changed the way educators view the relationship between research and practice.

• The Government Performance and Results Act (1993) required all agencies to not only state organizational goals and objectives in measurable terms, but also annually collect performance measurement and evaluation information as evidence of progress toward achieving those aims. All federal managers had to be able to communicate to Congress and the public what they were trying to accomplish, how they planned to achieve these ends, what indicators they would use to judge their performance, and how well they were doing with respect to anticipated results. A significant federal education action provided funds to public schools to reform their educational practices. But to receive the funds, the schools had to demonstrate that the reforms were proven practices – based on experimental control with comparisons to standards-based assessments.

• Perhaps the most sweeping federal initiative to influence research practice is the Elementary and Secondary Education Act referred to as No Child Left Behind (NCLB) (2001). This legislation requires the use of scientifically-based research to improve educational practice. The Act defines scientifically-based research as "rigorous, systematic, and objective procedures to obtain valid knowledge" about an educational program or practice. The expectation is that evaluations will be conducted of these programs using experimental and quasi-experimental methods to assess the impact of the programs with respect to intended results (see Chapter 4). Randomized designs and those using thoughtful matching techniques are the preferred research approach in NCLB (Slavin, 2002).

• The Education of the Handicapped Act, passed in 1975, was changed to the Individuals with Disabilities Education Act (IDEA) in 1990, and was reauthorized in 1997. IDEA (and its predecessor legislation) resulted in fewer students with disabilities being educated in separate schools or classrooms. The effect of this change has at least two methodological implications. First, identification of research subjects became more complicated, and second, placement in many schools resulted in an increase in the variability of contextual factors (Wang, Reynolds, & Walberg, 1990). The identification of the independent variable in studying the effects of educating students with disabilities in inclusive settings becomes a more complex issue, which is not satisfactorily resolved in most special education research (Gallagher, 1990; Wang et al., 1990).

The ultimate goal of these federal initiatives is to improve educational opportunities for all children, including those with special needs. The intent is to increase the number of special education graduates with the knowledge, skills, and values that they need to become productive citizens. The initiatives provide an excellent opportunity for researchers to play a significant role in the production of information that not only identifies successful practices, but also enables the sharing of these practices with others who face similar challenges. In this way, the initiatives fit nicely with the transformational worldview characterized throughout this text.

Programmatic Issues

The Office of Special Education Programs, U.S. Department of Education funded the IDEA Partnerships in October of 1998 to build capacity and develop leadership potential in their primary partner organizations and constituencies by modeling collaboration at all levels of partnership, creating and disseminating quality products that are user friendly, and creating national and public access to information in an audience-focused streamlined way (www.IDEAINFO.org). The IDEA Partnerships include families, advocates, teachers, local service providers and administrators, and state and national policymakers.

One significant outcome that the IDEA Partnerships achieved provides direction for current and future research in special education. Through collaborative needs assessments, the IDEA Partnerships identified five high-priority domains in which action was needed if educational opportunities and services for students with disabilities were to be improved. The domains are: Standards-Based Reforms, Personnel Development, Overidentification, Family Involvement, and School Climate and Discipline. The domains are described in a series of framing papers that may be accessed at http://www.ideainfo.org/summit.htm.

Standards-Based reforms. Standards-based reforms and their assessment programs have led to noteworthy improvements in educational opportunity for students through the alignment of educational practice to desirable educational outcomes. Yet, there are continuing challenges to ensure that all students, including those with disabilities, share in these benefits. Researchers must be able to inform policymakers and practitioners, as well as parents and advocates, about effective practices to include students with special needs in standards-based instruction and assessments. Research has demonstrated that the percentage of students with disabilities taking the assessments either through traditional means or through alternative assessments has been steadily increasing (Thompson & Thurlow, 2001). Yet, additional questions need to be addressed.

RESEARCH QUESTIONS TO THINK
ABOUT REGARDING STANDARDS-BASED REFORMS:

- What are the reasonable accommodations to make in curriculum and instruction to ensure the students acquire the necessary knowledge and skills to be able to perform on the assessments?

- For those students who cannot take the state assessments because of the limitations of their disability, what forms of alternative assessment approaches are reliable, valid, and fair?

Personnel Development. Having sufficient numbers of qualified professionals and paraprofessionals to provide special educational and related services has been an issue since the passage of PL 94-142, the Education for All Handicapped Children Act. Yet, our nation's schools continue to experience chronic shortages in personnel in the areas of instruction, related services, and program administration. Without qualified practitioners, educational opportunities for students with disabilities will never reach the level necessary to ensure educational success. Recruitment and retention of professionals in special education is of critical concern to federal, state, and local policymakers.

Research by Miller, Brownell, and Smith (1999) indicates that a number of factors influence decisions to continue in the field including working conditions, stress, and certification status.

RESEARCH QUESTIONS TO THINK ABOUT REGARDING PERSONNEL DEVELOPMENT

- What factors – personal and geographical – influence a person's decision to enter and stay in special education?
- What unique knowledge, skills, and values do these professionals require to be successful?
- Given the continued overrepresentation of minorities in special education, what practices will lead to the successful recruitment and retention of ethnically-diverse practitioners to the field of special education?
- The design and delivery of special education and related services is complex. How can research inform and improve the practice of cooperative teaching and collaboration within and across service domains?
- What role, if any, do economic and social trends play in recruitment and retention?

Overidentification. Like personnel issues, overidentification is not a new concern to special educators. Moreover, overrepresentation of culturally-diverse and linguistically-diverse students in special education is a fact based on both legal and research findings. On the one hand, overidentification can be traced to unfair, unreliable, and invalid assessment and diagnostic practices. On the other hand, disproportionality can result from a lack of cultural competency, understanding cultural diversity and being able to accommodate for the diverse needs and preferences of students who are culturally and linguistically diverse. While cultural competency has many different definitions, Hanley (1999), as cited in Edgar, Patton, and Day-Vines (2002), sees it as "the ability to work effectively across cultures in a way that acknowledges and respects the culture of the person being served" (p.10). According to Daugherty (2001), the number of ethnic minority group members will increase significantly in the future, and by the year 2020, the majority of school-age children in the United States will be from racial or ethnic minority groups. At the same time, the number of teachers and other service personnel who are European American comprise over 85% of our education workforce (Edgar et al., 2002). The resulting imbalance may lead to inappropriate referral decisions and placements in special education.

RESEARCH QUESTIONS TO THINK
ABOUT REGARDING OVERIDENTIFICATION

- How can research in special education lead to the development of more culturally and ethnically valid assessment instruments and processes?
- What role does cultural competency play in the decision to refer students for special education?
- How can teachers differentiate instruction so that students who are ethnically and linguistically diverse can benefit from their educational experiences?
- What role should families play in the design, implementation, and evaluation of educational programs for these students?

Family Involvement. Educators cannot and should not try to do the job alone when it comes to the education of students with special needs. They should form performance partnerships with parents aimed at achieving the shared goal of creating effective educational practices that will lead to better results for students. With the support of federal legislation, forming these partnerships is not only required but facilitated through the direction provided by the legislation and guidelines. Parents provide a rich source of information about the strengths and needs of their children. They can be a resource to the design and delivery of special educational and related services. Recent reports (Davies, 1996; Lewis & Henderson, 1997) indicate that parents and families are essential to the success of recent school reform initiatives. Yet, parental involvement remains a challenge today.

RESEARCH QUESTIONS TO THINK ABOUT
REGARDING FAMILY INVOLVEMENT

- What factors drive and restrain successful parental involvement? While research in special education has been a significant resource to our knowledge in this area, more needs to be done, particularly when dealing with culturally-diverse and linguistically-diverse students and families.
- Does the involvement of families in the prereferral process increase the validity of the decision making?
- What strategies work best to modify parental, teacher, and administrator attitudes to enhance functional family involvement?
- What new skills do parents, teachers, and administrators need to enable a positive working relationship that benefits children?
- How do state and local policies affect parental involvement?
- What strategies work best to enable schools to reach and involve traditionally underrepresented families?

School Climate and Discipline. Educating all children, including those with special needs, is most effective when carried out in a positive school climate. According to Sugai and Horner (2001), schools are not able to provide a full continuum of effective and positive learning experiences for their students. Many schools may lack the capacity to deal effectively with defiant and disruptive behavior. An emerging trend that is demonstrating positive results is entitled positive behavior support systems (PBS) (Sugai & Horner, 2001). The goal of PBS is to enhance the capacity of schools to educate all students, especially students with challenging social behaviors, by establishing an effective continuum of PBS systems and practices (Sugai & Horner, 2001).

Often the reason a student is referred for special educational services is because the student has been disruptive. Research reported by Sugai and Horner (2001) indicates that when PBS systems are in place, then there is not only a reduction in the number of referrals, but also an increase in the quality of referrals. These effects have been found to last over time when the practices are adopted PBS systems. A positive school climate is an important piece to the puzzle of effective school practice.

RESEARCH QUESTIONS TO THINK ABOUT REGARDING SCHOOL CLIMATE AND DISCIPLINE

- What specific practices will result in the development of a positive school climate and will also have positive effects on teacher, parent, and student behavior?
- What state and local policies are needed to support the systematic application of research-based practices that yield a positive school climate?

Total Inclusion Movement. Special education is embroiled in a time of change and reform that is an outgrowth of more than two decades of struggling with the implications of the original mainstreaming legislation. A strong voice from within the special education community is calling for total inclusion of students with disabilities, in the form of a merger of general and special education (Biklen, Ferguson, & Ford, 1989; Lipsky & Gartner, 1989), and general education is taking up this call as well (National Association of State Boards of Education, 1992).

Research Questions to Think About Regarding Total Inclusion

- What are effective practices for total inclusion based on specific types of disabilities?
- What are the factors that contribute to success in total inclusion programs? What are the barriers that must be overcome?

Contextual and Societal Trends

As Seelman (1999) noted about the demographics within the disability community, there is great diversity within the 20% of the national population that have disabilities. Women have higher rates of severe disabilities than men (9.7 vs. 7.7 percent), while men have slightly higher rates of nonsevere disability. Considering both sex and race, Black women have the highest rate of severe disability (14.3%), followed by Black men (12.6%). Rates of severe disability for men and women who are American Indian, Eskimo, or Aleut are nearly as high; persons who are American Indian have the highest rates of nonsevere disability. Researchers who undertake research with these populations need to be knowledgeable about the diversity within the community in order to be culturally sensitive in the interest of gathering valid research data and interpreting the results accurately.

RESEARCH QUESTIONS TO THINK ABOUT
REGARDING CONTEXTUAL AND SOCIETAL TRENDS

- What are effective instructional practices for students with disabilities whose native language is not English?
- What are the cultural factors that contribute to success for students from diverse ethnic or racial backgrounds?

Need for Additional Research

Over one decade ago, Wang et al. (1990) recognized the role that research can play in the complex challenges that face special educators. They stated:

The field of special education seems particularly open to theories and practices, even before they are thoroughly tested. There are millions of children whose problems have been diagnosed in terms of cognitive rigidity . . . Lack of sensory integration, perceptual problems, auditory sequencing difficulties, or unusual WISC profiles— all of which add up to zero or near zero validity when later tested for instructional relevance. The solution to these problems is a particular responsibility of the researchers in the special education community who should call for decent levels of evidence before practices are allowed to enter the field in broad ways. (p. 202)

The need for additional research should be a point of thoughtfulness at the end of every research study. Researchers should build their research on using the blocks of knowledge available from previous research, examine the contribution of the studies they have conducted themselves, and assess what is needed to further understand the issues of good practice. This topic is further explored in the final chapter of this book.

Steps Typically Followed in Conducting Research and the Organization of This Book

The typical process of planning and conducting a research study was used as the basis for organizing the information in this book (see Figure 1.1).

Figure 1.1   Steps in the Research Process

Step 1: Identify own worldview (Chapter 1)

Step 2: Problem sensing (Chapters 1, 2, 3, and 10)

Step 3: Literature review; research questions (Chapter 3)

Step 4: Identify design (quantitative/qualitative/mixed/program evaluation) (Chapters 2, 4, 5, 6, and 7)

Step 5: Identify and select sources of data (Chapter 8)

Step 6: Identify and select data collection methods/instruments (Chapter 9)

Step 7: Data analysis, interpretation, reporting, and identifying future directions (Chapter 10)

We recognize that the research process is never as linear as it is portrayed in Figure 1.1 and (especially with qualitative and mixed methods designs) the process can be very iterative in nature. However, our goal is to depict the typical steps in conducting research, even though a researcher may be doing footwork that more resembles the cha-cha than a straightforward stroll.

Research in special education is used to explore the use of the literature review, to define the theoretical framework and to identify research questions, variables, and the most appropriate approach to the research (Chapters 1, 2, and 3). Specific implications of quantitative, qualitative, mixed methods, or evaluation-based designs are critically evaluated in special education research (Chapters 2, 4, 5, 6, and 7). Issues such as the identification of subjects, the definition of populations, the heterogeneity of subjects, appropriate sampling techniques, and ethics (Chapter 8), and reliability, validity, and accommodations for populations with disabilities are examined for data collection (Chapter 9). Data analysis and interpretation issues are discussed in terms of appropriate use of analytic methods and the impact of analytic technique and results on conclusions and on future directions for research (Chapter 10).

The reader who is interested in actually planning a research study can use the organizational framework in this text in conjunction with any of the research book references presented earlier in this chapter to plan and conduct a research study.

QUESTIONS AND ACTIVITIES FOR DISCUSSION AND APPLICATION

1. What myths in education do you know about that influenced educators to behave in ineffective ways (e.g., physical punishment is a good way to discipline)?

2. How has research been helpful to you in your work?

3. What is your opinion as to the usefulness of research to the parent, teacher, counselor, or administrator in special education?

4. What issues can you identify that are in need of additional research?

5. What trends are occurring in special education that can influence research methodology and topics?

6. What trends are occurring outside of special education that can influence special education research methodology and topics?

7. What questions are being asked or assertions made with respect to the design, delivery, and/or outcomes of special education in your school or school division, by whom, and for what purposes?

2

Program Evaluation

Prospective special education teachers need to apply the instructional practices they are learning in order to be more effective teachers of students with special needs. Recognizing this, Levin et al. (2002) developed a teacher preparation curriculum that incorporated problem-based learning (PBL) strategies that encourage preservice teachers to apply what they were learning to solve complex, real-world problems associated with teaching students with disabilities. They evaluated the effectiveness of the new program by administering writing samples that collected student reactions to situationally-based problems and administering surveys on beliefs about inclusion. As a result of the evaluation, the authors concluded that the PBL experiences were effective in enhancing the application of the practices they were learning. They used the information for improving the program and as evidence for others involved in preservice education to adopt the program.

IN THIS CHAPTER

- Program evaluation is defined.
- The various purposes of evaluation are presented.
- A method for describing the program to be evaluated is offered.
- Different types of evaluation questions are set forth.
- Standards for evaluating the evaluation are discussed.

Evaluation is the systematic investigation of the merit or worth of an object for the purpose of reducing uncertainty in decision making about that object (Mertens, 1998). Evaluators often use the terms *merit* and *worth* synonymously. However, it is useful to contrast the two to focus the intent of evaluation more broadly (see below).

> Merit focuses more on the effectiveness of the program to achieve its aims while worth focuses on the broader impact of the program. Does achieving its aims add value to the community. According to Patton (1997)
>
> "Merit refers to the intrinsic value of a program, for example, how effective it is in meeting the needs of those it is intended to help. Worth refers to extrinsic value to those outside the program, for example, to the larger community. A welfare program that gets jobs for recipients has merit for those who move out of poverty and worth to society by reducing welfare costs." p. 85

The object of the evaluation may be a program, product, process, or policy, among other things. The important aspect of this definition is that evaluation is focused on a particular object and it is purposeful, affecting the way people think about the action and/or changing their behavior in relation to the object. Most would agree that research is a process that brings data to bear on a problem. What distinguishes research from evaluation is that research puts greater emphasis on the generation of knowledge, while evaluation uses the knowledge to inform decisions within a specific context. According to Rossi, Freeman, and Lipsey (1999), "program evaluation is the use of social research procedures to systematically investigate the effectiveness of social intervention programs that is adapted to their political and organizational environments and designed to inform social action in ways that improve social conditions" (p. 20). Scriven (1991) emphasizes the utility of evaluation when he talks about the "two arms" of evaluation — the collection of evaluation information and the valuing of that information using values and standards applied by those interested in the program. Evaluation information that ends with the collection of information is useless; the information has to be interpreted in the context of the program's intentions. It is at this point judgments can be made of the program's merit and worth.

Our purpose in this chapter is to expose the reader to some of the basic steps for the design, conduct, and report of educational evaluation studies. There are several excellent texts on program evaluation that are available to the reader who is interested in finding out more on this topic. A list of references is provided in Table 2.1. Stufflebeam (2001) presents a comprehensive discussion of various approaches to program evaluation.

Steps to Design Conduct and Report Evaluations

In Chapter 1, the basic steps to design and conduct research were presented as a framework for this text. These same steps are followed in

Table 2.1   Evaluation References

On-line Resources:

National Science Foundation. (1997). *User-friendly Handbook for Mixed-methods Evaluations.* Contains information on designing, conducting evaluation, and integrating quantitative and qualitative techniques for outcome evaluations; "practical rather than technically sophisticated."
URL: http://www.ehr.nsf.gov/EHR/REC/pubs/NSF97-153/start.htm

Trochim, W. M. (1999). *The Research Methods Knowledge Base.*
URL: http://trochim.human.cornell.edu/kb
Also available in print as: Trochim, W. (2001). *The research methods knowledge base* (2nd ed.). Cincinnati, OH: Atomic Dog Publishers.

U.S. General Accounting Office. (2000). *GAO Policy and Guidance Materials.* Contains information on evaluation synthesis, designing evaluations, case study evaluation, and prospective evaluation methods.
URL: http://www.gao.gov/policy/guidance.htm

W. K. Kellogg Foundation. (1998). *Evaluation Handbook.* Outlines a blueprint for designing and conducting evaluations, either independently or with the support of an external evaluator or consultant.
URL: http://www.wkkf.org/Pubs/Tools/Evaluation/Pub770.pdf

Text Resources:

Fetterman, D. M. (2001). Foundations of empowerment evaluation. Thousand Oaks, CA: Sage.

Scriven, M. (1991). *Evaluation thesaurus* (4th ed.). Newbury Park, CA: Sage.

Worthen, B. R., Sanders, J. R., & Fitzpatrick, J. L. (1997). *Program evaluation: Alternative approaches and practical guidelines.* New York: Longman.

program evaluation. There are some differences that should be highlighted. A listing of the elements of an evaluation plan is displayed in Table 2.2.

Step 1. Identify the Purposes of the Evaluation

What distinguishes evaluation is its intention – the evaluator collects and analyzes program information that is then interpreted to gain an assessment of the program's merit or worth. This assessment is used by the evaluator and persons who have an interest in the program to make decisions on the future of the program. There are several reasons why an evaluation is conducted.

Program Improvement (formative evaluation). Evaluation is often aimed at testing a theory of change. The underlying assumption is that if the teachers get appropriate training, then they will acquire new skills leading

Table 2.2   Elements of the Evaluation Plan

The Evaluation Plan

Without a plan, the evaluation will face many false starts. The evaluation plan should include at least the following components:

Purpose of the evaluation

Role expectations for evaluators, program staff, participants, and key stakeholders

Program description (Logic Model)

Evaluation questions

Evaluation design, including data collection strategies

Data analysis plan

Report plan

Meta-evaluation

Management plan and budget

---

to a change in their behavior resulting in a reduction in their referral rate. In real life, things rarely work out as planned. In fact, programs are usually not implemented as designed, typically because of contextual constraints (e.g., teachers' schedules are too full to allow them to participate at the anticipated levels). On the other hand, the program may be implemented as designed, but the expected changes are not observed. In this case, the program may need to be tweaked a little – perhaps adding individual technical assistance to teachers participating in the seminar to assist them in applying new skills. Formative evaluation seeks to collect information that will help program staff make mid-course corrections in the program design and/or delivery that will increase the probability of success – reducing the rate of referral. Formative evaluation is usually focused on new programs or existing programs that are in transition. The formative evaluator needs to collect several different types of information in support of program improvement: information on outcomes, participant feedback, program implementation, and possible contextual influences.

Program Accountability (summative evaluation). The design and delivery of the seminars requires the expenditure of resources – the school division's as well as the teachers' time and effort – that is, resources that could be directed to other division needs. The reduction in referral to special education was deemed important by the director. Evaluation may be directed at determining if these expectations were met. In the end, was the program worth the expenditure of resources? Is the program achieving the ends for which it was funded? Should it be continued? One purpose of evaluation is to establish evidence not only that the intended results were achieved, but that the program caused these changes. Summative evaluation should not be conducted until a program reaches stability – when formative evaluation indicates that additional change is not required.

Identify New Program Directions (needs assessment). There is life after the evaluation. The evaluation information may not only support that the need has been addressed – referrals reduced–but also provide information about needs. For example, the evaluation may uncover a need to train teachers to work more effectively with parents to improve collaboration between home and school leading to increased student performance in the classroom resulting in decreased school dropout and truancy.

Dissemination of Promising Practices. Schools across the country face similar problems. It is important to share promising practices with those who are confronted with the same challenges. Evaluation can be aimed at creating information that will support the decisions of potential adopters of the promising practice – one that has achieved success over repeated administrations in a particular context. Potential adopters require four pieces of evaluation information. First, they need evidence that the program actually will solve the challenge they face. Second, they need information about how the program works to bring about those changes, including areas in which there is flexibility in implementing the program – for example, reducing the number of seminars without losing the final result. Third, the potential adopter needs to know how much the program will cost to start up – purchasing training materials, hiring the consultant – and operate – release time for teachers. Finally, the adopter needs information about factors in the receiving context that could influence the success of the program when implemented. As noted earlier, the school board may have implemented a new policy restricting the number of referrals by each teacher. If the receiving division does not have that policy in place, it is unlikely to see similar results.

Policy Formation/Assessment. The evaluation study may be commissioned to determine the capacity to meet the needs of a particular group for the purposes of deciding if a policy should be put in place to enable or ensure that services get to the right people in the right way and at the right level. In the late 1960s, several evaluation studies were undertaken to identify the extent to which educational and related services were being provided appropriately to school-age students with disabilities. As a result of these studies, in part, Congress decided that policies had to be developed (PL 94-142) to ensure that these students received the services to which they were entitled. Since that time, hundreds of studies have been conducted to assess the degree to which the new policy was yielding the intended results. Many of these were designed to ascertain the degree to which the policy was implemented as designed, while others were addressing the impact on the policy in meeting the needs of students with disabilities. Policy evaluation can examine the need for policy, the level of implementation of a new policy, or the effectiveness of the new policy in achieving its intentions.

Other purposes for evaluation are discussed in the evaluation texts cited in Table 2.1 and in Stufflebeam (2001).

Step 2. Identify the People
Involved in the Evaluation (Stakeholders)

What is a stakeholder? Program evaluations are conducted to answer the question who needs to know what about a program, when, in what format, and with what frequency. The audience of the evaluation information may be internal, external, or both. Internal audiences include program staff. External audiences include program participants and those affected by the program, as well as policymakers and funding agency representatives that need to make decisions about the program. Rossi, Freeman, and Lipsey (1999) provide an excellent review of the types of stakeholders that might be considered in a program evaluation and their roles in the evaluation. They note that stakeholders should be thought of as those people not only affected by the program, but also those involved with the evaluation of the program.

Evaluation approaches have evolved in recent years that support the active engagement of stakeholders in all phases of the evaluation. They are based on the assumption that increased involvement of stakeholders increases the relevancy of the evaluation and its utility for the stakeholder. In Chapter 9, the concept of social validation is introduced in which researchers are encouraged to engage the research participants or their advocates in an assessment of the worth of the study in relation to their needs and well-being. Similarly, participants in an evaluation should be given the opportunity to reflect on the design of the evaluation. Participatory evaluation (Patton, 1997) calls for close and continuous involvement in the design, implementation, analysis, interpretation, and reporting phase of the evaluation to enhance the utility of the evaluation.

Empowerment evaluation (Fetterman, Kaftarian, & Wandersman, 1996) takes participatory evaluation to another level. While empowerment evaluation emphasizes collaboration between the stakeholders and evaluator, those who advocate for this approach would suggest that the role of the evaluator is more consultative and facilitative. Indeed the role of the evaluator is to enhance the capacity of the program staff in the design, implementation, and use of evaluation information for program management and communication with external stakeholders.

Based on the principles of the transformative paradigm, Mertens has proposed the Inclusive Evaluation Approach (Mertens, 2003a & b). Members of the community impacted by the evaluation would be involved to some degree in the methodological decisions relevant to the conduct of the evaluation. The emphasis is on deliberate inclusiveness of groups that have historically experienced oppression and discrimination on the basis of gender, culture, economic levels, ethnicities/races, sexual orientation, and disabilities, with a conscious effort to build a link between the results of the evaluation and social action. To this end, the inclusive evaluator attempts to address power imbalances in society by being inclusive of all relevant stakeholders in a way that authentic and accurate representations of their viewpoints are considered.

Step 3. Describe the Program to Be Evaluated

It might be said that it is an evaluation axiom that you should not evaluate a program that you do not know. In our opinion (there are other approaches, see Stufflebeam, 2001), program evaluation that is not guided by an understanding of what the program is trying to do, for whom, and using what strategies might be misguided and may result in an invalid portrayal of the program's performance.

Assessing the Program's Theory of Change. Every program has an implicit theory of change that is represented by a series of if, then statements. If we have these resources, then we can translate them into these activities for these program participants. If these program participants receive these activities, then they will change their knowledge, skill, and/or values. If they gain new skill, knowledge, and/or values, then they will change their behavior. If they change their behavior, then they will achieve the aims of the program.

For example, suppose that a local special education director has determined that teachers in the school district consistently refer a significantly higher number of students to the school child study team as possibly requiring special education services than the state average. Thus, the problem to be addressed is the abnormally high referral rate. The director decides to address the problem through a new training program described in a recent journal. The training program is based on the assumption that teachers who know how to diversify instruction to meet the unique characteristics of their students and who can create a positive classroom climate tend to refer students for special education less frequently. The special education director hires a nationally recognized consultant and purchases the training materials used in the research presented in the recent journal (the resources). The consultant uses the materials to conduct monthly seminars (the activities) for all teachers in the director's district. The theory is that if the teachers are exposed to the seminars, then they will learn new skills related to differentiated instruction and improving classroom climate. If they learn the new skills, then they will differentiate instruction and create a more positive school climate, leading to a reduction in their perceived need for referring students for special education. The evaluation will be designed to test the hypothesis: If teachers participate in the seminars, then they will decrease their rate of referral.

One purpose of evaluation could be to assess the quality of the theory of change. An important step in evaluation is to make explicit the theory of change using a technique for describing the program such as logic modeling (McLaughlin & Jordan, 1999). A Logic Model presents a plausible and sensible model of how the program will work under certain conditions to solve identified problems (Bickman, 1987). Patton (1997) refers to a program description such as this as an "espoused theory of action," that is, stakeholder perceptions of how the program will work. Evaluators are often called upon to collect information that attests to the validity of the espoused theory of change. Does previous research support the theory of change? Is it reasonable to expect the proposed outcomes to occur given the activities described?

It is important to note that as Bickman suggests, programs are delivered under specific conditions, within a certain context. These conditions are both antecedent and mediating. Antecedent conditions are those factors that exist when the program is designed–the entering skills and values of the teachers participating in the training, the characteristics of their students and the community in which they live, and policies that guide the design and implementation of education in the school division. Mediating factors are those that occur as the program is being implemented – such as changes in staff (the special education director leaves) and changes in school policy (the school board sets a limit on the number of students who can be referred by one teacher). Both antecedent and mediating factors can influence (positively or negatively) the outcome of the program. The evaluator must ask if it is reasonable to expect the proposed outcomes to occur given the activities described and given the conditions under which the program is implemented.

A simple logic model is set forth in Figure 2.1. Note that the model has three basic elements: The program that is delivered, the people who receive the program, and the program results. The arrows that connect the elements in the logic model indicate that there is a logical flow, an interrelationship from one element to the next. This is the theory of change. If we implement this program, for these people, we will achieve the desired result. The evaluator and the staff work together to develop the underlying rationale for the connections. The evaluator asks, "Why do you believe this program will lead to the intended outcomes for these participants?"

We will be discussing the evaluation questions that might be asked about a program. But it is useful to note that Wholey (cited in Wholey et al., 1994) views program evaluation as having two foci: the measurement of program performance, including resource levels, program activities, and program outcomes, and the testing of the relationships between the three elements of program performance. Developing a logic model and the underlying assumptions informs the evaluation team about how the program works to achieve its intentions and informs the evaluator about what to ask about the program.

Step 4. Develop Evaluation Questions

Evaluation questions serve as the bridge between the purpose of the evaluation and the data collection, analysis, and reporting phases of the

Figure 2.1

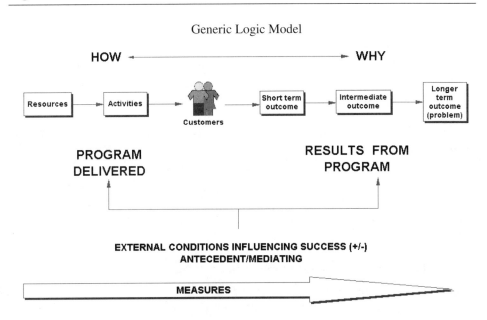

Generic Logic Model

EXTERNAL CONDITIONS INFLUENCING SUCCESS (+/-)
ANTECEDENT/MEDIATING

MEASURES

evaluation. Just like research questions, evaluation questions communicate the intent of the evaluation and the information required to serve that intent. Unlike research, the need for evaluation is unlikely to belong to the evaluator, but rather to the program staff or an external stakeholder such as an administrator, policymaker, or funding agency that may employ the evaluator to conduct the evaluation. Thus, in framing the evaluation questions, the evaluator must consult with stakeholders to ensure the relevancy of the evaluation effort to their needs.

TYPES OF QUESTIONS

Impact Evaluation. Impact evaluation is designed to assess the degree to which an intervention causes the intended results – the test of the program hypothesis. At least three pieces of information are required: observations of performance on a dependent variable(s) that serves as an indicator(s) of the expected result, implementation evaluation information that can attest to what happened to the participants, and contextual information that could serve as rival explanations for observed changes. In order to provide convincing evidence, the evaluation should not only provide evidence of change in the strategic result – reduction in referral rate, but also provide evidence of the intermediate outcomes – change in teacher knowledge and changes in teacher behaviors. The primary interest in impact evaluation is not only in observing the expected change, but also being able to explain why the result was achieved. More about this topic will be presented in Chapter 4.

Sample impact evaluation questions include:

Did the reading program lead to improved reading performance of fifth grade students with learning disabilities?

Did teachers who participated in a collaborative teaching workshop exhibit increased episodes of collaboration six months after the workshop?

Do parents who participate in school governance exhibit a higher level of satisfaction with the school and a higher level of participation in school-based activities?

Evaluators have recognized that successful evaluation does not just happen. Evaluation for program improvement requires the measurement of program performance – resource expenditures, program activities, and outcomes – and testing the causal assumptions linking these elements. Prior to conducting a program evaluation, it is important to perform an evaluability assessment to identify possible impediments to the evaluation. These might include:

1. Evaluators and intended users fail to agree on the goals, objectives, side effects, and performance criteria.

2. Program goals and objectives are found to be unrealistic given the resources available.

3. Relevant information on program performance is not available.

4. Administrators on the policy or operating level are unable or unwilling to change the program on the basis of evaluation information (Wholey et al., 1994).

Performance Evaluation. Public, private, and not-for-profit programs are encouraged and often required to report on program performance to external stakeholders. Managers of these programs need performance information to manage for results – to identify what is working and not working and make mid-course corrections to improve performance and increase the likelihood for success. A program's performance spectrum includes resources, activities, outputs, and outcomes. In the early 1990s, accountability advocates called for a focus on outcome data as opposed to reports of resources expended, activities implanted, or outputs generated. Outcomes are measures of actual changes in program participants while outputs are variables produced by the program to bring about those changes – number of teachers attending seminars on differentiated instruction. Recently, evaluators, program managers, and policymakers are seeing the need to have a more balanced approach to performance measurement to meet the needs of both internal and external users of performance information for both program accountability and program improvement.

Examples of performance evaluation questions include:

Did the program hire certified teachers as specified in their proposal to the funding agency?

Are students being involved in 60 minutes of individualized instruction daily as set forth in the research plan?

Did students' scores on the math assessment increase?

Process Evaluation. There are times when an evaluation may focus only on the program processes – the actions necessary to achieve desired results. The evaluation question might be, "What is being done to whom, by whom, and how well?" This is an important question in special education because of the specific regulations under which the programs are to be implemented. On the one hand, the theory is that if the program is in compliance, then these procedures have to be followed. The regulations serve as the standard. The evaluation question is, "Are the regulations followed?" On the other hand, the regulations are based on best practice, so the theory might be, "If the regulations are followed, then students with disabilities will prosper." If it is true that the regulations are research-based, then measuring the implementation will provide evidence that students with disabilities will be better off. Of course, this is a testable hypothesis.

Examples of process evaluation questions include:

Did students who are fourteen years of age receive a transition assessment?

Are parents involved in the development of their child's Individual Education Plan (IEP)?

Are students who have been selected to participate in a new program for teaching social skills attending at the levels intended in the research plan?

Cost Evaluation. As noted previously, potential adopters require information on the start-up and operational costs of the program to be adopted. Thus, one aim of program evaluation might be to document the costs associated with the implementation of a program. Another type of cost evaluation, cost-benefit evaluation, is more difficult but equally important. In this type of evaluation, the question is, "Does Program A that achieves the same results as Program B cost the same to start up and operate?" The difficulty of this type of evaluation is in finding a program that achieves the same results and then being able to compare costs.

Examples of cost evaluation questions are:

What are the start-up and operational costs of the new program to reduce school dropout? What does it cost to train the teachers who will be running the dropout program? What are the costs associated for running the after school program?

Given two programs that both demonstrate a reduction in school dropout, are the start-up and operational costs different for the programs?

Step 5. Data Collection, Analysis, and Reporting

In evaluation, the steps for design, data collection, analysis, and reporting parallel those in research. Therefore, the reader is referred to subsequent chapters on these topics for guidance.

Step 6. Management Plan and Budget

The management plan and budget are keyed to the evaluation questions. For each question, the evaluators identify who does what, when, and at what costs. For each question, there will be activities and costs related to information collection, data analysis, and reporting. In addition, there will be activities and costs related to the management of the evaluation and the conduct of the meta-evaluation (see following).

After the evaluation plan is completed, we like to conduct a force field analysis of the plan. A team of people composed of the evaluators and other stakeholders come together and ask the following questions:

- Given the purposes of the evaluation and the evaluation plan, what forces exist that could serve as bridges to the success of the evaluation?
- What barriers exist that might have a negative influence on the success of the evaluation as planned?

After the force field analysis, the group may decide to refine the plan, taking advantage of some of the opportunities and developing strategies that could address some of the barriers.

Evaluation is like a program. It is an intentional transformation of resources into specific activities to achieve a defined purpose. Like any program, the evaluation program should follow the plan and monitor and refine the model. Having a plan in place at the start is important, but be prepared to make mid-course corrections as the evaluation unfolds. Revisions in the plan are made based on the feedback from continuous meta-evaluation.

Step 7. Meta-evaluation — Assessing the Quality of the Evaluation Design, Implementation, and Use

The last step in planning the evaluation is to develop a meta-evaluation plan. The purpose of this plan is to develop an evaluation of the evaluation. Typical meta-evaluation questions at the evaluation design stage are:

- Is the design of the evaluation consistent with the needs of the evaluation audiences?
- Is the design of the evaluation technically sound in terms of proposed methodology for collecting information, analyzing, and interpreting evaluation information?
- Is the evaluation cost-efficient, providing an appropriate balance between the cost of the program and the cost of the evaluation?
- Does the evaluation ensure that the rights of the evaluation participants are protected?

As the evaluation unfolds, these same questions might guide the continuous monitoring of the evaluation project.

Program Evaluation Standards

The Program Evaluation Standards (Joint Committee on Standards for Educational Evaluation, 1994) provide guidance to evaluator and the evaluation consumer about designing, conducting, and reporting the evaluation of programs. A summary of the standards may be acquired through the American Evaluation Association (AEA) at www.Eval.org. There are four standards:

- *Utility*. There are seven utility standards designed to ensure that the proposed evaluation meets the needs of intended audiences and/or users. The utility standards require that the evaluator becomes aware of the stakeholders in the evaluation, determines what their information needs are, designs an evaluation responsive to these needs, and reports the evaluation findings clearly and in a timely fashion.

- *Feasibility*. There are three feasibility standards that not only address the cost of the evaluation, but also address the practicality of the evaluation, recognizing the need to reduce the burden of the evaluation on the evaluation participants and staff.

- *Propriety*. The eight propriety standards are to ensure that the evaluation is designed, conducted, and reported legally, ethically, and with regard for the welfare of those involved in the evaluation and potentially affected by the outcome of the evaluation.

- *Accuracy*. There are twelve accuracy standards designed to enable the collection of technically sound information. The standards reflect the criteria we present at the end of the chapters in this text. In the end, these standards require that the evaluator brings to light and communicates accurate information about the program's merit and worth.

Questions for Critical Analysis for Evaluation

These standards can be used to critically assess the quality of evaluation studies. Questions to ask for critical analysis are included in Table 2.3.

Ethics and Evaluation: The Guiding Principles

Another important resource for designing high quality evaluations is the Guiding Principles for Evaluators (American Evaluation Association, 1995), also available through the American Evaluation Association. There are five guiding principles:

Table 2.3   Questions for Critical Analysis Based on Evaluation Standards
(Mertens, 1998, pp. 244-247)

These questions are designed to parallel the Standards and to address issues
raised by the construct of multicultural validity as it was described by Kirkhart
(1995).

Utility

1. *Stakeholder identification.* Were the people involved in or affected by the
   evaluation identified?
2. *Evaluator credibility.* Is the evaluator perceived to be trustworthy and
   competent to perform the evaluation?
3. *Information scope and selection.* Was the information collected broadly
   selected to address pertinent questions about the program and responsive
   to the needs and interests of clients and other important stakeholders?
4. *Values identification.* Were the perspectives, procedures, and rationale used
   to interpret the findings carefully described, providing a basis for value
   judgments that was clear?
5. *Report clarity.* Did the evaluation reports clearly describe the program
   being evaluated, including its context and the purposes, procedures, and
   findings of the evaluation, so that essential information was provided and
   easily understood?
6. *Report timeliness and dissemination.* Were significant interim findings and
   evaluation reports disseminated to intended users so that they could be
   used in a timely fashion?
7. *Evaluation impact.* Was the evaluation planned, conducted, and reported in
   ways that encouraged follow-through by stakeholders so that the
   likelihood that the evaluation was used was increased?

Feasibility

1. *Practical procedures.* What evidence is there that the evaluation was
   conducted in a practical way, keeping disruption to a minimum?
2. *Political viability.* What evidence is there that the evaluation was planned
   and conducted with anticipation of the different positions of various
   interest groups? What evidence is there that the cooperation of the
   various interest groups was obtained? What evidence is there that possible
   attempts by any of these groups to curtail evaluation operations or to bias
   or misapply the results were averted or counteracted?
3. *Cost-effectiveness.* What evidence is there that the evaluation was
   conducted in an efficient manner and produced information of sufficient
   value to justify the resources expended?

Propriety

1. *Service orientation.* What evidence is there that the evaluation was designed
   to assist organizations to address and effectively serve the needs of the
   full range of targeted participants?

2. *Formal agreements.* What evidence is there that a formal agreement for the evaluation work was agreed to by formal parties?
3. *Rights of human subjects.* What evidence is there that the rights and welfare of the people participating in the evaluation were respected and protected?
4. *Human interactions.* What evidence is there that the evaluators respected the dignity and worth of the people associated with the evaluation?
5. *Complete and fair assessment.* What evidence is there that the evaluation was complete and fair in its examination and recording of strengths and weaknesses of the program being evaluated?
6. *Disclosure of findings.* What evidence is there that the full set of evaluation findings along with pertinent limitations were made accessible to the persons affected by the evaluation and any others with expressed legal rights to receive the results?
7. *Conflict of interest.* What evidence is there that any conflict of interest was dealt with openly and honestly, so that it did not compromise the evaluation processes and results?
8. *Fiscal responsibility.* What evidence is there that the evaluator's allocation and expenditure of resources reflected sound accountability procedures and expenditures were accounted for and appropriate?

Accuracy

1. *Program documentation.* What evidence is there that the program being evaluated was described and documented clearly and accurately?
2. *Context analysis.* What evidence is there that the context in which the program exists was examined in enough detail, so that likely influences on the program could be identified?
3. *Described purposes and procedures.* What evidence is there that the procedures of the evaluation were monitored and described in enough detail to be identified and assessed?
4. *Defensible information sources.* What evidence is there that the sources of information used in a program evaluation were described in enough detail, so that the adequacy of the information could be assessed?
5. *Valid information.* What evidence is there that the information-gathering procedures could ensure validity of the interpretations for their intended uses?
6. *Reliable information.* What evidence is there that the information-gathering procedures could ensure that the information obtained was sufficiently reliable for the intended use?
7. *Systematic information.* What evidence is there that the information was collected, processed, and reported in a way that allowed for systematic review and correction of errors?
8. *Analysis of quantitative information.* What evidence is there that the quantitative information was appropriately and systematically analyzed so that evaluation questions could be effectively answered?

(Continued)

Table 2.3 Continued

9. *Analysis of qualitative information.* What evidence is there that the qualitative information was appropriately and systematically analyzed so that evaluation questions could be effectively answered?

10. *Justified conclusions.* What evidence is there that the conclusions reached in the evaluation could be explicitly justified?

11. *Impartial reporting.* What evidence is there that the reporting procedures guarded against distortion caused by personal feelings and biases of any party to the evaluation?

12. *Meta-evaluation.* What evidence is there that the evaluation itself was formatively and summatively evaluated against these and other pertinent standards? Can stakeholders closely examine the evaluation's strengths and weaknesses?

Methodological Validity

1. *Face validity.* Do the items on the measurement instrument appear relevant to the life experiences of persons in a particular cultural context?

2. *Content validity.* Do the measurement items or tools have content relevance?

3. *Criterion-related validity.* Have the measures selected been validated against external criteria that are themselves culturally relevant?

4. *Construct validity.* Are the constructs that are used developed within an appropriate cultural context?

5. *Generalization.* Have threats to generalization of causal connections been considered in terms of connections across persons and settings, nonidentical treatments, and other measures of effects?

Interpersonal Validity

1. *Personal influences.* What are the influences of personal characteristics or circumstances, such as social class, gender, race and ethnicity, language, disability, or sexual orientation in shaping interpersonal interactions, including interactions between evaluators, clients, program providers, consumers, and other stakeholders?

2. *Beliefs and values.* What are the influences of the beliefs and values of the evaluator and other key players in filtering the information received and shaping interpretations?

Consequential Validity

1. *Catalyst for change.* What evidence is there that the evaluation was conceptualized as a catalyst for change (e.g., shift the power relationships among cultural groups or subgroups)?

2. *Unintended effects.* What evidence is there of sensitivity to unintended (positive or negative) effects on culturally different segments of the population?

Multicultural Validity

1. *Time.* Were the time and budget allocated to the evaluation sufficient to allow a culturally sensitive perspective to emerge?
2. *Cultural sophistication.* Did the evaluator demonstrate cultural sophistication on the cognitive, affective, and skill dimensions? Was the evaluator able to have positive interpersonal connections, conceptualize and facilitate culturally congruent change, and make appropriate cultural assumptions in the design and implementation of the evaluation?
3. *Avoidance of arrogant complacency.* What evidence is there that the evaluator has been willing to relinquish premature cognitive commitments and to be reflexive?

- *Systematic Inquiry.* Evaluators conduct systematic data-based investigations about the program being evaluated.
- *Competence.* Evaluators provide competent performance in the design, implementation, and reporting of the evaluation.
- *Integrity/Honesty.* Evaluators ensure that the evaluation is conducted with honesty and integrity in its entirety.
- *Respect for People.* Evaluators respect the security, dignity, and self-worth of the respondents, program participants, clients, and other stakeholders with whom they interact.
- *Responsibilities for the General and Public Welfare.* Evaluators articulate and take into account the diversity of interests and values that may be related to the general and public welfare.

The Program Evaluation Standards and the Guiding Principles for Evaluators should be used by the evaluator in developing and implementing the evaluation study. Conducting the meta-evaluation at the design stage not only ensures that a worthwhile evaluation has been constructed that is likely to produce the information needed by users, but also will increase the confidence of those associated with the evaluation. Conducting the meta-evaluation across the life cycle of the evaluation will enable the evaluation.

QUESTIONS AND ACTIVITIES FOR APPLICATION AND DISCUSSION

1. Compare and contrast the purposes and methods of research and evaluation.

2. Discuss the similarities and differences between the concepts of merit and worth.

3. Compare and contrast performance measurement and impact evaluation.

4. Identify a program in which you are involved. Carry out the following activities:
   a. Develop an evaluation plan that could guide the evaluation of the program.
   b. List and discuss how the plan addresses the Program Evaluation Standards and the Guiding Principles for Evaluators.

5. Locate an evaluation of a special education program in the literature. Evaluate the study using the Program Evaluation Standards and the Guiding Principles for Evaluators. Find some partners and role-play different perspectives on the evaluation – evaluator, staff member, participant, and stakeholder. Identify ways in which you would improve the evaluation.

3

Literature Review

Jason Smith is a faculty member in the Department of Special Education in the College of Education who teaches methods courses for preservice teachers who will be teaching students with learning disabilities. One of the contributions that he has made to his field is to conduct a meta-analysis of effective practices for teaching writing to students with learning disabilities.

Laura Jones is a doctoral student in learning disabilities who is interested in doing her dissertation in the area of teaching writing to students with learning disabilities. As she begins to plan her study, she asks herself several questions. What have others found with respect to variables that should be considered in teaching writing? In what ways have others designed research to study interventions for teaching writing? What measures might be used to assess writing skills for this group?

These two scenarios present two purposes for conducting the literature review. On the one hand, the completed review can be a very useful product for the field. On the other hand, the review of literature serves as an essential resource for planning, conducting, interpreting, and reporting research in special education. It is difficult to think of a researcher undertaking a research project without some specific purpose in mind. One of the primary purposes of research is to generate information that will increase understanding and identify successful practices or products. The researcher does not start from ground zero; there is a prior knowledge base established by other researchers. It is doubtful that there is any topic in special education that has not been addressed in some research endeavor. The professional literature serves as a major resource to researchers as they plan, implement, interpret, and report their research. The objective of this chapter is to orient the reader to the strategies associated with the conduct and use of the literature review. The information in this chapter serves as a bridge to subsequent chapters which describe other steps in the research process.

IN THIS CHAPTER

- The purposes of conducting the literature review and sample research questions and hypotheses are presented.
- Sources from which the literature can be drawn are identified.
- Search procedures for identifying and selecting appropriate literature are explained.
- Various procedures the researcher can employ to aggregate the literature selected for review are discussed.
- Questions for critically analyzing literature reviews in research are provided.

PURPOSES OF THE LITERATURE REVIEW

Remember your last vacation? If you are like most people, you probably spent substantial time planning your trip. You considered what you wanted to accomplish, your destination, what you would do during your vacation, and the items you needed to do these things. While for some people research is not a vacation, it does require planning if it is going to generate the required information. Just like vacation planning, personal experience is a valuable resource in planning research, but even the vacation planner goes beyond experience to consult travel brochures and maps. A major resource for the researcher at the planning stage of research is the professional literature.

Summarize Extant Research. The researcher may approach the literature with a number of purposes in mind. The intent may be to summarize the extant research to inform the reader of what is known about the subject, that is, what research has already been conducted. A by-product may be a publication that could become a resource to practitioners. The review may identify how the results of research might be applied in the delivery of services to persons with disabilities. For example, Vaughn et al. (2000) reported on a synthesis of research on higher-order processing and problem solving, reading comprehension, written expression, and grouping strategies. The purpose of their article was to present the results of studies that examined the relationship between these variables and improved reading performance for students with disabilities. Their work provides both researchers and practitioners insights into these relationships. As discussed later in this chapter, a powerful tool for summarizing extant research findings is meta-analysis.

Gaps in Knowledge Base. A second important purpose of the literature review is the identification of weaknesses or gaps in the current knowledge base. For example, O'Donnell and Livingston (1991) conducted a review of research on the relationship between low vision and the cognitive, motor, and social development of young children. The authors cited research that supported various approaches and optical aids that might be used by practitioners to enhance development in these areas. O'Donnell and Livingston identified a gap in the knowledge base in that previous researchers had not studied the effects of using low vision optical devices on the cognitive development of infants with low vision.

Thompson, Blount, and Thurlow (2002) provided a very useful review of research related to the effects of accommodation in large-scale tests on the scores of students with disabilities between 1999 and 2001. They reached the conclusion that at least three accommodations showed a positive effect on student test scores across at least four studies: computer administration, oral presentation, and extended time. They provided an extensive list of topics in need of additional research based on their review of the current literature, including the effects of accommodations under more carefully defined conditions, the desirability and perceived usefulness of accommodations by students themselves, and increased research in the subject areas that are required by NCLB, such as science.

The literature review informs the researcher of the results of previously conducted studies. The review may be used to inform practitioners of successful practices, and it may also enable the researcher to identify the next logical step in the research chain. This need for further research may go beyond omissions by previous researchers to new ways of addressing the research problem and different measurement and analysis techniques.

Interpretation of Findings. While the literature review is a major resource to researchers who are playing out their role as planners, there is a third purpose of the literature review. Just like being on a vacation, things do not always go as planned in research. It is often necessary to return to the literature throughout the research to obtain information to help explain expected and unexpected findings. Levin, Hibbard, and Rock (2002) examined the effect of using problem-based learning on the learning and attitudes of preservice teachers. In discussing the implications of their findings, they presented other factors that might have contributed to the observed results. In particular, they were concerned that the trainers might have influenced the outcome because of their background and approach differences. They discussed this possibility and cited previous research as indicating that instructor effects may not have been a problem in their research.

In another study, Favazza et al. (2000) studied the factors that influenced the acceptance of young children with disabilities by their peers. In discussing their findings, the authors cited the importance of teacher characteristics in the formation of attitudes toward students with disabilities. In support of this conclusion, they cited several previous studies that had examined the role of teachers in promoting social acceptance and integration.

The researcher can be thought of as a problem solver. Because the goal of the research is to increase understanding, the problem is a gap in the knowledge base. To solve the problem, the researcher must establish an empirical information base from which to draw conclusions and make recommendations about the problem.

Conceptual Framework. The literature helps the researcher construct a theoretical or conceptual framework. The framework becomes the standard for the proposed research, a statement of what the researcher expects to observe as the research project unfolds. It communicates expected outcomes, activities or interventions necessary to achieve these outcomes, and resources that must be available to support the intervention. The conceptual framework tells the researcher what information to collect, that is, what should be measured to increase understanding about the problem addressed in the study. More important, the conceptual framework provides a thorough description of the underlying logic of the proposed research – why a particular intervention might lead to these specific outcomes for this population under these conditions.

One example of a conceptual framework was that developed by the National Longitudinal Transition Study of Special Education Students (NLTS) to explain the transition experiences and outcomes for youth with disabilities (DeStefano & Wagner, 1991). SRI is currently conducting the National Longitudinal Transition Study-2 (NLTS2) for the Office of Special Education Programs (OSEP), U.S. Department of Education (Wagner, 2003). NLTS and NLTS2 have been designed to serve as a framework for understanding and predicting the relationship between school-based special education experiences and postschool outcomes. Researchers interested in studying relationships in this domain could use the NLTS framework as a guide for designing and interpreting their research. The school-based experiences might be thought of as measures of the independent variables that lead to expected results – the dependent variable. The interrelationships between and among these variables present an outcome structure that could be used to design, analyze, and interpret a study of the effects of school-based experiences on postschool outcomes. Another conceptual framework was developed by the National Center on Educational Outcomes at the College of Education, University of Minnesota, to explain educational outcomes for children and youth with disabilities (Ysseldyke, Thurlow, Bruininks, Gilman, Deno, McGrew, & Shriner, 1993). This group was established to provide leadership in the development of educational outcomes for all students with disabilities.

Research Questions and Hypotheses

The literature review serves as a foundation for forming research questions. Hedrick, Bickman, and Rog (1993) suggest that the research questions operationalize the objectives of the proposed research. Research questions focus the research hypotheses and clarify what information needs to be collected from what sources and under what conditions. Simply stated, a hypothesis is an if, then statement. For example, a hypothesis could state that if subjects are exposed to a particular intervention, then they will behave in a certain predictable manner. Kerlinger (1973) states that "the hypothesis is a conjectural statement, a tentative proposition, about the relationship between two or more phenomena or variables" (p. 12). Typically, researchers use the research question to direct their research rather than the hypothesis, unless there is sufficient previous research to justify forming the hypothesis.

Framing the research question can be a difficult task for beginning researchers. Hedrick et al. (1993) present a taxonomy for categorizing research questions that includes four categories of questions: descriptive, normative, correlative, and impact. Each is briefly discussed within the context of research in special education.

Descriptive research questions are designed to produce information about what is happening in relation to the target of the research. For example, the researcher might want to describe certain characteristics of the participants in an intervention or the prevalence of a particular disability within a specific domain. Such a research question might ask: What is the participation rate of students with disabilities in the state's standards-based assessments?

Normative research questions go beyond description, requiring that the information generated in response to the descriptive research question be compared to some standard or expected observation. Because special education has minimum requirements regarding most aspects of the service delivery system, a normative research question might ask: Were individual education plans (IEPs) in place before the placement was made, as is required by the minimum service delivery requirements?

We noted that a great deal of research is conducted to identify relationships to enable the explanation of how specific phenomena covary. One avenue for examining relationships is the **correlative research** question. As Hedrick et al. (1993) point out, data derived in response to such questions indicate the strength and direction of a relationship between two or more variables, not causality. For example, the special education researcher might ask: What is the relationship between instructional setting (mainstream vs. self-contained) and participation rates in the state standards-based assessment process? A finding of a strong relationship between setting and participation rates would lead to further study about the facets of setting that were related to participation and perhaps the development of an intervention to increase participation rates across settings.

Impact research questions are the last category offered in the Hedrick et al. (1993) taxonomy. Here the researcher's aim is to identify effects, that is, to establish causal links between an independent variable (the intervention) and a dependent variable (the anticipated change). Wehmeyer et al. (2000) examined the effect of a self-determined learning model on the academic achievement and self-determination of students with disabilities. The purpose of the study was to determine the impact of the new model on the performance of students with disabilities. Their hypothesis was, "If students with disabilities are exposed to the new model, then they will show higher gains in academic achievement and self-determination than students with disabilities who were not exposed to the model."

In sum, the literature review serves many purposes. It establishes a historical perspective on the intended research and provides a vision of the need for additional research. But how does the researcher identify the salient literature to include in the review? There are several tools available to researchers to assist them in their review of the literature.

RESOURCES TO SUPPORT THE LITERATURE REVIEW

Locating sources for the literature review is the first challenge for the prospective author. Critically analyzing the research articles and reports and aggregating the information into a usable form are the next challenges. The purpose of this section is to provide insights into the location of the literature. We should note, however, that while the literature is a primary information support, it is historical by nature. Therefore, researchers are well advised to consult other researchers and practitioners in the field of interest. According to Hedrick et al. (1993), such discussions may reveal current trends and issues or new information which has yet to be found in the literature. Attending professional conferences, such as the annual meeting of the American Educational Research Association, the American Evaluation Association, or the Council for Exceptional Children, where research is reported provides an excellent opportunity for such dialogue. Most disability areas are represented by a professional organization that not only produces journals, but also may hold professional meetings at which current research and practice are presented. These professional associations would be good sources of information.

Secondary Sources

Often a literature review begins with reading secondary sources, that is, a synthesis of research findings on a particular topic. Any publication that is written by an author who did not conduct the primary (original) research is considered a secondary source. Literature reviews are considered secondary sources, as are textbooks and reference books. We have previously sighted some examples of research syntheses and will reference others when meta-analysis is discussed. An excellent example of a secondary source that could be used by the researcher in the planning phase of the research is a piece by Cronis and Ellis (2000) in which they present a brief history of special education and forecast emerging trends such as inclusion, research-to-practice, and personnel preparation. Woodward & Reith (1997) present a review of nearly twenty years of research on the uses of technology in special education. Their review addresses both instructional and assessment domains and provides insights into both practice and future research. Ysseldyke (2000) published his reflections on twenty-five years of research on assessment and instructional decision making. He provides many insights into issues around assessment, use of data-based decisions by professionals in special education, the problem with stereotypes in the disability community, psychometric issues around identification, and the importance of the political process in bringing about change. Gersten, Baker, and Lloyd (2000) also provide much guidance in thinking about research issues in special education in their review of literature on designing high-quality research in special education and the use of experimental designs. They discuss the problems with confounding variables, treatment fidelity, and comparisons groups. Such a literature provides the "big picture" of research methods in special education. Last, Gersten et al. (1997) present a review of research in special education aiming to bridge the gap between research and practice. The article sets forth roles and responsibilities researchers might adopt to encourage the translation of research into practice and identify gaps that might be filled through continually improving research practice in special education. All these are examples of secondary sources in which the authors review the work of other researchers and identify potential next steps in both research and practice.

Primary Sources

Primary sources include publications that are prepared by the researcher who conducted the research. Because this type of report contains the details describing how the research was conducted by the persons who conducted the research, it is considered good practice to base the review of literature on citations from primary sources including research journals, dissertations, or final reports of research projects. There are a number of journals presenting research that could serve as a resource to researchers who are contemplating investigations of topics associated with persons with disabilities. Several journals that might serve as a resource to the researcher interested in special education are listed in Table 3.1. Other important sources include final reports from research projects supported through public and private funding agencies, as well as reports to Congress by federal agencies. For example, the U.S. Office of Special Education Programs submits an Annual Report to Congress on the status of service delivery programs for students with disabilities (U.S. Department of Education, 2001a) and publishes a data dictionary that includes definitions of key terms in special education legislation (U.S. Department of Education, 2001b).

Table 3.1   Selected Journals Containing Special Education Resource Information

American Annals of the Deaf

American Journal on Mental Retardation

Annals of Dyslexia

Australasian Journal of Special Education

Behavioral Disorders

British Journal of Special Education

Career Development for Exceptional Individuals

Education and Training in Mental Retardation

Exceptional Children

Exceptionality: A Research Journal

International Journal of Disability, Development and Education

Journal of Autism and Developmental Disorders

Journal of Deaf Studies and Deaf Education

Journal of Early Intervention

Journal of Learning Disabilities

Journal of Special Education

Journal of Speech and Hearing Research

Journal of the Association for Persons with Severe Handicaps

Learning Disability Quarterly

Mental Retardation

Remedial and Special Education

Research in Developmental Disabilities

Volta Review

Databases

Conducting a review of literature can be exhausting; however, the development of computerized databases has eased the process. For an overview of various databases, look in OCLC FirstSearch (which is a search engine for various databases). FirstSearch lists various databases by topic, including one for education. That list can be found at: http://www.oclc.org/firstsearch/databases/bytopic.htm#education. The main databases are ERIC, Education Index/Abstracts/Full Text, PsycINFO, and psycARTICLES (see Table 3.2 for brief descriptions of the available databases). The databases can generally be searched for free at many libraries. If you do not have access to such a library, then they can be searched on-line,

Table 3.2   Electronic Databases Useful for Special Education Research

Databases, Web addresses, and Descriptions

ERIC (Educational Resources Information Center): Contains over one million abstracts of journal articles and research reports on education-related topics; some full text documents are available. Web address: www.eric.ed.gov. ERIC is also available at many libraries or on CD-ROM. Most ERIC documents are available in print or microfiche in libraries. If the library offers E*Subscribe, you can get electronic versions of the documents for free. If not, you can go to the E*Subscribe service at www.edrs.com where you can purchase paper or electronic copies. If you do not have access to such a library, print copies of journal articles can be purchased through such article reprint services as Ingenta at www.ingenta.com.

Exceptional Child Education Resources: ERIC also maintains a database for the Council on Exceptional Children called ECER. Web address: http://ericec.org/ericecer.html. It contains only citations and abstracts, not full text.

Education Abstracts Full Text: Indexes about 500 core journals and monographs in education. The Full Text version of this database contains a mixture of abstracts and full text for many journals published since 1994. Web address: http://www.hwwilson.com/databases/educat.cfm

PsycINFO: This is a product of the American Psychological Association; however, both members and nonmembers can search the database and purchase articles. Web address: http://www.apa.org/psycinfo/about/questions.html#1

PsycARTICLES: This is a product of the American Psychological Association, and it includes the full text articles of 49 journals related to psychology. Web address: http://www.apa.org/psycarticles/. The database can be searched by American Psychological Association members and by nonmembers (for a small fee).

but there is generally a fee associated with obtaining documents this way. Cooper and Hedges (1994) provide a comprehensive review of literature search sources that furnish access to journals, books, unpublished technical reports, conference papers, and government publications. An excellent resource guide and process is also offered for identifying fugitive literature.

An essential first step in the process is generating a list of key words that will guide the search through the various written and electronic references. These key words are topic-oriented or subject-oriented and are used to navigate indexes to the resources to identify relevant articles, reports, texts, and so on. Identifying key words is an emergent process. The researcher may start by generating the key words based on experience and previous readings. After some useful references have been located, the researcher may modify the list by dropping those that did not yield appropriate citations and adding new words suggested by other authors. The development of key word lists is made easier by consulting various thesauri linked to reference indexes, such as the *Thesaurus of ERIC Descriptors* (Houston, 2001) and the *Thesaurus of Psychological Index Terms* (American Educational Research Association, American Psychological Association, & the National Council on Measurement in Education, 2001).

The Web sites associated with each database contain excellent instructions and examples on how to improve your search results. Some databases provide the full text of articles and include instruction on how to access those articles directly on-line in the database. If there is not full text access, articles may be available through an article reprint service, such as Ingenta. If an article is not available at your own library or through one of these services, you can also ask the librarian to acquire articles through interlibrary loan.

REPORTING THE LITERATURE REVIEW METHOD

Many times authors do not include a description of the method they used for their literature review. This is problematic in that it is more difficult for the reader to judge the quality of the report without knowing how and where the authors searched, what terms they used in their search, and what rules they used for including or excluding studies. Thompson, Blount, and Thurlow (2002) provide an excellent example of reporting on their literature review method (see Table 3.3).

AGGREGATING INFORMATION FOR A LITERATURE REVIEW

Once located, the literature must be critically reviewed. The criteria presented at the end of each chapter in this book can be used to critically review special education research. Cooper (1989) provided another framework for critical analysis of research, as well as a variety of methods for aggregating the results of studies in a literature review. The purpose of this section is to provide insights into the analysis and synthesis of literature from two perspectives: integrated literature review and meta-analysis.

A study by Morrison and D'Incau (2000) provides an example of critically reviewing the existing research to inform the focus and design of their research. The authors were interested in the factors that contribute to the expulsion of students, particularly students with special needs, from school. They indicated that even though expulsion from school resulted in a substantial social and personal impact on students, "research focused on

Table 3.3   Method Used in Literature Review: An Example (Thompson, Blount, & Thurlow, 2002)

The primary purpose of the accommodations research conducted over the past three years has been to determine the effect of accommodations use on the large-scale test scores of students with disabilities.

Method

Four major databases were searched to identify research on test accommodations published from 1999 through 2001: ERIC, PsychInfo, Educational Abstracts, and Digital Dissertations. Research papers were also obtained at major conferences. Additional resources for identifying research included:

Behavioral Research and Teaching at the University of Oregon: http://brt.uoregon.edu/

Education Policy Analysis Archives: http://epaa.asu.edu

National Center for Research on Evaluation, Standards, and Student Testing: http://www.cse.ucla.edu/

Wisconsin Center for Educational Research: http://www.wcer.wisc.edu/testacc/

Several search terms were used. The terms were varied systematically to ensure the identification of all research on changes in testing, published from 1999 through 2001. Search terms included:

accommodation
large-scale testing accommodations
test accommodations
test adaptation
test changes
test modifications
standards-based testing accommodations
state testing accommodations

A decision was made to limit the selection of publications to empirical research. Included within this realm are studies with samples consisting of preschool, kindergarten through high school, and postsecondary students. The focus of the empirical research was not limited only to large-scale testing, but also included studies that incorporated intelligence tests and curriculum-based measures (CBM). We decided to focus on testing accommodations as opposed to instructional accommodations, although there is some overlap between these purposes in the literature. We did not include any conceptual or opinion pieces in this analysis.

this phenomenon is surprisingly sparse." They go on to cite research that demonstrates that the frequency of expulsion from school has increased significantly. Next, they present a discussion of the variables studied in previous research and the results. Finally, they identify a gap in the literature that would help practitioners better understand the phenomenon of expulsion. "What has not been examined in the literature is the extent to which the expulsion offense is predictable and therefore preventable." Next, the authors provide an in-depth discussion of variables that might influence the expulsion behavior and present a theory that might support the prediction process. Thus, their review of the literature demonstrated an important problem, what was known and unknown about a specific aspect of the problem, and identified where their research would fit in the picture.

THE INTEGRATED LITERATURE REVIEW

The integrated literature review is a process that requires the researcher to capture all the relevant literature, especially primary sources, critically analyze it, and produce a written representation of the current knowledge about a certain topic and conclusions that can be drawn from that knowledge base. Typically, the researcher looks at the evidence that supports various conclusions and areas needing further research, as well as research paths that have proven to be blind alleys. Further, the reviewer investigates the common and unique research approaches, exploring ways in which they were productive or unproductive. Cooper's (1989) guidelines can be used to determine potential threats to the validity of conclusions drawn from integrated reviews and for making decisions about the inclusion of articles in the review. The reader is referred to the section in this chapter that addresses meta-analysis for an example of the methods and criteria that might be used in developing an integrated literature review.

Edyburn (2000) provides an interesting modification of the Cooper approach to creating an integrated literature review. He noted that typically the integrated literature review is based on an in-depth review of a specific research problem across time. Yet for some research fields, such as special education, that are relatively young, it might be more useful to conduct an integrated review and synthesis of research reported in one year, asking the question, "What have we learned lately?" Edyburn focused on special education technology and conducted a comprehensive review of the literature published on special education technology in 2000. The steps used by Edyburn to select and code articles to include in the synthesis are summarized as follows:

- Review the journals indexed by ERIC and the holdings of up to three libraries for groups of journals that might contain research in the target problem area.

- Conduct manual searches of the tables of contents of the journals in the selected areas. Computer searches were not employed because of the time lag for entering the articles in the database.
- Select articles to review based on relevance, in this case, articles that addressed technology with students with disabilities in instructional settings.
- Code articles selected by category, for example, type of disability, age, type of technology.
- Conduct a meta-analysis.

Where the integrated research is based on a conceptual synthesis of research findings, the meta-analysis approach uses additional analyses to aggregate the findings of studies and reach conclusions (Glass, McGraw, & Smith, 1981). Meta-analysis is a quantitative synthesis of the existing research. Using primary source information from the literature, the meta-analyst establishes empirical evidence to increase understanding about a particular theory. Effect size is a statistic that is calculated to standardize the effects of treatments across studies. The exact way to do the calculations is explained in Chapter 10 of this text. Additional information can be found in Cooper and Hedges (1994) and Gall, Gall, and Borg (2003).

In meta-analysis, the researcher locates studies that have attempted to establish a causal relationship between some intervention and an outcome. Gersten and his colleagues have conducted several exemplary meta-analyses of special education research (Gersten & Baker, 2001; Swanson, 2001; Swanson & Hoskyn, 1998; Vaughn et al., 2000). The methodology for collecting data (research articles/reports) and conducting, analyzing, and interpreting the syntheses is presented in detail by these authors. Basically the process includes the following elements (Swanson, 2001):

- Conduct a search of on-line data bases (see those cited previously) using key words.
- Follow up with a manual search of relevant journals.
- Select articles using specific criteria, for example:
  o Study provides a good description of intervention that is targeted in the synthesis.
  o Study includes valid, reliable, objective measures of important dependent variables.
  o Study uses participants who are within the required age range, disability type, and so forth.
  o Study includes experimental and comparison group, preferably using random assignment or matched pairs.
  o Study provides sufficient information to enable the application of synthesis statistics.
  o Study occurred in required timeframe.

- Code selected articles and check for interrater reliability.
- Check the internal validity of the selected study (see Chapter 4).
- Conduct synthesis analyses (effect sizes).

Scruggs and Mastropieri (1998) present a meta-analysis of single-subject research. Their review provides a rationale for conducting meta-analyses and sets forth examples for conducting such reviews. One important point they make in support of meta-analysis is that it focuses on replications of individual research and creates a cross-research picture that may be more convincing than singular research initiatives. Finally, they provide a critique of the practice of meta-analysis in single-subject research.

There are both driving and restraining forces to using meta-analysis. While it does offer a systematic and objective method of aggregating the results of a large number of studies on a specific topic, this approach also suffers from the same threats that are faced in integrative research efforts, that is, the exhaustive nature of the retrieval process and the diversity of research quality in the studies selected. One problem with meta-analysis is that the literature tends to have a publication bias against neutral or negative studies, those in which the hypotheses failed to be supported. Thus, the meta-analyst and the consumer of the meta-analysis must be concerned about studies that have been conducted but not published because of neutral or negative results. Kavale (1984) and Guskin (1984) provide a useful discussion of the potential problems associated with employing meta-analyses in place of the integrated review procedures described by Cooper.

QUESTIONS FOR CRITICALLY ANALYZING THE LITERATURE REVIEW

1. Is the review current, using research that is recent enough to have applicability to the proposed research?

2. Is the review based predominantly on primary research, rather than on secondary or opinion pieces?

3. Does the review establish a need for the study?

4. Does the review provide a critical analysis of existing literature, recognizing the strengths and weaknesses of current research?

5. Is the research review objective, free from the biases of the reviewer?

6. Does the review provide enough information to support the research theoretical framework and research questions posed?

7. Does the review provide sufficient information to guide the research procedures, including the identification of subjects and selection of data collection and analysis processes, as well as appropriate reporting strategies?

QUESTIONS AND ACTIVITIES FOR DISCUSSION AND APPLICATION

1. What are the purposes of the literature review?

2. How do the three different types of literature sources compare?

3. What are the essential steps in the review process?

4. What are the commonalities and differences between the integrated literature review and the meta-analysis?

5. How does the literature review relate to the other steps in the research process—selection of sample, identification of the research design, information collection and analysis strategies, the discussion of findings, conclusions, and recommendations?

6. Conduct an integrated literature review and apply the criteria for critical analysis found at the close of each chapter in this text (or use those provided by Cooper, 1989).

4

Quantitative Research Methods: Questions of Impact

Quantitative research methods are commonly used to determine if an intervention led to a desired outcome. For example, Bottge (1999) wanted to determine if changes in mathematics instruction for middle school students with various types of disabilities would demonstrate improved test scores in computation, word problem, and contextualized problem tests following exposure to an experimental treatment. The intervention consisted of two video-based, contextualized mathematics problems that were used as the basis of instruction. The videos depict real-life problems that involve mathematics such as having enough money to buy a pet and to buy construction materials to make a cage for it. Students in the control group were given instruction in standard single-step and multistep word problems. After ten days of instruction, the researcher administered three different mathematics tests to see if the intervention had been successful.

IN THIS CHAPTER

- Quantitative research approaches are discussed in terms of the philosophical assumptions associated with them.
- The importance of quantitative methods that focus on measuring the impact of an intervention in special education is explored.

- Experimental, quasi-experimental, and single group designs are illustrated, along with an explanation of internal and external validity.
- For each approach, challenges associated with the use of quantitative designs in special education are discussed.
- Questions for critical analysis of each of the quantitative approaches are provided.

This chapter is designed for both the producer and the consumer of research. As a potential producer of research, your worldview, initial conceptualization of your research problem, and readings of related literature may have led you to conclude that a quantitative approach to research is the most appropriate method to address your research questions. As a consumer of research, you can use this chapter to identify the designs used in extant research studies and their corresponding strengths and weaknesses.

The most simplistic definition of quantitative research is the systematic collection of data that results in the quantification of characteristics of participants in the study. There are many types of quantitative research, three of which are explored in this chapter: experimental, quasi-experimental, and single-group designs. Four additional quantitative approaches are described in Chapter 5: causal comparative, correlational, single-case, and survey research approaches.

PHILOSOPHICAL ASSUMPTIONS ASSOCIATED WITH QUANTITATIVE RESEARCH

Quantitative research is rooted in the positivist/post-positivist paradigm, which holds that the purpose of research is to develop our confidence that a particular knowledge claim about educational or psychological phenomena is true or false by collecting evidence in the form of objective observations of relevant phenomena (Gall, Gall, & Borg, 2003). Research design can be defined as a process of creating an empirical test to support or refute a knowledge claim. The assumption is made that a researcher can capture "reality" or "truth" within a certain level of probability. Thus, if two programs are compared and a statistically significant difference is calculated on the outcome measure, then the "truth" is that one method produces higher levels of skills or knowledge than the other. The assumption is also made that the best way for the researcher to obtain this knowledge is to maintain a stance of objectivity, which is achieved by maintaining a distance from the people involved in the programs. Methodologically, the gold standard for this paradigm is defined by use of randomized experimental designs. (These terms are explained in the next section in this chapter.)

The researcher must maintain a careful balance because there are at least three types of information that must be considered when testing for impact: (1) evidence of implementation fidelity with respect to independent variable(s), (2) possible antecedent and mediating contextual factors, and (3) documentation of a change in the desired outcome (e.g., knowledge, skills, behavior, or attitudes).

Before researchers can establish the impact of an experimental treatment, they must provide evidence of what treatment was actually implemented. As Erickson and Gutierrez (2002) state, "A logically and empirically prior question to 'Did it work?' is What was the 'it'?—'What was the 'treatment' as actually delivered?'" (p. 21). At first, this may seem like a simple matter of providing sufficient description of the treatment as outlined by the researcher. However, treatments are often implemented by people other than the researcher and sometimes implemented in many locations simultaneously, thereby making it impossible for the researcher to verify that the treatment was implemented as intended.

The term "treatment integrity" means that treatments are implemented in ways that researchers intended. Ysseldyke (2001) identified the achievement of treatment integrity as one of the most difficult challenges for researchers in special education. Discrepancies occur for a number of reasons, ranging from variations in school policies across sites to individuals' desires to do only those things that appear to be less work than what they are currently doing. In their major study of a Learning Information System, Accelerated Math, Lemkuil, Ysseldyke, Ginsburg-Block, and Spicuzza (in press) reported that the system to track student performance and progress in mathematics worked better in some classes than in others. The extent to which the system worked was correlated directly with the integrity of implementation. Ysseldyke provides some insights into a researcher's experience with treatment integrity in his comments found in Figure 4.1.

There are a variety of ways for researchers to both increase the probability of treatment integrity and check to see how successful they are in that endeavor. First, researchers can train the implementers of the treatments very carefully. Second, they can collect data as to the integrity of the implementation in a number of ways. Erickson and Gutierrez (2002) suggest that a considerable portion of the research budget should be devoted to documenting the treatment as delivered. In order to provide an answer to the question "What was the treatment specifically?," qualitative research methods will need to be employed (see Chapter 6). Observation and teacher logs are common ways to gather evidence on the integrity of the treatment. Finally, researchers can analyze the data within groups to determine if there are patterns of differential impact in the experimental group. They would then need to determine what contextual factors other than the treatment might account for the differences in performance.

Researchers in the interpretive/constructivist and transformative paradigms have critiqued the post-positivist stance of valuing experimental, quantitative approaches on a number of principles. Three of these are discussed here as a way of stimulating thinking in the design of quantitative research studies. First, researchers who focus on the reduction of a complex social phenomenon to one or more numbers that can be statistically

Figure 4.1 An Experienced Researcher Looks at Treatment Integrity

A big concern in impact research is addressing the issue of intervention integrity. I have conducted many studies of students with disabilities, and I have supervised the work of a large group of colleagues and students conducting research in applied settings with students with disabilities. Repeatedly, we have much difficulty ascertaining the extent to which we got treatment integrity or intervention integrity or fidelity of treatment (these terms are all used) in the treatment groups we have compared. A classic example is a very large mathematics study we just completed. In one study, we had over 2,000 students in the treatment group. The results seemed "strange," and so we looked at indices of implementation. We looked at the numbers of mathematics problems students actually did. We learned that teachers had not implemented the treatment with 187 students. These were students who completed no practice problems and did no work in mathematics. Yet, had we left them in the experimental group, we would have significantly altered our interpretations.

My graduate students repeatedly tell me, "Jim, the teacher is really doing a lousy job of implementing the treatment," or "Mr. Smith could be effective doing just about anything," or "I really had bad luck with my study; my random assignment of teachers to conditions ended up with nearly all of the really effective teachers in the control group."

In our research on inclusion, we had a few teachers who engaged in "malicious compliance." They went through the motions of the treatments we put in place, but they sure looked and talked as if they had made up their minds that what we were asking them to do was really not a good idea and they were out to show us that this was the case. Well, sorry to harp on this for so long, but this is a message I share intensely now with those I train. I believe it is a critical issue that has impacted research findings in special education for a very long time.

—J. Ysseldyke,
personal communication,
March 23, 2003

analyzed run the risk of overlooking important variations in terms of implementation of treatment and characteristics of study participants that may have explanatory power for the results (Erickson & Gutierrez, 2002). Second, maintaining a distance from the group being studied may result in inaccuracies of understandings that could be corrected by having a closer, personal relationship with members of that group. Involving members of the targeted group in the study planning, conduct, and interpretation of results might lead to very different understandings. Finally, denial of treatment is a major issue that has been highlighted by transformative scholars. The Helsinki Declaration (Okie, 2000), an international accord for research ethics, includes in its 32 principles the statement that "the benefits, risks, burdens and effectiveness of a new method should be tested against those of the best current prophylactic, diagnostic, and therapeutic methods." This has been interpreted to mean that the control group should receive the best available alternative. Denial of treatment (as in the provision of no treatment) is only permissible if there is no known alternative treatment.

Importance of Quantitative Research Focusing on Impact for Special Education

Both political and methodological arguments can be used to affirm the importance of quantitative methods in special education. As noted in Chapter 1, federal passage of the No Child Left Behind (NCLB) Act includes provisions for evaluating the effectiveness of school-based practices using "scientifically based research" that uses "rigorous, systematic and objective procedures to obtain valid knowledge" (U.S. Congress, 2001). Thus, the political climate is supportive of the use of experimental or quasi-experimental designs, preferably with random assignment to groups. A related implication is that the probability of obtaining funding for innovative programs will be increased if this method is chosen. Methodologically, the claim is made that ". . . when well-specified causal hypotheses can be formulated and randomization to treatment and control conditions is ethical and feasible, a randomized experiment is the best method for estimating effects" (Feuer, Towne, & Shavelson, 2002, p. 8). Shavelson (2002) extends this point to conclude that ". . . the experiment is the design of choice for studies that seek to make causal conclusions, and particularly for evaluations of education innovations" (p. 18).

Experimental, Quasi-Experimental, and Single-Group Designs

A research design basically specifies who gets (or got) what treatment and when. It reflects selection, assignment, treatment conditions, and measurement. The issue is control in all of these domains. Researchers choose their designs based not only on their worldviews and research questions, but also on the logistics of their research settings. Three broad categories of research designs are discussed in this section: experimental, quasi-experimental, and single-group designs. We discuss one example of each type of design; the reader is referred to the general research methods texts referenced in Chapter 1 for more in-depth discussions of these design options.

To depict the features of each design, a coding system is used with the following symbols:

R—Random assignment of participants to conditions

X—Experimental treatment (intervention)

O—Observation of the dependent variable (e.g., pretest, posttest, or interim measures)

The independent variable is the variable that is manipulated (e.g., teaching strategy for teaching reading for students with disabilities). For example, a researcher could compare two teaching methods: new and traditional. The new method would be given to the experimental group and would be called the experimental treatment (X). The traditional method would be given to the control group. The dependent variable is the variable that is affected by (depends on) the independent variable (e.g., academic achievement, reading achievement gains in students with disabilities, or demonstration of acquired teaching skills).

Experimental Designs

True experimental designs use comparison groups and random assignment of participants to conditions or levels of treatment. One such design used in special education research is discussed here.

Pretest-Posttest Experimental Design. This design includes a control group and randomized assignment to two or more groups. Participants in each group receive a pretest before being exposed to the intervention and a posttest after the intervention. Bottge (1999) used a four-group design to investigate the effect of two different methods of teaching mathematics concepts to middle school students with various types of disabilities (learning disabilities, speech and language, emotional disability, and attention-deficit disorder). His independent variable was teaching method and the dependent variables were several measures of mathematics skills, including fraction computation, word problems, and contextualized problems. He cited research that suggested students can better generalize their mathematics skills to other situations if they have a sense that solving the problem is important and they have been provided with an opportunity to develop an intuitive, yet tentative solution. He combined this information to test the effect of contextualized problem solving (X_{CP}) with the more traditional teaching of word problems (X_{WP}). He was only able to randomly assign the students with disabilities from the remedial mathematics class to the two conditions. Therefore, this part of his study exemplifies a true experimental design. A simplified version of his design looks like this:

$$R \ O \ X_{CP} \ O$$

$$R \ O \ X_{WP} \ O$$

The Rs indicate that individuals were randomly assigned to one of the two treatment groups. The first O on each line indicates that a pretest was given to each group. The Xs indicate the treatment condition. The final Os indicate the posttest.

As mentioned previously, it is sometimes very difficult to implement a completely randomized experimental design because of logistical and ethical problems. Shavelson (2002) described his difficulties and eventual solution to problems associated with finding schools that would agree to participate in a random experimental study of his Success for All program. Initially, they offered each school $30,000 to participate in the study, but few schools agreed. They were either unwilling to take a chance on being assigned to the control group for three years or they could not afford the program costs beyond the $30,000 incentive. They were finally able to attract enough schools when they changed the offer to allow schools to use Success for All in either grades K-2 or 3-5, at no cost. In another study of preschool programs, they allowed the schools to use the program for free in either the 2002-2003 or 2003-2004 school year, with random assignment to the two start dates. Thus, the 2003-2004 group served as the control group in 2002-2003. The provision of treatment now or later made the use of randomized groups acceptable to the schools.

If experimenters are unable to randomly assign participants to conditions, then they may choose a quasi-experimental approach. Note that treatment conditions may be randomly assigned to groups.

Quasi-Experimental Designs

Quasi-experimental designs are those that are "almost true" experimental designs, except that the researcher studies the effect of the treatment on intact groups, rather than being able to randomly assign participants to the experimental or control groups. One quasi-experimental design commonly used in special education research is briefly described here.

Nonequivalent Control Group Pretest-Posttest Design

Bottge (1999) also had two classes of students who were enrolled in prealgebra. These students could not be randomly assigned as individuals to treatments because of the students' schedules; therefore, he randomly assigned the entire class to a treatment. This example illustrates a legitimate research design and also why experimental designs are difficult to implement in special education research because of barriers to randomization. (Bottge was lucky in that he was able to randomly assign the classes to treatments. In many school-based research studies, this is not possible, and it introduces additional threats to the validity of the study.)

As with experimental designs, quasi-experimental designs can involve more than two groups, and their control group can receive an alternative treatment (as opposed to no treatment). In the Bottge study, the prealgebra classes were assigned as intact groups to either the Contextualized Problem Group or the Word Problem Group. Thus, a simplified version of the design for this study was:

$$O\ X_{CP}\ O$$
$$\overline{O\ X_{WP}\ O}$$

Notice that there is no R in front of the two lines that depict the groups because the students could not be randomly assigned to conditions. The dotted line is used between groups in the symbolic representation of quasi-experimental designs (or nonequivalency).

If it is not possible to use comparison groups, researchers may choose to use a single-group design or attempt to control for group differences using statistical controls discussed later.

Single-Group Designs (Nonexperimental)

While this design does have many weaknesses, Gall, Gall, and Borg (2003) state that it is justified under circumstances in which the researcher is attempting to change attitudes, behavior, or knowledge that are unlikely to change without the introduction of an experimental treatment. One preexperimental single-group design commonly used in special education research is briefly described here.

One-Group Pretest-Posttest Design

This design is often used to test effects of curriculum interventions. For example, Englert, Mariage, Garmon, and Tarrant (1998) explored how well mildly disabled students who had participated in an Early Literacy Project had maintained their gains in reading performance over time. The researchers administered a pretest of students' reading performance, implemented the treatment, and then used a posttest of reading ability. This design is represented as follows:

$$O\ X\ O$$

Despite the weaknesses associated with this design, it may be necessary to use it in a situation in which it is not possible to have a control group because the school does not allow differential provision of services. It is especially important for the experimenter to examine the experimental conditions for rival hypotheses and competing explanations when using a single-group design.

Internal and External Validity

Within the post-positivist tradition, two tests of knowledge claims exist: (1) Is the knowledge claim true in this situation (internal validity)? and (2) Is the knowledge claim true in other situations (external validity or generalizability)? In the next section, we discuss the terms *internal validity* and *external validity,* ways to minimize threats to internal and external validity by using various research designs, and reasons why it can be difficult or impossible to apply these designs in special education research.

Internal Validity

Internal validity means that the changes that are observed in the dependent variable are due to the effect of the independent variable and not some other unintended variables (known as extraneous variables). If extraneous variables are controlled, then the results are assumed to be due to the treatment and, therefore, the study is said to be internally valid. Extraneous variables that are not controlled become rival or competing explanations for the research results. Nine of the extraneous variables that can threaten internal validity are defined with examples (Campbell & Stanley, 1963; Cook & Campbell, 1979).

Threats to Internal Validity

History: events that happen during the course of the study that can influence the results. Such events could include things such as changes in schedules/cycles or time of the school year at which the intervention is tried, for example, doing a study at the beginning of the year versus holidays versus at the end of the year.

Example: You are studying the effect of an integration program on people's attitudes toward individuals with disabilities. During your study, the mayor of the city declares it "Persons With Disabilities Capabilities Week," and the city is blanketed with a media campaign extolling the capabilities of persons with disabilities. This event could have an impact on people's attitudes, and it is not the treatment that you have in mind.

Maturation: biological or psychological changes in the participants during the course of the study, such as becoming stronger, more coordinated, or tired as the study progresses.

Example: You may be interested in the development of social skills in children with severe disabilities who are integrated into their neighborhood schools. Generally, as children mature (i.e., grow older), their social skills improve. How would you know whether the change in their social skills was the effect of integration or simply that the children had become more mature?

Testing: Participants may become "test-wise" by having taken a pretest that is similar to or the same as the posttest. Single-group designs are especially vulnerable to testing, history, and maturation because of a lack of a control group.

Example 1: The participants know what to expect, learn something from the pretest, or become sensitized to what kind of information to tune in to during the study because of their experience with the pretest.

Example 2: A researcher wants to examine a new process for improving general education students' attitude toward their peers with disabilities. A pretest is administered that asks several questions about their attitudes.

Instrumentation: another threat to validity in studies that use both pretests and posttests or in observational studies in which the researcher serves as the data collection instrument. It arises when there is a change in the instrument during the course of the study.

Raters/observers tend to get better as time goes by. Therefore the scores they obtain are different from those obtained earlier because of this learning.

Example: If a pretest and a posttest were used, it is possible that one test might be easier than the other. Thus, changes observed on the dependent variable would be due to the nature of the instrument and not the effect of the independent variable.

Statistical Regression: occurs when the researcher uses extreme groups as the participants (i.e., students at the high or low end of the normal curve).

Example: If you select students who score at the 25th percentile on an achievement measure and then test them again on a similar measure at the conclusion of the study, their scores could increase simply because of statistical regression, rather than because of your treatment. This is due to the role that chance and error play in test scores. We cannot measure achievement with 100% precision. Therefore, there is always an element of error in any measurement. If we have selected students from the bottom of the normal curve, then by chance it is most likely that their scores will go up. (Because they are already at the bottom, it is unlikely that they will go down.) Statistical regression is a particular problem in special education research, especially when researchers try to use the original test data by which the students were selected or identified for special education as part of the study.

Differential Selection: If participants with different characteristics are in the experimental and control groups, then differences in performance on the dependent variables may be due to group differences and not necessarily due to the treatment or independent variable. Quasi-experimental designs are especially vulnerable to differential selection because of the lack of randomized assignment.

Example: In Bottge's (1999) study, the prealgebra students were assigned to treatments as intact groups. A pretest of mathematics skills revealed that the students assigned to the experimental treatment group had a higher average score than did those in the control group. The author mentions this as a possible limitation in interpreting the study's results.

When differential selection is a threat to validity, it is necessary to collect as much information as possible about the background characteristics of the groups, so that the experimental and control groups can be compared for important preexisting differences.

Experimental Mortality: the effect of participants who drop out during the course of the study. It becomes a threat to validity if participants differentially drop out of the experimental and control groups.

Example: Suppose you have a new strategy for teaching reading to learning disabled students during a special summer program. The experimental group gets the new strategy, and the control group gets the traditional approach. During the study, many of the higher ability students drop out of the experimental group. At the end, the scores for the lower ability students are higher than those in the control group. Can you say that your program was successful? Maybe the answer is yes; maybe the answer is no. It could be that the program is successful for the lower ability students but is dreadfully boring for the higher ability students.

Experimental Treatment Diffusion: People will talk, and if the ideas sound interesting, they might just try to use them themselves. If the treatment group is in proximity to the control group, it is possible that the control group participants might learn about the independent variable and begin using some of the ideas themselves.

Example: Teachers might hear about a unique approach in the staff lounge and try it, not being aware that they are part of a study. This would cloud the effect of the treatment. The researcher should conduct observations of selected classes to determine if the control group has become contaminated and also conduct interviews with the participants to determine their perceptions of what they were doing. Wilson and Sindelar (1991) addressed this problem by assigning participants to treatment groups by school, so that within-school contamination would be avoided.

Compensatory Rivalry by the Control Group: Some individuals who think that their traditional way of doing things is being threatened by a new approach may try extra hard to prove that their way of doing things is best.

Example: This threat is also known as the John Henry effect, based on the folktale of the railroad worker who was pitted against a machine. John Henry wanted to prove that man was superior to the machine, so he tried extra hard. He did beat the machine, and then he died. (Let this be a warning to the control group.) The researcher should also be aware that control groups can sometimes become disgruntled or demoralized because they are not chosen for the "new" program, and they actually perform worse than normal.

Design Considerations and Internal Validity

One of the main reasons that research that uses an experimental design is held in such high regard is because the design itself controls so many of the threats to validity. For example, Bottge's (1999) study demonstrated the use of experimental design to control internal threats to validity with the students who were randomly assigned in the remedial mathematics class. By the use of randomly assigned experimental and control groups, he was able to control the effects of history, maturation, testing, instrumentation, and differential selection. His use of a pretest provided insights into initial characteristics of the participants and thus controlled for the effects of experimental mortality (i.e., he would know the characteristics of the participants who dropped out of his study and could compare them to those who completed it, if necessary). The researcher always needs to be aware of what is going on in and around the study that might influence results.

External Validity or Generalizability

External validity is the extent to which findings in one study can be applied to another situation (Gall, Gall, & Borg, 2003). If the findings from one study are observed in another situation, then the results are said to be generalizable or externally valid. The concept of population validity (i.e., to whom you can generalize the results) is described in Chapter 6. Bracht and Glass (1968) described another type of external validity, termed ecological validity, which concerns the extent to which the results of an experiment can be generalized from the set of environmental conditions created by the researcher to other environmental conditions.

Threats to Ecological Validity

Explicit Description of the Experimental Treatment: The independent variable must be sufficiently described so that the next researcher could reproduce it. This a common criticism of special education research, particularly as it applies to studies of alternative teaching methods or placements.

Example: Asking the question, "Is placing a student with a disability in an inclusive setting effective?" is really absurd without more definition because there are so many ways that inclusion can be implemented.

Good examples of descriptions of treatments can be found in Englert, Mariage, Garmon, and Tarrant's (1998) description of the Early Literacy Project, as well as in Bottge's (1999) description of the Contextualized Problems Treatment.

Multiple-Treatment Interference: If participants receive more than one treatment, then it is not possible to say which of the treatments or which combination of the treatments is necessary to bring about the desired result.

Example: Fuchs, Fuchs, and Thompson (2002) describe three methods of teaching reading for kindergartners with disabilities in mainstream classrooms. The treatment consisted of two main parts: (1) Phonological Awareness (PA) or the capacity to blend, segment, rhyme, or in other ways manipulate the sounds of spoken words and (2) Peer-Assisted Learning Strategies for Kindergartners (PALS), a beginning decoding program. The researchers wanted to tease out the effects of using PA and PALS; therefore, they had three groups: one group that received only PA, a second group that received PA and PALS, and the control group used the standard language arts curriculum.

Hawthorne Effect: The idea of receiving special attention, of being singled out to participate in the study, may be enough motivation to change behavior. The Hawthorne effect derives from a study at the Western

Electric Company (Roethlisberger & Dickson, 1939) of changes in light intensity and other working conditions on the workers' productivity. The researchers found that it did not matter if they increased or decreased the light intensity; the workers' productivity increased.

Example: Suppose a group of parents were selected to participate in a new study to enhance their skills for helping their children with their homework. If parents have experienced a high level of frustration in the past, they might be delighted to have any kind of guidance in the provision of homework help. Thus, the treatment itself might be less relevant than just knowing they were in a study focused on a problem they really want to solve.

Novelty and Disruption Effects: A new treatment may produce positive results simply because it is novel, or the opposite may be true. A new treatment may not be effective initially because it causes a disruption in normal activities, but once it is assimilated into the system, it could become quite effective.

Example: In total inclusion schools, teachers and administrators often express a high degree of concern over the implications of having children with severe disabilities in their "regular" education classes. This concern can have a deleterious effect on the success of the inclusion program, quite apart from the actual strategies being used in the inclusion process.

Experimenter Effect: The effectiveness of a treatment may depend on the specific individual who administers it (e.g., the researcher or the teacher). The effect would not generalize to other situations because that individual would not be there.

Example: This can be a problem when volunteer teachers are used in the study because they may be selected due to their willingness to accept students with disabilities in their classes. In Bottge's study (1999), the special needs teacher chose to teach the remedial contextualized problem group because she wanted the opportunity to approach problem solving in a new way. In the Fuchs et al. (2002) study, the teachers were randomly assigned to the treatment and control groups. In the Englert et al. (1998) study, one teacher agreed to use the experimental approach because she thought it was a more exciting approach to teaching and learning than her former attempts to deliver literacy instruction which she characterized as boring or not meeting the needs of her individual students.

Pretest/Posttest Sensitization: Participants who take a pretest or posttest may perform differently from students who never take pretests or posttests. Students who take a pretest may be more sensitized to the treatment than individuals who experience the treatment without taking a pretest. This is especially true for pretests that ask the participants to reflect on and express their attitudes toward a phenomenon.

Example: Students in regular classrooms might be asked, prior to a study of peer tutoring for students with disabilities, "How do you feel about working with students who have disabilities?"

Posttest sensitization is similar to pretest sensitization in that simply taking a posttest can influence a subject's response to the treatment.

Taking a test can help the subject bring the information into focus in a way that participants who do not take the test will not experience. So, in the next replication, if the test is not given, the results may be different. Potential adopters need to know this.

Other Threats to Validity

Two other threats to validity deserve mention here because of their prevalence in special education research because individualization and modifications are part of the special education culture. The first is **treatment fidelity,** in which the implementer of the independent variable (e.g., a teacher, counselor, or administrator) fails to follow the exact procedures specified by the investigator for administering the treatments (Gall, Gall, & Borg, 2003). Researchers should try to maximize treatment fidelity by providing proper training and supervision and to assess it by observations or teachers' logs.

Englert et al. (1998) trained the teachers in the experimental techniques and provided opportunities to practice the strategies prior to implementing them in the study. In addition, they conducted weekly on-site observations and gave feedback to the teachers on a regular basis. They also had biweekly meetings with the teachers in small groups to share teaching experiences.

In the Fuchs et al. (2002) study, they gave the teachers monthly calendars and asked the teachers to record the activities they implemented and when they did them. They also used an observational checklist, and staff rated the teachers on how well they implemented the strategies. The staff who did the observations had been trained to a level of 100% agreement, using videotapes prior to the classroom observations.

The second problem concerns the **strength of the experimental treatment.** An experiment to determine the effectiveness of an innovative teaching strategy can last for a few hours, days, weeks, months, or years.

It is not reasonable to expect that students' learning and attitudes can be impacted by an experiment of short duration. This does not mean that the approach is not effective, but simply that it was not tried long enough. Change with special education students is often slow. Usually students in need of special education services are identified because they are progressing slowly. Measures must be sensitive to small changes and be taken over long time periods to show effects. Another similar challenge is that sometimes the effect of the intervention is not realized for some time after the intervention, after a second intervention that adds the missing piece.

Challenges to Using Experimental Designs in Special Education

Special education students are very heterogeneous, as are the settings in which they receive services. Many challenges face the special education researcher who would like to use an experimental design. Several of these factors are discussed in Chapter 6 in a discussion of the protection of human participants in research, including the distribution of students in diverse settings, school policies restricting differential treatment, difficulty in identifying appropriate comparison groups, small sample sizes, sampling bias, and ethical considerations. Feminists and other transformative researchers have raised questions about the ethics of depriving one group of participants (the control group) of a treatment that is expected to have positive effects (Guba & Lincoln, 1989; Reinharz, 1992). Because of these problems, some researchers have turned to single-subject designs (described in Chapter 5) and qualitative designs (see Chapter 6).

Feuer et al. (2002) recognize that experimental designs are not always feasible. They provide the example of studying the effect of teacher salary on drop-out rates and suggest that teachers would reject the practice of assigning them randomly to different salaries.

Questions for Critically Analyzing Experimental, Quasi-Experimental, and Single-Group Designs

Internal Validity

1. History. Could events (other than your independent variable) have influenced the results?

2. Maturation. Could biological or psychological changes in your participants (other than those associated with your independent variable) have influenced the results?

3. Testing. Could the participants have become "test-wise" because of the pretest?

4. Instrumentation. Was there a difference between the pretests and posttests?

5. Statistical Regression. Were extreme groups used?

6. Differential Selection. Did the experimental and control groups differ in ways other than exposure to the independent variable?

7. Experimental Mortality. Did participants drop out during the study?

8. Experimental Treatment Diffusion. Were the treatment and control groups close enough to share ideas?

9. Compensatory Rivalry by the Control Group. Did the control group try extra hard? (Were they disgruntled or demoralized?)

External Validity (Ecological Validity)
(See also the section on Population Validity in Chapter 8.)

1. Was the experimental treatment described in sufficient detail?

2. Were multiple treatments used? Did they interfere with each other?

3. Was the Hawthorne effect operating?

4. Was the treatment influenced by being novel or disruptive?

5. What was the influence of the individual experimenter?

6. Were the participants sensitized by taking a pretest or posttest?

Other Criteria

1. Were steps taken to ensure the treatment was implemented as planned?

2. What was the influence of the strength of the treatment?

3. Was anyone denied treatment? Was it ethical to deny the treatment to the control group? Was the best known available treatment provided to members of the control group?

4. Was the community impacted by the results of the study involved in the decision to participate in the study? Did they agree to be in either the experimental or control group? Were they fully informed as to the consequences of participation?

5. If the study reveals superior outcomes for members of the experimental group, what is the moral responsibility of the researchers and program personnel to attend to the deficits that are documented in the control group?

QUESTIONS AND ACTIVITIES FOR DISCUSSION AND APPLICATION

1. Find a study that used an experimental design that is related to a topic of interest to you. For that study: (1) identify the research approach that is used, (2) identify the independent and dependent variables, (3) draw the design that was used, and (4) critique the study, using the appropriate criteria.

2. Find a study that did not use an experimental design. Redesign the study so that it could be an experimental example. Discuss problems in the redesign and how you would address those.

3. Using the proper symbols (R, X, and O), draw the design for the following study.

   Fuchs, Fuchs, and Fernstrom (1992) addressed the problem of reintegrating special education students into mainstream classrooms. Their purpose was to implement and validate a process by which pupils with mild and moderate disabilities (learning disabilities, behavior disorders, and language impairments) could be transitioned into regular mathematics education classes. Their experimental treatment was a process for readying students to transition, using a curriculum-based measurement system that included goal setting, repeated measurement on goal material, feedback to the teachers to adjust their instructional programs, and transenvironmental programming that included skill training for the transitioning student. Their dependent variables included mathematics achievement scores, time spent in special education mathematics, and teachers' ratings of the students and the program. They had three groups of students: students in special education mathematics classes who received the experimental treatment and were transitioned into regular mathematics classes, control students in special education mathematics classes who did not receive the treatment and followed the school's typical process for reintegration, and Low Achieving Peers (LAPs) who were identified by their teachers as representing their lowest acceptable mathematics group in the regular mathematics classroom.

Based on statistical analysis, the authors concluded that the experimental students' pretreatment to posttreatment performance improved significantly as compared to the control group. Further analysis indicated that the experimental group's improvement occurred while the students were in the experimental treatment condition (i.e., preparing for transition) and that their progress ceased after they entered the regular education classes.

4. Apply the questions for critical analysis to the extent possible to the Fuchs et al. (1992) study previously described in number 4. If sufficient information is not given in the summary of the study, explain how the authors could have addressed the threats to validity relevant to this design.

5. Recall the ethical concerns discussed earlier in this chapter in terms of: (1) problems associated with focusing on the reduction of a complex social phenomenon to one or more numbers that can be statistically analyzed which creates a risk of overlooking important variations in terms of implementation of treatment and characteristics of study participants that may have explanatory power for the results (Erickson & Gutierrez, 2002), (2) maintaining a distance from the group being studied may result in inaccuracies of understandings that could be corrected by having a closer, personal relationship with members of that group (involving members of the targeted group in the study planning, conduct, and interpretation of results might lead to very different understandings), and (3) denial of treatment and the Helsinki Declaration (Okie, 2000) that "the benefits, risks, burdens and effectiveness of a new method should be tested against those of the best current prophylactic,

diagnostic, and therapeutic methods." This has been interpreted to mean that the control group should receive the best available alternative. Denial of treatment (as in the provision of no treatment) is only permissible if there is no known alternative treatment.

Using these three ethical concerns, critique an experimental research study. Support your conclusions with evidence from the article.

5

Other Quantitative Approaches: Causal Comparative, Correlational, Single-Case, and Survey Research

Quantitative approaches to research other than randomized or matched experiments have great value for special educators and the people they serve. Shavelson (2002) recognized that correlational and descriptive research is essential in theory building and in suggesting variables worthy of inclusion in experiments. They can explore variables that go beyond overall program impacts. In contexts in which experiments are impossible to implement, correlational or descriptive studies can provide valuable insights.

IN THIS CHAPTER

- Four other quantitative approaches to research are explained and illustrated with examples from special education contexts, including causal comparative, correlational, single-case designs, and survey research.

- For each approach, strategies and challenges associated with the use of quantitative designs in special education are discussed.
- Questions for critical analysis of each of the quantitative approaches are provided.

CAUSAL COMPARATIVE AND CORRELATIONAL RESEARCH

The principal announced to the faculty that the school would participate in a research study to compare the effect of a new strategy for teaching reading to learning disabled and nondisabled students. In order to control for differential selection effects, all the names of the students in the school would be put in a hat and then randomly assigned to the learning disabled and nondisabled groups. Of course, this example is absurd. You cannot assign people to different disability conditions. There are many characteristics of individuals besides presence or absence of a disability that are not manipulable, such as existing abilities or attitudes, gender, ethnicity, age, conditions of living, or parents' background.

When studying such characteristics, a researcher can use a causal comparative or correlational approach. These types of research are quite common in special education research because of the frequency of comparison of persons with disabilities and persons without disabilities. While both approaches explore cause-and-effect relationships among variables, neither involves the experimental manipulation of treatment variables; therefore, the results cannot be used as proof of a cause-and-effect relationship. For example, blind children were compared with sighted children for their ability to identify vocal expressions of emotion (Minter, Hobson, & Pring, 1991). When the researchers found that the sighted children were more successful in correctly identifying the emotions, they did not conclude that blindness causes an inability to recognize emotions. Rather, they explored alternative (competing) explanations, such as cognitive differences, age, and time spent in residential schooling. In both types of research, it is important not to assume causality and to explore alternative hypotheses for explaining the study's results.

The main difference procedurally between causal comparative and correlational research is in the way the independent variable is operationalized and the types of analyses that are done with the data. In causal comparative research, the researcher makes group comparisons (e.g., hearing vs. deaf) and thus typically uses statistics that reveal whether a statistically significant difference exists between the groups. Correlational research provides an estimate of the magnitude of a relationship between two or more variables (e.g., relationship between

---

Box 5.1   Causal Comparative Research

Steps for Conducting Causal Comparative Research

Step 1. Identify a research problem or question.
Step 2. Select a defined group and a comparison group.
Step 3. Collect data on relevant independent and dependent variables and on relevant background characteristics.
Step 4. Analyze and interpret the data.

---

degree of hearing loss and academic achievement) and therefore uses correlational statistics.

A study of early literacy by Englert, Mariage, Garmon, and Tarrant (1998) provides an example of the steps in conducting causal comparative research. They identified their research question as: How effective is the Early Literacy Program approach for readers who entered school with differing levels of literacy knowledge? For this problem, the children were divided into four different levels of literacy knowledge based on pretesting their knowledge of initial word recognition ability.

Because causal comparative research compares the performance of two (or more) intact groups, the threat of differential selection must be addressed. If the two groups differ significantly on characteristics other than the independent variable (i.e., presence or absence of disabling condition), then it might be other (nonexperimental) characteristics that explain the difference between the groups. This is one of the reasons it is so important for researchers to collect and report information about the independent and dependent variables and on relevant background characteristics.

Englert et al. (1998) address the contextual and background characteristics relevant to their study in several ways. They provide a lengthy and well-referenced theoretical rationale for the early literacy intervention that was used with all of the children in the study. They also provide details as to the setting of the schools (urban in a high poverty area) and the children's disabilities (LD, emotional impairments, and mental impairments), grade level (first, second, and third), and gender (67% boys; 33% girls). The dependent measures were posttests on the SORT (a word recognition test) and on the Durrell Analysis of Reading Difficulty (Durrell & Catterson, 1980). The Durrell consists of having the students read a set of passages graduated in difficulty and thus provides an opportunity to measure reading proficiency in context as opposed to the SORT which simply requires the student to be able to recognize a word.

The Englert et al. team analyzed their data by comparing the four levels of readers on the SORT and Durrell at the end of the school year. They

---

Box 5.2

An Example - Defining the Groups in a Causal Comparative Study:
   Four groups of students were formed based on their scores on a test of their sight word recognition performance on the graded words lists of the Slosson Oral Reading Test (SORT; Slosson, 1963):

Level 1 readers: the lowest readers (nonreaders) who recognized 1 or fewer words on the initial administration of the SORT (0.0 reading-grade level).

Level 2 readers: students who were showing an emerging awareness of words (emergent readers) who recognized between 2 and 11 words on the SORT (0.1-0.5 reading-grade level).

Level 3 readers: students who recognized 12 to 31 words on the SORT (beginning readers; 0.6-1.5 reading-grade level).

Level 4 readers: students who recognized more than 31 words (early fluency; 1.6 reading-grade level and above). (Englert et al., 1998)

---

reported that gains were made across all four levels. However, Level 1 readers exhibited the lowest gains, followed by Level 2 readers. Results were generally consistent for both dependent measures. They concluded that students who began the year with the least literacy knowledge made fewer gains per year than slightly more advanced readers. They hypothesized that differences in background knowledge such as word and phoneme awareness and decoding might explain the differences in the children's achievement. Additional research is needed to determine what effective instructional strategies would look like for the lowest level readers.

Correlational studies can be either prediction studies or relationship studies. In prediction studies, the researcher is interested in using one or more variables (the predictor variables) to predict performance on one or more other variables (the criterion variables). For example, kindergarten test scores can be used to predict first grade test scores if there is a strong relationship between the two sets of scores. In prediction studies, it is important to be aware of any other variables that are related to performance on the criterion variable. Relationship studies usually explore the relationships between measures of different variables obtained from the same individuals at approximately the same time to gain a better understanding of factors that contribute to making up a more complex characteristic.

One advantage of correlational research is that several variables can be included in one study (more easily than in experimental or causal

---

Box 5.3   Steps in Correlational Research

Step 1. Identify an appropriate problem or question.
Step 2. Identify variables to be included in the study.
Step 3. Identify appropriate research participants.
Step 4. Collect quantifiable data.
Step 5. Analyze and interpret the results.

---

comparative designs). However, the choice of variables should be done using a theoretical framework, rather than a shotgun approach[1] (Gall, Gall, & Borg, 2003). When a number of variables are included, then more complex procedures such as multiple regression must be used for analysis.

Calderon and Greenberg's (1999) study of maternal and child adjustment in families with a school-age child with a hearing loss provides an example of how to conduct correlational research. They identified their problem as: What factors differentiate between those children and families that adjust well and those who do not in order to derive implications for more effective services? Previous research identified many variables that influence a family's adjustment, such as demographic characteristics, problem-solving skills, and presence of supportive relationships. The research participants were chosen from four school districts in a metropolitan area. The participants' children had to have a hearing loss that was severe to profound and be between the ages of eight and fifteen years.

The researchers collected quantifiable data for the demographic characteristics of the mothers and their children and to assess levels of stress and coping resources. For example, they used the Life Events Survey (Sarason, Johnson, & Siegel, 1978) to obtain a life stress index that indicates the overall negative life stress experienced by the mothers. A standardized problem-solving task was also conducted with the mothers to measure their ability to conceptualize alternative means of solving interpersonal dilemmas concerning their children. Children were independently rated by their teachers using questionnaires that assessed the child's socioemotional adjustment. The maternal personal overall adjustment was measured, as well their adjustment specific to their deaf or hard-of-hearing child.

Using multiple regression analysis, the researchers were able to control for such factors as the child's age, degree of hearing loss, and gender. They then tested for the effects of four coping resources (problem-solving skills, social support, utilitarian resources, and general and specific beliefs) on maternal and child outcomes. They reported two interesting findings. A significant relationship was found between the mothers' social support and their adjustment to their deaf or hard-of-hearing child, no matter how severe the loss or how high the negative level stress index. Also, mothers who scored as better problem solvers had children who were rated by teachers as having better socioemotional adjustment. The researchers hypothesized that this relationship may be due to the parents' provision of a model for their children in appropriate problem-solving techniques or giving their children direct instruction in problem solving.

Challenges and Paradigmatic Perspectives for Causal Comparative and Correlational Research

Causal comparative and correlational research are rooted in the philosophical assumptions of the post-positivist paradigm. Hence, they generally follow the philosophical assumptions associated with that worldview. Transformative paradigm scholars have raised important points to think about regarding these approaches. For example:

1. **Group Differences.** Causal comparative studies rely on finding differences between or among groups, while correlational studies depend on finding differences based on a characteristic that is manifested to differing degrees in different people. Thus, both are essentially looking for group differences. Transformative scholars suggest that researchers be aware of a potential bias in the literature that might lead the reader to believe that two groups are more different than they really are (Campbell, 1988; Shakeshaft, Campbell, & Karp, 1992). Campbell (1988) attributes the abundance of group difference research to two factors: (1) Group difference studies (and she was specifically talking about gender differences) are based on research designs borrowed from agriculture in which a study is designed to investigate differences in effect of treatments on variables such as crop size and quality. Such an approach fails to accommodate the needs of a researcher who is exploring the complexity of human beings in that it does not allow an examination of similarities and differences; and (2) it is common practice in research journals in education and psychology to publish studies in which statistically significant differences are found. Therefore, studies in which groups are found to be similar would not be published.

2. **Group Identification.** A second area of challenge for the researcher is the definition of who belongs in which group. This is a problem not only for disability research, but also for race/ethnicity and class. Problems associated with determining a person's disability condition, particularly with regard to learning disabilities, are discussed in the section on sampling in Chapter 8.

3. **Fallacy of Homogeneity.** Stanfield (1993a) discusses the fallacy of homogeneity – that is, assuming similarities within racial and ethnic groups on other characteristics, such as socioeconomic class. The parallel issue in disability research would be the caution that not all people who share a disability condition are the same. For example, not all blind people are alike, not only in terms of their ability to see, but also in terms of all the other characteristics that are used to describe a person and that influence

Box 5.4   Four Statistical Notes Concerning Correlational Research

Note 1.   It is important to realize that the correlation coefficient can range between plus and minus 1.00. The closer the correlation coefficient is to plus or minus 1.00, the stronger the relationship. A positive correlation means that the two variables increase or decrease together. For example, a positive correlation might exist between age and reading skills for deaf children, meaning that older children tend to exhibit higher reading skills. A negative correlation means that the two variables differ inversely, that is, as one goes up, the other goes down. For example, reading skills may be higher for children with less severe hearing losses; that is, as hearing loss goes up, reading skills go down. If the correlation coefficient is near zero, then no relationship exists. For example, lip reading ability might be unrelated to reading skills in deaf children.

Note 2.   When a correlation coefficient is squared, it tells you the amount of explained variance. For example, Kraus, Upshur, Shonkoff, & Hauser-Cram (1993) obtained a correlation coefficient of .45 between the intensity of parent group participation and perceived helpfulness of the peer social support for mothers of infants with disabilities. The conclusion is reached that mothers who attended more of the parent group sessions reported significantly more social support from peers. When the correlation coefficient is squared, it is .20, thus indicating the 20% of the variance related to gains in perceived social support from peers could be attributed to increased attendance at the sessions.

Note 3.   The order of entry for variables in multiple regression equations is important. When the predictor variables are correlated (a situation called collinearity), then the amount of variance that each independent variable accounts for can change drastically with different orders of entry of the variables. While there is no "correct" method for determining the order of variables (Kerlinger, 1973), the researcher must decide on a rationale for entry. If the researcher is interested in controlling for the effects of background characteristics before testing the effects of a treatment, then it makes sense to enter the background characteristics first (as did Calderon and Greenberg). Then the treatment variable will explain what is left of the variance.

Note 4.   The size of the obtained correlation coefficient is, in part, determined by the standard deviation of one or more variables entered into the correlation. If one or more variables has a small standard deviation, the coefficient will be low because of this and may not reflect the true relationship.

their knowledge, skills, abilities, or attitudes. Researchers must be sensitive to the many ways that people with disabilities can differ and include that in their work.

4. **Post Hoc Fallacy.** The post hoc fallacy states that causality is incorrectly attributed to a specific characteristic that differentiates members of two groups. For example, it is not the person's dyslexia that causes him or her to not be able to spell. If a person with dyslexia cannot spell, then the hypothesis could be tested related to appropriate instructional strategies that would be effective in teaching such a person that skill. If group differences are found, the researcher must be careful not to attribute the cause of the difference to the presence or absence of the disability. Rather, competing explanations should be explored to determine causative factors.

Questions for Critically Analyzing Causal Comparative and Correlational Research

1. Is a causal relationship assumed between the independent (predictor) variable and the dependent (response) variable? What unexpected or uncontrollable factors might have influenced the results? What competing explanations are explored?

2. How comparable are the groups in causal comparative studies?

3. Could a third variable cause both the independent (predictor) and dependent (criterion) variables?

4. After the initial groups were defined, were subgroup analyses conducted, based on age, sex, socioeconomic status (SES), or similar variables?

5. For correlational studies, what was the rationale for choosing and entering predictor variables? What was the percent of variance explained by the predictor variables?

6. If a predictive relationship was studied, was the test the only criterion used to select participants? Would combining the test with other screening criteria improve its predictive validity? (A predictive validity coefficient of about .8 is needed for an accurate prediction.)

7. What is the reliability of the criterion variable (as compared to the test used to make the prediction)? Is there a restricted range for the criterion variable?

SINGLE-CASE RESEARCH

Single-case research is an experimental technique where one participant (or a small number) is studied intensively. The focus of the study is to document the change in a specific targeted behavior that results from an intervention applied to a single individual. The intervention can then be applied to other individuals, but always with the intent of observing a change in that specific behavior in the person being studied. Single-case research should not be confused with case study research which is discussed in the chapter on qualitative methods (see Chapter 6). Specifics on how to design and conduct such research can be found in Barlow and Hersen (1984), Bullis and Anderson (1986), Odom (1988), and Tawney and Gast (1984). The work of Garfinkle and Schwartz (2002) will be used as a basis to illustrate the various single-case designs (see Table 5.1). They studied the effectiveness of a peer imitation intervention on four preschool children, three with autism and one with developmental delays. The intervention was implemented as part of the integrated classroom during regular small group activity. Data were collected at small group and free playtime to assess the implementation and effectiveness of the intervention. The behaviors of interest included peer imitation behaviors, nonimitative social behavior, and nonsocial engagement. Results of the intervention indicate that the participants increased peer imitation behaviors in small group and in free playtime settings. Increases were also seen in social behavior (both in proximity to peers and in number of interactions) as well as in levels of nonsocial engagement.

Two basic types of single-case designs will be discussed here: withdrawal and multiple baseline designs.

Withdrawal Designs or A-B-A-B

Withdrawal designs are based on the logic that if you can establish consistency in behavior before an intervention (A), then any change in behavior after the intervention is probably due to the treatment (B). In order to test that inference, the treatment is then withdrawn (A), the behavior is observed to determine if there is a change in the direction of the original baseline, and then the treatment is reinstated (B).

For example, Garfinkle and Schwartz (2002) measured the preschool children's number of peer imitation behaviors prior to the intervention (A) for children with autism and/or developmental delays. The teachers then gave instructions to the group that established one child as the leader and that all the other children should imitate the leader. The teacher then prompted the children to imitate the leader during the small group activity. During this intervention phase (B), observers counted the number of peer imitation behaviors that occurred. The intervention was then stopped to count the number of peer imitation behaviors that occurred without the intervention (A). If the researchers had asked the teachers to provide additional training to the children to encourage positive peer imitation, then this could constitute reintroduction of the intervention and would be labeled B. (They did not take this step in their reported research.) Peer imitations

Table 5.1   Single Case Study: Increasing Social Interaction for Children with Autism

---

Purpose: The researchers wanted to determine the effectiveness of a peer imitation intervention on increasing social interaction for children with autism and developmental delays.

Participants: Four boys between the ages of 5 years 5 months and 3 years 7 months were chosen to be included in the study. Three of the boys exhibited the symptoms of autistic behavior, and the fourth had been diagnosed as being developmentally delayed. All the boys exhibited difficulty in appropriate ways to initiate social interactions with adults and their peers. For example, one boy screamed to get attention, and another boy would say, "Come on," each time he wanted attention.

Independent Variable/Treatment: The intervention was small group peer imitation training. It had four steps: (1) The teacher instructed the small group that they would engage in an activity or game and they needed to pick a leader for the activity. The group then was supposed to imitate the leader. (2) The group decided who would be the leader. The children were asked to volunteer, and the teacher asked children to volunteer if they had not done so already. (3) The teacher gave encouragement and guidance to the students to follow the leader. (4) The teacher praised the children for imitating the leader. This continued until all members of the group had imitated the leader. When the activity was completed, the group engaged in another activity until every child had the opportunity to be the leader twice. The activity sessions lasted approximately 10 minutes each over a five-month period, approximately four times per week.

Data Collection: The researchers counted the number of peer imitation behaviors that occurred at least once per week during small group activities in order to assess the effects of the independent variable. The day was randomly selected but rotated so that the data represent a cross section of the behavior that occurred. Observations were made for 5 minutes. The timing of the observation within the small group period was also rotated so those data were not always collected during the same 5-minute period of the 10-minute treatment session. The data were recorded live using a 10-second interval observation system. The observers were cued to the intervals by an audiotape through an earphone.

Dependent Variables: The observers counted several behaviors including: (1) the number of peer imitations during small group session and (2) social initiations that were nonimitative verbal and nonverbal behaviors directed at peers in an attempt to gain a social response. Initiations were recorded only at the start of the interaction.

Reliability: Interobserver agreement was determined by having two observers independently, but simultaneously, code behaviors. Observers were trained before the baseline period. After studying the coding system and practicing with it, observers worked together until they achieved a high interobserver agreement rate (85%). During the experimental part of the study, interobserver agreement was monitored and calculated to be at a very high level (98%).

Source: Adapted from Garfinkle & Schwartz, 2002.

were scored when the target child copied a peer's behavior, in the same context as the original behavior and in a time immediately after the original behavior with or without prompting from the teacher. Data were collected once per week and continued over a five-month period.

This is a strong design because baseline data are provided, the behavior to be measured is specific and observable, observations were made over a considerable period of time, observations were continuous and frequent, and the researcher included a withdrawal phase to demonstrate the treatment's effectiveness. The definitions of the behaviors provided in the research article are not very specific. However, the researchers did report that they were able to reliably count the behaviors. Therefore, the implication is that they had a definition that was specific enough to count the individual behaviors. The observations were made weekly over a five-month period. They also demonstrated the effectiveness of the treatment by withdrawing the intervention and continuing to count behaviors.

Data analysis for single-participant designs typically takes the form of graphs and tables of frequencies, rather than the use of statistics that are designed to aggregate over a group of people in a study. Therefore, an example of single-participant data analysis is presented in this chapter rather than in Chapter 10 where more general analytic tools are described. A graph is displayed in Figure 5.1 that illustrates how data from an A-B-A-B design can be analyzed. The data in the graph are loosely based on the work of Garfinkle and Schwartz, but they are based on a fictitious student named Ariel.

Assume that the researchers in the fictitious study have counted the number of Ariel's peer imitative behaviors in a 5-minute period, weekly over four weeks. They then calculated that there would be thirty data recording opportunities for each 5-minute period (six 10-second intervals/minute for five minutes). They could then calculate the percentage of observation intervals in which the child demonstrated the target behavior. For example, Ariel showed 0% peer imitation during baseline. During the first week of intervention, the rate of the target behavior rose to 30% of the possible observation intervals in the 5-minute period. The graph illustrates a very low response rate for peer imitation during the baseline period, with a gradual increase and plateauing of the behavior through the intervention period. When the intervention is withdrawn, the behavior decreases and then increases again when the intervention is reinstated. Thus, the researchers in this fictitious study could conclude that the treatment was effective for increasing peer imitative behaviors for this individual student.

Multiple Baseline Designs

Sometimes it is not possible to withdraw a treatment because of ethical reasons or to observe a change in behavior after the treatment is withdrawn because a skill has been learned or an attitude has changed which

Figure 5.1   A – B – A – B Design Data Display

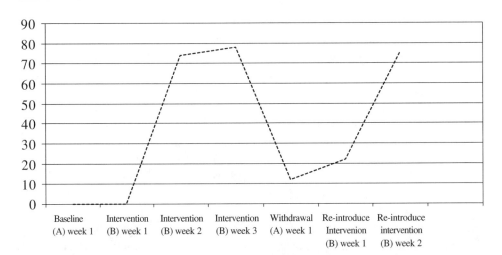

cannot be unlearned by removing a treatment. Under these conditions, researchers have turned to multiple baseline designs. There are three types: across behaviors, across participants, and across situations.

Multiple Baseline Across Behaviors. In this design, the researcher chooses two different behaviors (e.g., peer imitations and nonimitative social initiations) to target for change. A baseline is established for both behaviors, and then an intervention is implemented for the first behavior. If a change is observed in that behavior, then the intervention is applied to the second behavior. In some studies, the two behaviors are measured simultaneously to demonstrate the effect of the intervention across behaviors. This is what happened in the Garfinkle and Schwartz (2002) study. The observers counted both the peer imitation behaviors and the nonimitative social behaviors for the children. (Nonimitative social behaviors were defined as verbal and nonverbal behaviors directed at peers in an attempt to gain a social response.) This gives added credibility to the inference that the treatment is effective.

In a fictitious extension of the Garfinkle and Schwartz study, the researcher could have implemented a training program to increase both peer imitation and nonimitative social behaviors. If they had done so, the data resulting from that hypothetical study could be displayed as in Figure 5.2. This graph could be interpreted as supporting the effect of the intervention on both types of behaviors, as a very low level of responding is seen for both behaviors during baseline. Once the intervention is introduced, both behaviors tend to increase gradually and finally plateau after several weeks.

Multiple Baseline Across Participants. In this design, the researchers use one (or more) behavior(s) and try to establish a change using the same independent variable with more than one participant. Again, in the Garfinkle and Schwartz study, they implemented the treatment with four

Figure 5.2 Multiple Baseline Across Behaviors

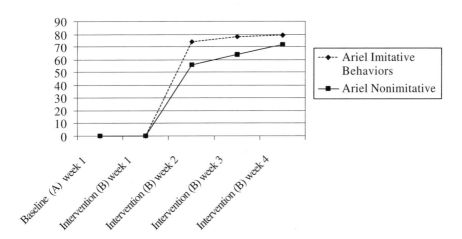

participants, thus replicating their results. A graph based on two fictitious students, Ariel and Zen, illustrates the typical method for displaying results in a multiple baseline across participants study (see Figure 5.3). In the fictitious example, the treatment seems to be more effective for Ariel than Zen. A critical reader might ask the following questions: What is the difference between the two children that might help explain the differential effects? What are the characteristics of the children in this study that might explain the effects, as opposed to generalizing it to other types of children?

Multiple Baseline Across Situations. In this design, the researcher chooses one behavior, one independent variable, and one participant and attempts to change that participant's behavior in two or more situations. For example, if you have a participant who does not complete her homework in mathematics and reading, you can choose completion of homework as the target behavior. The independent variable might be the use of token reinforcements for every day of homework completion. You would establish baseline for both behaviors and then implement the treatment for homework completion in reading class. Once a change in behavior has been observed and stabilized, the treatment can be implemented in the mathematics class.

In the Garfinkle and Schwartz study, the researchers measured behavior change during small group time as well as during free playtime. If the researchers had deliberately tried to change peer imitative behaviors in both settings, a sample graph, using fictitious data, such as that seen in Figure 5.4 could be used to display the results. The critical reader might ask questions about studies that use multiple baselines across situations such as: How are the two situations different? What kinds of activities typically occur in each setting? Is there equal opportunity for behaviors such as peer imitation to occur in both settings? Would an individual child

Figure 5.3   Multiple Baseline Across Participants

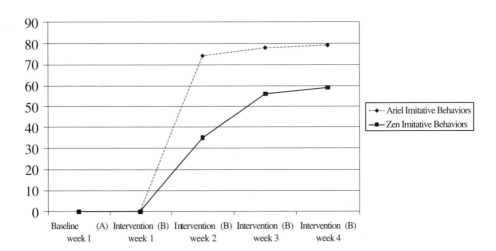

be more inclined to exhibit the target behavior in one setting or the other? Do the two settings (e.g., small group time and free playtime) always follow each other? Is there an ordering effect due to social engagement being more intense for a period of time, with a need for disengagement afterward?

Questions for Critically Analyzing Single-Case Designs

1. Is the behavior specific and observable (e.g., self-concept and anxiety are too broadly defined, although they can be operationalized in a specific, observable way)?

2. Does the researcher provide baseline data?

3. Are the observations as continuous and frequent as possible?

4. Is a series of observations made over some period of time in order to determine both the degree and direction of change?

5. Did the author investigate the reversal effect, that is, the removal of the treatment and return to baseline behavior? Did the researcher then reinstate the treatment and observe improved behavior? (Note: It is not always possible to reverse a learned behavior; therefore, the researcher may choose to use a multiple baseline design as an alternative.)

6. Does the researcher repeat the procedure with three or four participants with similar results (multiple baselines across participants)? Can the effect be attributed to the uniqueness of the participant?

Figure 5.4 Multiple Baseline Across Situations

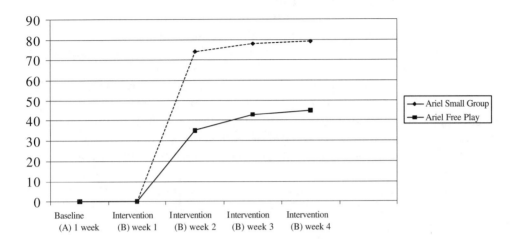

7. Does the researcher use multiple baselines across behaviors?

8. Does the researcher use multiple baselines across situations?

SURVEY RESEARCH

Survey research can be thought of as either a method of data collection that can be used with other research designs (e.g., causal comparative or correlational designs) or a descriptive research design in itself. Because of the design issues related to survey research, we chose to discuss this approach to research in this chapter on quantitative methods rather than in the data collection chapter (see Chapter 9). (It should be noted that surveys that collect qualitative data by such means as records review or interviews are discussed in Chapter 6.) Surveys can be used to help people tell their stories, too.

Survey research has the advantage of allowing the researcher to collect information from a large number of people, in contrast to experimental research in which the size of the sample is usually more limited. Survey research can be associated with disadvantages if it relies on self-report or reports of uninformed proxies, is retrospective, or suffers from response bias from poorly worded questions. We do not attempt to teach the reader how to design a survey research study here because many good texts are available for that purpose (see Dillman, 2000; Fowler, 1993; Gall, Gall, & Borg, 2003). Rather, we concentrate on such issues related to survey research with special populations as who to collect data from, how to do it, design considerations, and response rate.

Two major surveys involving children and youth with disabilities serve as examples of conducting research with special education populations.

First, the National Longitudinal Transition Survey of Special Education Students was conducted by SRI from 1985 through 1993. SRI is currently conducting the National Longitudinal Transition Study-2 (NLTS2) for the Office of Special Education Programs (OSEP), U.S. Department of Education (Wagner, 2003). The design of NLTS2 reflects a careful alignment with the first National Longitudinal Transition Study (NLTS). By including many of the same research questions and data items that appeared in NLTS, the new study will provide important information about the ways in which secondary education and results and postschool experiences have changed for youth with disabilities in the previous decade or more.

NLTS2 is a ten-year study of the experiences of young people who were thirteen to seventeen years old and receiving special education in the 2000-2001 school year. The sample size is approximately 13,000 youth who were chosen to be a nationally representative sample of youth with disabilities in that age group for that group as a whole, as well as representing each of the federal special education categories for disabilities (see Chapter 8).

The NLTS2 conceptual framework and research questions are designed to allow analyses of the relationships between NLTS2 data and data generated by OSEP's Special Education Elementary Longitudinal Study (SEELS). This six-year study, following a group of students in special education (6 to 12 years old as of September 1, 1999), is assessing the experiences and achievements of students as they transition from elementary school to middle school and middle school to high school. The overlap of NLTS2 and SEELS students in high school will permit statistically linking the early school factors measured in SEELS with postschool experiences measured in NLTS2.

Second, the Annual Survey of Hearing Impaired Children and Youth is conducted by Gallaudet University's Center for Assessment and Demographic Studies. Data collected by the survey include demographic, audiological, and educationally related information about the students and program information about the schools they attend (Gallaudet Research Institute, 2001). The 1999-2000 Annual Survey database contains information on 43,861 school-age children (ages birth to 21), reported as attending either a residential school for deaf students, a day school for deaf students, or a local school (public or private) designed to serve hearing students.

Design Considerations

In survey research, the researcher has a choice from among simple descriptive, cross-sectional, and longitudinal approaches. The simple descriptive approach is a one-shot survey for the purpose of describing the characteristics of a sample. The cross-sectional design involves examining the responses of different groups of participants at one point in time (e.g.,

---

Box 5.5   Steps in Conducting Survey Research

Step 1. Decide on the survey design: simple descriptive, cross-sectional, or longitudinal.

Step 2. Design the questionnaire:
Outline the topics to be covered
Decide on the degree of structure in the questions (open or closed-ended)
Generally avoid psychologically threatening questions
Avoid double negatives, jargon, and biased questions
Decide on the format for the questionnaire

Step 3. Pilot test the questionnaire with representatives of target participant group: Select a pilot group; ask the group to review the instrument and give you feedback on it; revise as necessary (tailor the survey content and procedure to the target participant)

Step 4. Prepare a letter of transmittal

Step 5. Conduct the survey
Send out an advance letter if possible
Enclose the questionnaire and transmittal letter for mail surveys
Supervise the data collection
Send at least three follow-ups to nonrespondents
On third follow-up, send new survey
Control processing errors (clean the data set)
Analyze and report the results

---

first, third, and fifth grade students). Longitudinal designs survey one group or cohort of participants at different points in time (e.g., one year after leaving school, two years after leaving school, and three years after leaving school). Cross-sectional designs have the advantage of collecting information in a shorter time frame. The disadvantage is that the experience of the students who are now in the fifth grade may have been different in the first grade, as compared to students who are now in first grade. The advantage of longitudinal research is that it follows the same (or highly similar) participants over a period of time. The disadvantage is that it takes a long time to do it, and conditions may not be the same for students who are graduating three years later. Short of a time warp, there is no easy solution to these problems, other than acknowledging the limitations of individual studies.

In longitudinal research in special education, it is important to be aware that progression from one grade to another may not be the most appropriate way to measure passage of time. The students' Individual Education Plans often define goals for individual growth rather than progression from grade to grade; thus, longitudinal research with these populations would more appropriately focus on age, rather than grade.

Sources of Information

When you conduct a survey, you can collect information from the participants themselves, from another person (such as a parent or responsible adult), or by examining records (such as a student's file). Your choice of information source depends on the nature of the person's disabling condition and the type of information you are collecting (DeStefano & Wagner, 1991). If the child has moderate to severe disabilities, it may be necessary to ask the parent or responsible adult for the information (or, in the case of deaf students, to use a qualified interpreter). When youths are still in school, the parent or responsible adult may be the best source of information because he or she still has frequent contact with the child. The type of information also influences the choice of information source. For example, parents would most likely be aware of whether their older child is employed and what type of job he or she has. They may even be aware of how much the child is being paid; however, parents are a less reliable source for attitudinal information such as the child's satisfaction with the job.

School records can provide good information in some instances, such as what classes the child actually took. For example, DeStefano and Wagner (1991) reported that parents may not be aware that their child took vocational training, though it is reflected on the school record. On the other hand, school records reflect a sizeable number of students who cannot be accounted for in terms of school completion. Such students are typically reported as "withdrawn," "moved," or "status unknown." Students in these categories accounted for more than 13% of secondary school dropouts with disabilities in the 1986-1987 school year (U.S. Department of Education, 1989). Even parents can be confused by what constitutes graduation from high school. The NLTS revealed that 60% of parents whose children had "aged out" reported that their children had graduated (DeStefano & Wagner, 1991).

Data Collection Methods

In survey research, the researcher has a choice of mail, telephone, personal interviews, e-mail or Web-based surveying, or a combination of these as a method of collecting data. Which method is used depends on the nature of the data collected, cost factors, and the size and characteristics of the sample. The NLTS2 is using multiple methods of data collection, including telephone interviews with parents and youth, surveys of school staff while youth are in secondary school, direct assessments of academic skills and knowledge, and collection of transcripts. It is often advisable to

---

Box 5.6   Steps specific to telephone or personal interviews

Step 1. Prepare for the interview:

Learn the local language that is used to describe the variables of interest to you.

If possible, hold an introductory meeting to share the purpose, discuss confidentiality issues, and get assurance that the person wants to participate. Then schedule the interview.

Review your interview guide and pretest your interview procedures.

If you are training interviewers, be sure they are very familiar with the instrument and procedures and allow them to practice until they can perform at the desired level.

Step 2. Starting and conducting the interview:

Start by establishing rapport.

Sequence questions from the general to the specific.

Ask for examples, contrasting views, and clarification.

Record the interview if possible and always take notes.

Step 3. Concluding the interview:

Ease into the conclusion by summarizing what you have heard.

Explain what you plan to do with the data.

Thank the person for participating.

Probe gently (Did I miss anything?).

Follow-up if possible with a phone call or letter thanking the person and asking for any needed clarifications.

---

conduct in-person interviews to supplement telephone interviews in areas with high rates of nonresponse.

Bowe (1991) adapted the mail survey method for use with blind participants. He sent the questionnaire to the participants and then telephoned, asking them to arrange for a sighted reader's assistance or to use a magnifying glass to read the print. He achieved a 49% response rate using this method. Freeman, Goetz, Richards, and Groenveld (1991) also conducted a survey with blind participants, but they used a lengthy individual interview that was fifteen pages long, in a semistructured format. They reported an 85% response rate and an interesting response to the methodology:

Nearly every interviewee told us they welcomed the opportunity that the intensive semi-structured interview offered them to share information and feelings, often for the first time. . . . It is doubtful that responses to a written questionnaire or standardized test scores (while useful) would have generated similar results. (p. 369)

Web-based Surveys

There is also a growing number of software development systems designed specifically for Web-based surveying (Solomon, 2001). Examples include Perseus's Survey Solutions for the Web, Creative Research System's The Survey System, and Survey Said™ Survey Software. These packages tend to offer features specific to survey research. Examples include managing the distribution of e-mail cover letters, built-in statistical analysis and reporting capabilities, and automatic tracking of people who have responded, coupled with the ability of sending out follow-up e-mail reminders to those who have yet to respond. They also have HTML editors that allow you to simplify and streamline the process of developing and formatting the question response fields.

According to Dillman (2000), there is an increasing trend toward self-administered surveys. This movement has been influenced by advances in technology including computer-assisted telephone interviews, e-mail, and Web-based surveys. As with any data collection technique, there are potential barriers to obtaining useful information. One threat associated with Web surveys is coverage – making certain that all possible respondent groups are represented in the survey sample frame. Obviously, persons without access to a computer could not be included, and thus, there most likely would be bias in the interpretation and use of the results. Dillman suggests that researchers use a mixed method survey approach to address this threat – using mail and telephone surveys and personal interviews along with Web surveys (Dillman, 2000).

E-mail and Web surveys are similar in that they both rely on the Internet and computers for the collection of information. E-mail surveys are much less interactive and restrict the options for responding to the survey. They are often text messages delivered as part of an e-mail or as an attachment to an e-mail. On the other hand, Web surveys present the researcher with a high level of creativity in designing the questions and response options. Drop-down lists of response choices make it possible to provide a variety of options and enable easy coding and analysis strategies. Web surveys also allow the researcher to scan in pictures or link audio or film clips to the survey, providing capabilities that could not easily be achieved with paper surveys.

The capacity to creatively design the survey may provide useful ways to adapt the survey to meet the restrictions that might be encountered in surveying a person with specific disabilities. Persons with low incidence disabilities–blindness, severe physical disabilities, and hearing impaired – may be able to respond more effectively to the Web survey. On the other hand, the technical sophistication of the survey may prevent some from participating. Again, the mixed-mode process suggested by Dillman may be the best answer for acquiring the amount and quality of information needed to answer the research questions.

Fortunately, along with the increased trend toward self-administered Web-based surveys, there has been an increase in the number of resources available for constructing, administering, and analyzing the surveys. All one has to do is conduct an Internet search to find resources for Web surveys. One such survey resulted in over 10,000 hits. We recommend that the researcher consult Dillman's (2000) 29 principles for designing and conducting Web surveys to help the researcher navigate these resources.

Response Rates

In survey research, a response rate is calculated based on the number of completed questionnaires or interviews, as compared to the number that were initially distributed or attempted. For example, Freeman et al. (1991) had phone numbers for 81 participants and completed interviews with 69 participants, for a response rate of 85%. In follow-up studies in special education, response rates range from 27% to 91%, with a reasonable expectation of 50% (Bruininks & Thurlow, 1988). Many factors affect response rate, but particularly in special education, the nature and severity of the youths' disability is a factor. DeStefano and Wagner (1991) reported a lower response rate for participants with milder disabilities and recommended pilot testing instruments and procedures as a way to increase response rates, that is, try out the questionnaire with a small sample to be sure it is appropriate for that audience.

Cook and colleagues (2000) conducted a meta-analysis of factors influencing response rates in Internet-based surveys. They found three factors that increased response rates. Follow-up contacts with nonrespondents, personalized contacts, and contacting sampled people prior to sending out the survey were the three dominant factors in higher response rates. Kittleson (1997), in a study of e-mail-based surveying, found it was possible to double the response rate with follow-up memos. As with mailed surveys, repeated follow-ups have diminishing returns and at some point risk irritating potential respondents without noticeably increasing response rates. Additionally, Dillman, Tortora, Conrad, and Bowker (2001) found that relatively plain Web surveys that load quickly resulted in higher response rates than "fancier" surveys that take longer to load.

Response rate is also influenced by the ability to locate respondents and obtain data (DeStefano & Wagner, 1991). When participants are in school, there is not much of a problem. Once the child has left school, there can be a problem trying to locate people through school records. Some schools do not record parents' names or students' telephone numbers, or they require parental consent to reveal students' names in special education. Sometimes you can use community agencies to locate individuals with moderate to severe disabilities, or you can locate them through student-friend networks, community colleges, adult education programs, former teachers, or neighborhood canvasses. When planning a longitudinal study, Edgar (1988) recommended getting permission to maintain contact before the student leaves school, obtaining the student's Social Security number and names and addresses of extended family members and close friends, and maintaining periodic contact with the students or the family.

Response rate influences the generalizability of the findings, in that there may be a systematic bias in terms of those who do not respond to the survey. It is important in survey research to conduct a follow-up of a sample of nonrespondents to determine how they differ from respondents. This can be done using school records in terms of background characteristics or by conducting a limited telephone interview with a small sample of nonrespondents, for example, 10%. These differences, if any, should be reported as part of the limitations of the study.

Challenges and Paradigmatic Perspectives in Survey Research

Survey research is generally rooted in the post-positivist tradition, with the exception of open-ended interviewing which is more closely aligned with the interpretive/constructivist paradigm. Transformative scholars have raised issues related to survey research that can stimulate researchers' thinking. For example:

1.   Concerns have arisen because surveys typically rely on responses to fairly simple questions that can be numerically coded. Thus, there is concern that complex issues will be oversimplified by reducing them to a limited number of questions and response options. Some researchers try to address this concern by asking many questions that attempt to get at some of the details of the events and by including participants' verbatim comments in the text. Some researchers have turned to interviewing as their data collection method because it allows for freer interactions between the researcher and the interviewee and includes opportunities for clarification and discussion (Reinharz, 1992).

2.   Concerns have also arisen related to the appropriateness of surveys as a method of data collection for diverse cultural groups. Smith (1993) noted that traditional national surveys typically are underrepresented for African Americans by a factor of ten, based on their frequency in the general population. This is important for disability researchers to keep in mind as the field becomes more cognizant of the impact of racial and ethnic diversity in the population with disabilities. Sampling strategies can be modified to increase the probability of contacting members of racial/ethnic minority groups, alternate contact methods could be used such as going through churches or neighborhood associations, or random digit dialing could be used for telephone interviews with a higher proportion of the sample chosen for exchanges in areas with high Black density (Mertens, 1998).

3. Language difference between the researcher and the respondent is another serious issue. An instrument can be translated into other languages, but a careful assessment of the translation is needed. Typically a process of back translation is used in which a native speaker is asked to translate the instrument, and then the instrument is retranslated into the language of the source document to ensure that the original intent was preserved. Problems can arise despite these measures because some concepts are very difficult to translate cross-culturally. Researchers must be careful to base their interpretations of data in a thorough understanding of the culture that produced them.

4. Transformative scholars have also raised concerns related to the influence of the researcher's theoretical framework on the questions that are asked. For example, Oliver (1992) provided a contrast in questions that represent a "blame-the-victim" theory versus an emancipatory theory for surveying people with disabilities. He used sample questions from the Office of Population Census and Surveys in Great Britain as examples of questions that locate the problem of disability within the individual. For example: What complaint causes your difficulty in holding, gripping, or turning things? He contrasted that question with one that reflects the location of the problem elsewhere. For example: What defects in the design of everyday equipment like jars, bottles, and tins cause you difficulty in holding, gripping, or turning them? In other words, some questions place the problem in the person and their disability, while other questions ask about what failures in society's response to the disability are the cause of problems.

QUESTIONS FOR CRITICALLY ANALYZING SURVEY RESEARCH

1. Are biased questions asked (e.g., leading questions, questions that give a clue to the right or desired response)?

2. What was the influence of self-reporting on the survey? (With self-report, the participant tells you only what he or she wants you to know. Omissions or distortions can occur.)

3. What was the response rate? Was a follow-up done of nonrespondents? Were they similar to or different from respondents?

4. Does the researcher ask too many questions and thus impose an unreasonable burden on the respondent?

5. What is the effect of the type of options provided (e.g., free response, closed-end questions, or "happy" faces)?

6. If the desired respondent was not available, who answered the survey? Adequacy of proxies?

7. How were answers recorded (e.g., taped, notes, or self-report)?

8. If interviewers were used, were they trained?

9. Was the survey cross-sectional or longitudinal? If the survey was cross-sectional, what is the effect of different students at each grade level?

Questions and Activities for Discussion and Application

1. For the following study: (1) identify the research approach that was used and (2) critique the study, using the appropriate criteria.

   Pollard and Oakland (1985) examined the relationship between fifteen family, psychological, and demographic variables and reading and mathematics achievement for deaf children at a residential school. The variables were chosen because they "were thought to represent important child-related characteristics which may have had some influence on children's academic development" (p. 69). No previous research or theoretical framework was used as a rationale for the inclusion of variables related to mathematics or reading achievement. For mathematics achievement, the significant predictors were IQ and size of weekly allowance (a proxy for socioeconomic status). The research basically told us that children with higher IQs and from higher SES homes achieve higher in mathematics. This study is an example of the shotgun approach that entered variables into the equation without controlling for background characteristics first.

2. For the following study: (1) identify the research approach that was used and (2) critique the study, using the appropriate criteria.

   In the comparison of blind and sighted children discussed previously, Minter et al. (1991) matched the children on sex and age. On the age variable, they selected sighted children who were eighteen months younger than the same-sex blind children because of evidence that cognitive development of young, congenitally blind children tends to be delayed by about eighteen months, compared with their sighted peers. The researchers also administered a vocabulary test to determine if there were group differences in language ability.

3. Critique the following study, using the questions for critically analyzing survey research.

   Shapiro and Lentz (1991) adapted the survey research methods for use with a sample with learning disabilities. They first contacted their participants by telephone to tell them that a survey was coming and then mailed the survey. They then recontacted the participants by telephone, interviewing them while they had the survey in front of them. They were able to get an 88% response rate six months after graduation and a 72% response rate for 12-month and 24-month follow-ups.

4. For the following studies:

(1) identify the research approach that was used and (2) critique the study, using the appropriate criteria

Study #1: Winterling (1990) taught vocabulary words to a participant who was mentally disabled. He used three different word lists, thereby showing that the treatment was effective on the learning of different words in the same participant.

Study #2: Winterling (1990) used a multiple baseline, across-participants design by expanding his treatment for teaching vocabulary words to three participants with mental disabilities or learning disabilities.

5. For the following study: (1) identify the research approach that was used and (2) critique the study, using the appropriate criteria.

Meadow (1967) compared deaf children of hearing parents and deaf children of deaf parents on a number of dependent variables. She controlled group differences by two means: matching and screening. She first screened the sample to eliminate those with deaf siblings, minority group membership, secondary disabilities, deafened after the age of two years, and deafness resulted from maternal rubella, Rh incompatibility, or anoxia. The students from the two groups were then matched according to sex, age, IQ test score, degree of residual hearing, and family size. (Note: The reader is referred to general research methods texts regarding difficulties with matching, such as being able to match on IQ, but not on more pervasive differences in family background.) When her results indicated that deaf children of deaf parents were superior to deaf children of hearing parents on intellectual, social, and communicative functioning, she did not conclude that deaf children should be born to deaf parents. Rather, she explored such competing explanations as the effects of early exposure to manual communication and parental acceptance of deafness.

NOTE

1. This note is for those readers not schooled in the characteristics of different types of guns. A shotgun scatters the "shot" in a broad area; it does not hit a precise area. Thus, the likelihood of hitting something is increased with a shotgun, but it may not be the precise thing that you intended to hit. So in research, throwing a large number of variables into the equation may result in finding some that are significant. However, it is difficult to determine the meaning of a significant variable that does not have a theoretical rationale for being in the analysis.

6

Qualitative Methods

Parenting a child with disabilities such as blindness, cerebral palsy, or Down's syndrome is challenging. This challenge is increased for families who are non-English speaking or for whom English is a second language. Tellier-Robinson (2000) explored the experiences of such families in her dissertation research. She visited nine families in their homes, met all the members of the families, and spent time observing, talking with, or playing with the children with special needs and their siblings. She interviewed the families in the language of their choice, as well as teachers, school administrators, and social workers who worked in the community. The parents explained the difficulties they faced in being involved in their child's education in terms of the distance of the schools from their homes, work schedules that complicated attending school functions, and language barriers between themselves and school staff. She also reported that most of the children spoke two languages, thus suggesting that they were quite capable despite their apparent disabilities (Anzul, Evans, King, & Tellier-Robinson, 2001). This example illustrates the use of qualitative methods in special education.

IN THIS CHAPTER

- Qualitative research is defined and its typical characteristics are discussed.
- The importance of qualitative methods in special education research is explored.
- The philosophical assumptions of this approach are explained, along with methodological implications of those assumptions.

- Data collection strategies for qualitative research in special education are introduced.
- Questions for critically analyzing qualitative research are provided.

DEFINITION AND CHARACTERISTICS OF QUALITATIVE METHODS

Qualitative research has many possible definitions; however, it is generally thought of as an approach to research that uses methodologies designed to provide a rich, contextualized picture of an educational or social phenomenon (Denzin & Lincoln, 2000; Schwandt, 2001). There are many types of qualitative research and names that are used to describe these types. In fact, Tesch (1990) identified 26 different types in her analysis. Table 6.1 provides a description and examples of the following types: basic qualitative research, ethnography, phenomenology, grounded theory, and case study (Merriam, 1998).

Despite the differences among these approaches, several features tend to characterize most qualitative research. These include:

- The goal is to elicit understanding and meaning.
- The researcher is the primary instrument of data collection and analysis.
- Data collection includes field work.
- The analysis is typically done using an inductive orientation.
- The findings are richly descriptive, providing a full contextual picture of the phenomenon under study.

Note: Qualitative methods can also be used within the positivist paradigm, for example, if the researcher establishes predetermined, static questions to guide the research and/or converts the qualitative data to frequency counts, and so on. However, we focus on the use of qualitative methods within the interpretive/constructivist and transformative/emancipatory traditions because of the unique criteria for judging quality associated with such research.

IMPORTANCE OF QUALITATIVE METHODS IN SPECIAL EDUCATION RESEARCH

Patton (2002) suggested using qualitative methods under the following conditions:

1. The program emphasizes individualized outcomes.

2. Detailed, in-depth information is needed about certain clients or program.

Table 6.1   Types and Examples of Qualitative Research Approaches

Ethnography: This approach can be defined as a research method designed to describe and analyze practices and beliefs of cultures and communities. Examples: Keller, Karp, and Carlson (1993) and Mertens (1992) studied community and school contexts for the integration of students with disabilities in total inclusion programs in their neighborhood schools.

Phenomenology: A phenomenological study focuses on the essence or structure of an experience (phenomenon). It is an attempt to be able to describe the meaning of an experience from the perspective of the person who experiences it. Example: Davidson and his colleagues (2001) investigated the problem of rehospitalization for people with schizophrenia from the viewpoint of its functionality to the persons with a mental illness.

Grounded Theory: The main differentiating characteristic for the grounded theory approach is that the researcher's goal is to develop a theory that is grounded in the data collected using qualitative methods (see Glaser & Strauss, 1967; Strauss & Corbin, 1998). Example: Szarkowski (2002) used the grounded theory approach to develop a theory of positive perspectives in raising a deaf child. Based on interviews, observations, and document reviews, she developed a model that explained theoretically how parents can view raising a deaf child in a positive light.

Case Study: A case study uses qualitative methods to obtain an extensive description of a single unit or bounded system, such as an individual, program, event, group, intervention, or community. The case study is one type of ethnographic approach that involves intensive and detailed study of one individual or of a group as an entity, through observation, self-reports, and any other means. Because of the emphasis on the individual, case studies have played a very important role in special education research. Examples: The reader interested in this methodology is encouraged to read Yin's *Case Study Research* (1998) and *Applications of Case Study Research* (1993). Stake (2000) also provides excellent guidance in the methods of case study research. Examples of case studies in special education can be found in Koppenhaver and Yoder's (1992) literature review of case studies related to individuals with physical disabilities and Ferguson's (1992) case study of six students with severe autism. Evans (1995; 1998) conducted a case study of one deaf girl in a hearing family to determine the nature of her communication experiences and language development.

3. The focus is on diversity among, idiosyncrasies of, and unique qualities exhibited by individual people, groups, organizations, and/or institutions.

4. No standardized instrument is available that can validly and reliably measure program outcomes.

Table 6.2   Examples of Quantitative and Qualitative Subject Descriptions

In a quantitative survey study, the subjects were described as follows:

"These children were identified as learning disabled in accordance with criteria (which closely resemble the federal criteria) set forth by the Delaware Department of Public Instruction." (Bear, Clever, & Proctor, 1991, p. 414)

In a qualitative study, the description read:

One student . . . "had a reading deficit. He had a tough time decoding words, although his spelling and writing were pretty good. He always seemed to understand what he had read, but if he had to read material, he struggled, slowly, missing key vocabulary words." (Davis & Ferguson, 1992, p. 126)

Many of the criteria that establish the appropriateness of choosing qualitative methods parallel the conditions in special education.

In special education, low incidence conditions, such as deaf-blindness, cause sample sizes to be either restricted or small. This issue is discussed in Chapter 8 in the section on the identification and selection of subjects. In special education, the subjects are unique with diversity across categories of disabilities, as well as within them. Two descriptions of students in quantitative and qualitative studies (as presented in Table 6.2) demonstrate the difference in focus for these two types of studies. Qualitative studies tend to provide more detail about the uniqueness of the students' disabling conditions than do quantitative studies.

In special education, each student's program, by definition, is deliberately designed to be unique in order to satisfy that student's needs. This is reflected in the requirements of the Individuals with Disabilities Education Act (IDEA), including an Individualized Education Plan (IEP) for school-age students, an Individual Family Service Plan (IFSP) for children from birth through three years old, and an Individual Transition Plan (ITP) required for all individuals by their sixteenth birthday. By definition, if not by legal mandate, the programs for special education students are diverse and idiosyncratic.

Peck and Furman (1992) explored the importance of qualitative research in special education in terms of the philosophy of science, the need for more holistic analysis of problems in policy and practice, and increased attention to descriptions of the world, as experienced by individuals, in the analysis of issues in special education. They identified several substantive contributions that qualitative research has made to special education.

First, qualitative researchers have identified the fundamental roles of ideology, organizational dynamics, and the social/political process in shaping policy and practice in special education. Peck and Furman's analysis suggests that the most fundamental problems constraining the inclusion of children with disabilities in regular classes are less technical than political in nature. Therefore, focusing on the instructional process affecting children's behavior is less useful than addressing political issues. They contend that adherence to the positivist tradition of research is likely to lead researchers away from asking some critical questions about why children with disabilities are not succeeding in school. This ability to provide insight into the social/political process is one that has been emphasized by feminists as well (Reinharz, 1992).

Second, Peck and Furman noted the value of constructing some sense of the insider's view. They noted that qualitative research has enabled the development of professional interventions in special education that are responsive to the cognitive and motivational interpretations of the world held by children, parents, and professionals. For example, definitions of aberrant or inappropriate behaviors can be reframed in terms of their functional meaning for a child.

Third, qualitative methods have led to insights into the cultural values, institutional practices, and interpersonal interactions that influence special education practice. For example, placement and categorizing children in special education are subject to these influences and can be understood only through a research process that can look at different levels of social ecology.

PHILOSOPHICAL ASSUMPTIONS AND METHODOLOGICAL IMPLICATIONS IN SPECIAL EDUCATION RESEARCH

The qualitative approach to research is rooted in several rich philosophical traditions. The interpretive/constructivist and the phenomenological philosophical orientations underlie what is typically thought of as qualitative research (Schwandt, 2000; Merriam, 1998). More recently the transformative/emancipatory philosophical orientation has brought a shift in perspectives in some special education research (Clough & Barton, 1998; Mertens, 1998; Pugach, 2001). The assumptions associated with these philosophical stances are explained as follows.

First, the interpretive/constructivist paradigm purports that reality is created as a result of a process of social construction; that is, there is no one reality that is waiting to be "discovered," as is believed in the positivist paradigm (Guba & Lincoln, 1989). For example, the concept of "disability" is a socially constructed phenomenon that means different things to different people. The methodological implication of having multiple realities is that the research questions cannot be definitively established before the study begins; rather, they will evolve and change as the study progresses. In special education research, the concept of multiple realities and social construction of reality also mean that the perceptions of a variety of types of persons must be sought. For example, Crowley (1993) used extensive interviews and classroom observations to explore multiple perspectives of practices that help or impede the learning of students with behavioral disorders in mainstream settings (including the opinions of the students themselves). Reiff, Gerber, and Ginsberg (1993) constructed a definition of learning disability from the perspective of insider adults with learning disabilities that focused on the academic areas of reading and writing, rather than on the vocational and social dysfunctions found in many traditional definitions.

In the transformative/emancipatory paradigm, the assumption is also that reality is socially constructed. However, there is a greater emphasis on the impact of historical, social, and cultural determinants of the definitions. The focus rests on ways to identify the constructions from the viewpoints of those with a disability within a larger cultural context. In addition, researchers who work from this perspective explicitly acknowledge that issues of discrimination and oppression must be addressed. For example, there has been convincing evidence supporting overrepresentation of students of color and low socioeconomic class in special education placements (Pugach, 2001; Scheurich, 2002). These researchers suggest that disability in and of itself is not the issue, but rather the larger question of institutionalized racism and classism in the schools and in our society. Therefore, research needs to examine the complicated relationships and intersections of disability and race, gender, class, culture, and language.

Second, the interpretive/constructivist paradigm assumes that the inquirer and inquired-into are interlocked, each affecting the other through the process of their mutual interaction. Thus, the qualitative researcher rejects the notion of objectivity that is espoused by the positivist and opts for a more interactive, personally involved style of data collection. For example, one special education teacher conducted a qualitative research study in collaboration with a university researcher, in which she discussed with her students with mild learning disabilities how they could more effectively respond to the demands in the mainstream classroom (Davis & Ferguson, 1992). She then used their ideas to structure the intervention that was the focus of her qualitative study.

In the transformative/emancipatory paradigm, there again is agreement as to the importance of an interactive relationship between the researcher and those with disabilities. However, there is also a critical examination of issues of power and control of the research process and the interpretation of the results from the viewpoint of people with disabilities.

Third, the interpretive/constructivist believes that facts are products of social construction; therefore, the values surrounding any statement of "facts" must be explored and made explicit. The concept of least restrictive environment (LRE) in special education exemplifies the connection between facts and values. The federal government defined LRE as inclusion of students with disabilities in regular education classes as much as possible, as long as their needs can be met in that environment. However, deaf advocates contended that because of communication barriers and even with qualified interpreters that inclusion in regular education would be socially isolating. Hence, there was a more restrictive placement for deaf students than one in which the primary language was sign-based, and they were surrounded by people who were deaf and competent signers.

In the transformative/emancipatory paradigm, much emphasis is placed on ways to legitimately involve people with disabilities in the research process. Methods of interviewing, observation, and document review are used, but there is a directive to provide the research participants with control over the processes and products of the research (Swain & French, 1998).

Pugach (2001) provided a list of thought provoking questions that would be pursued if researchers set a high priority on social justice in special education. She wrote:

- Who will tell the disciplined stories, for example, of school cultures that regularly enable teachers to place African American males into special education or of special education teachers who do not work aggressively to stem this practice?
- Who will study the experiences of Native American students who are identified as having a disability and how this interacts with their lives both on reservations and in urban communities where so many Native Americans live?
- As students of color move increasingly into middle class communities and schools, who will study the degree to which they find themselves in special education and why? (p. 450)

An additional question that might be posed is: Who will study the impacts of programs for students with disabilities in rural and inner-city environments?

QUALITATIVE METHODS AND DATA COLLECTION STRATEGIES

Because there is no one correct method for conducting qualitative research, Bogdan and Biklen (1998) recommend that researchers describe their methodology in detail. They offer a framework for structuring and conducting a qualitative research study that provides one approach for designing and conducting such a study. The reader who intends to conduct a qualitative research study is referred to other texts that explore this topic in more depth (Denzin & Lincoln, 2001; Guba & Lincoln, 1989; Patton, 2002; Yin, 1993, 1994).

Typically, qualitative researchers use three main methods for collecting data: observation, interviews, and document and records review.

Observation

Spradley (1980) outlined five types of observation based on degree of participation of the observer:

1.   Nonparticipation: The lowest level of involvement is usually accomplished by watching a videotape of the situation. For example, a researcher could ask a teacher to turn on a video camera at selected times when a student with disabilities is in her class. The researcher would then review the videotape at a later time.

2.   Passive participation: The researcher is present, but does not interact with the participants. Keller (1993) used this approach in observing a girl with Down's syndrome who was integrated in a regular education classroom.

3.   Moderate participation: The researcher attempts to balance the insider/outsider roles by observing and participating in some, but not all of the activities. Keller (1993) used this approach when he taught three lessons in the sixth grade classroom in which the girl with Down's syndrome was integrated.

4.   Active participation: The researcher generally does what the others do but does not participate completely. Mertens (1991a) used this approach in a study of gifted deaf adolescents in a summer enrichment program. She was with the students all day in the classroom, on field trips, and at meals. However, she did not sleep in the students' dorms at night and thus was not involved in their "after dark" activities.

5.   Complete participation: The researcher becomes a natural participant, which has the disadvantage of trying to collect data and maintaining a questioning and reflective stance. This approach was used by Ferguson, who was a special education teacher for students with learning disabilities (Davis & Ferguson, 1992). She continued with her role as the special education teacher while collecting qualitative data by observation and interviews.

Table 6.3 provides a description of the observation methodology used in Morse's (1994) study of a classroom team servicing special education students with multiple disabilities. Morse explained that her observations also included attendance at different types of meetings, such as informal, unplanned chats in the parking lot at the end of the school day, regularly scheduled once-per-week meetings with all the team members, and formal IEP meetings with team members and parents. She audiotaped and transcribed all the IEP and other formal planning meetings.

Interviewing

Interviews in a qualitative study are typically done with an unstructured or minimally structured format. Interviewing can be conducted as a

Table 6.3   Sample Description of the Observation Methodology (Morse, 1994)

For four months, I observed an average of two days per week in the classroom; then, I continued to observe once a month and to attend meetings on three specific children for another five months. I would arrive at 7:30 A.M. and leave when the staff left, usually between 3:00 and 4:00 P.M. In the classroom, I was both participant and nonparticipant. From the beginning, it seemed appropriate to help set up activities, have snacks and lunch and go to the playground with the staff and children, and clean up accidents. I could join any activity or be a nonparticipant and watch; listen; take notes . . . (pp. 44-45)

part of participant observation or even as a casual conversation. The questions emerge as the researcher is sensitized to the meanings that the participants bring to the situation. As the study evolves, interviewing can become more structured and formal. Morse (1994) provides an example of the types of individuals she interviewed in her study of children with multiple disabilities and the team that served them (Table 6.4).

Interviewing students with disabilities can present challenges because of the capabilities or communication needs of the respondents. For example, Ferguson (1992) conducted a case study of autistic students in which he interviewed adults who had various connections to autistic individuals at the school, including regular and special education teachers, administrators, and support staff. He commented, "Because of the limited verbal skills of the students in Mel's class, I did not conduct formal interviews with any of them. I did have short, informal conversations with the students when I was there doing observations" (p. 166).

Mertens (1991a) interviewed gifted deaf adolescents and found that it was necessary to train herself to take notes while watching the respondents in order to not miss any of their signs. She found that she could accommodate this situation by using a clipboard that was tilted enough for her to see, with her peripheral vision, that the writing was going onto the right part of the page. She also paused between questions to finish writing each response and then spent time immediately after each interview, filling in any holes that had been created by this interview process.

Swain and French (1998) conducted interviews with visually impaired students and adults. The interviews were open-ended which allowed the participants to control somewhat the direction of the questioning, as well as to end an interview if they felt uncomfortable.

Document and Records Review

All organizations leave trails composed of documents and records that trace their history and current status. Documents and records include not

Table 6.4   Example of Interview Procedures in Morse's (1994) Study of Children with Multiple Disabilities

I interviewed the teacher, other members of the classroom team, consultants, parents, nurses, physicians, and administrative personnel . . . I conducted my first two audiotaped interviews with the preschool coordinator and the support teacher five weeks after the study began. . . . To obtain additional information, clarify issues, and verify that my findings truly reflected the perspectives of the people I had interviewed, I conducted follow-up interviews, either formal audiotaped interviews or telephone interviews. I had formal follow-up interviews with the preschool coordinator, the classroom teacher, the consulting psychologist, the speech therapist, and one child's parents and had telephone interviews with the classroom teacher, the preschool coordinator, the consulting psychologist, and a physician. (p. 46)

only the typical paper products such as memos, reports, and plans, but also computer files, tapes (audio and video), and artifacts. Advances in digital photography and video hold great potential as data sources as well. It is to these documents and records that the qualitative researcher must turn in order to get the necessary background of the situation and insights into the dynamics of everyday functioning. The researcher cannot be in all places at all times; therefore, documents and records give the researcher access to information that would otherwise be unavailable. In special education research, documents that might be important include report cards, special education files, discipline records, IEPs, IEP meeting minutes, curriculum materials, and test scores.

In Morse's (1994) study of children with multiple disabilities and their service team, she examined the following documents: cultural artifacts, such as children's files, school brochures, newspaper articles, personnel procedures, written communications, and family picture albums. She also obtained permission from the parents to review the daily notes to and from the school and home which were kept in a home-school communication book for each child. The notebooks contained a chronology of events such as doctor's appointments, special family events, and negotiations over how to coordinate the management of a particular problem. She found this to be a valuable resource that revealed many of the parents' and staff's hopes and fears. She also kept a log of her own reactions, feelings, and insights about the events as they occurred.

CRITICALLY ANALYZING QUALITATIVE RESEARCH

Criteria for judging the quality of qualitative research that parallel the criteria for judging positivist, quantitative research have been outlined by a number of writers (Guba & Lincoln, 1989; Mertens, 1998). Guba and Lincoln equate credibility with internal validity, transferability with external validity, dependability with reliability, and confirmability with objectivity. They added the additional category of authenticity for qualitative research. In this section, each criterion is explained, along with ways to enhance quality in special education research.

Credibility

Guba and Lincoln (1989) identified credibility as the criterion in qualitative research that parallels internal validity in positivist research. Internal validity means the attribution within the experimental situation that the independent variable caused the observed change in the dependent variable. In qualitative research, the credibility test asks if there is a correspondence between the way the respondents actually perceive social constructs and the way the researcher portrays their viewpoints. A number of research strategies can be used to enhance credibility, including:

Prolonged and Substantial Engagement. There is no hard-and-fast rule that says how long a researcher must stay at a site. When the researcher has confidence that themes and examples are repeating instead of extending, it may be time to leave the field. Keller (1993) observed the girl with Down's syndrome from January through June of one year.

Persistent Observation. The researcher should observe long enough to identify salient issues. The researcher should avoid premature closure, that is, coming to a conclusion about a situation without sufficient observations. Keller (1993) had more than eighty contacts with the school or the staff over a six-month period.

Peer Debriefing. The researcher should engage in an extended discussion with a disinterested peer of findings, conclusions, analysis, and hypotheses. The peer should pose searching questions to help the researcher confront his or her own values and to guide the next steps in the study. Keller (1993) shared the narratives from his field notes with two other researchers involved in the school. Often, the researcher may decide to return to the field to ask new questions, perhaps more focused as a result of the dialogue with a colleague.

Negative Case Analysis. Working hypotheses can be revised, based on the discovery of cases that do not fit; however, it should not be expected that all cases will fit the appropriate categories. Guba and Lincoln (1989) state that when a "reasonable" number of cases fit, then negative case analysis provides confidence in the hypothesis that is being proposed. For example, suppose a researcher sees a pattern emerging which suggests that a top-down approach to a total inclusion program creates resistance in the school staff (Mertens, 1992). The researcher could seek additional data for negative case analysis from a school that used a bottom-up approach to total inclusion. If resistance was identified in that setting as well, the researcher would need to revise the emerging hypothesis that administration style alone creates resistance. It may be one of many factors that contribute to resistance to change.

Progressive Subjectivity. The researcher should monitor his or her developing constructions and document the process of change from the beginning of the study until it ends. The researcher can share this statement of beliefs with the peer debriefer, so that the peer can challenge the researcher who has not kept an open mind, but has only found what was expected from the beginning. For example, a study of the social experiences of deaf high school students suggested that social isolation can be a very painful result of being the only deaf student (or one of a few) in a school (Mertens, 1989). The emotional strength of this finding might have left the researcher biased against the integration of students with disabilities into regular classes. Consequently, in Mertens' (1992) subsequent work in total inclusion research, she needed to discuss this personal experience at the beginning and throughout the duration of the study, so that she could keep an open mind and not be biased by previous experience.

Member Checks. This is the most important criterion in establishing credibility. The researcher must verify with the respondent groups the constructions that are developing as a result of data collected and analyzed. Member checks can be formal and informal. For example, at the end of an interview, the researcher can summarize what has been said and ask if the notes accurately reflect the person's position. Drafts of the research report can be shared with the members for comment. Morse (1994) discussed the themes and interpretations back to the respondents for them to correct and verify. In Swain and French's (1998) study with visually disabled people, early and late drafts of the findings were sent to the participants in an accessible format. They were invited to send comments in print, Braille, on audiotape, or by telephone. Their comments were taken seriously by the authors, and the drafts were amended accordingly. The researcher who can negotiate decision rules with a client prior to conflicts arising at the interpretation stage is in an advantageous position. If possible, it is highly recommended that this issue be discussed in the planning stages of the study, even before any data are collected.

Triangulation. Triangulation involves checking information that has been collected from different sources or methods for consistency of evidence across sources of data. Guba and Lincoln (1989) no longer support this notion of triangulation because it implies that it is possible (or desirable) to find consistency across sources, which contradicts the notion of multiple realities discussed earlier in this chapter. They say that triangulation can still be used to check on factual data (e.g., how many children are in a program), but they recommend the use of member checks for other types of data. In Morse's (1994) study of children with multiple disabilities and their service providers, she corroborated her findings by examining the results across multiple data sources, including the observations and interviews and the documents from the children's health, medical, and education files, emergency classroom procedures, and home-school communication books.

Transferability. Guba and Lincoln (1989) identified transferability as the qualitative parallel to external validity in positivist research. External validity means the degree to which you can generalize the results to other situations. They contend that in qualitative research that the burden of transferability is on the reader to determine the degree of similarity between the study site and the receiving context. The researcher's responsibility is to provide sufficient detail to enable the reader to make such a judgment. Extensive and careful description of the time, place, context, and culture is known as thick description. Mertens (1990a) studied the reasons that referrals were increasing to a special school that served several school districts in a rural area. She provided an in-depth description of the community in which the special school was located, as well as the sending and receiving schools, by means of demographic and observational data. She observed in all the schools and provided a description of the physical setup of the classrooms and the processes of instruction that were used. Thus, readers could determine how similar their own conditions were to those reported by Mertens. A thick description of the context was important because the rural nature of the community had an impact on understanding the reasons for the increased referrals (e.g., in terms of ability to attract and retain qualified special education staff and to provide services for students with low incidence disabilities in sparsely populated areas).

Dependability. Guba and Lincoln (1989) identified dependability as the qualitative parallel to reliability. Reliability means stability of observed changes over time in the positivist paradigm. In the constructivist paradigm, change is expected, but it should be tracked and be publicly inspectable. A dependability audit can be conducted to attest to the quality and appropriateness of the inquiry process. For example, Mertens (1991a) began a study of ways to encourage gifted deaf adolescents to enter science careers, with a focus on instructional strategies used in science classes. However, emerging patterns in the data suggested the importance of examining administrative practices that facilitated the acquisition of competent interpreters or teachers and staff who were deaf. This change of focus is acceptable and to be expected in qualitative research, but it should be documented.

Confirmability. Guba and Lincoln (1989) identified confirmability as the qualitative parallel to objectivity. Objectivity means that the influence of the researcher's judgment is minimized. Confirmability means that the data and their interpretation are not figments of the researcher's imagination. Qualitative data can be tracked to its source, and the logic that is used to interpret the data should be made explicit. Guba and Lincoln recommend a confirmability audit to attest to the fact that the data can be traced to original sources and the process of synthesizing data to reach conclusions can be confirmed. The confirmability audit can be conducted in conjunction with the dependability audit. Thus, a special education researcher's peers can review field notes, interview transcripts, and so on and determine whether the conclusions are supported by the data (Keller, 1993).

Authenticity. Authenticity refers to the presentation of a balanced view of all perspectives, values, and beliefs. It answers the question: Has the researcher been fair in presenting views? Among the criteria identified by Guba and Lincoln (1989) to judge the authenticity of investigations conducted within the constructivist paradigm were the following:

Fairness answers the question: To what extent are different constructions and their underlying value structures solicited and honored in the process? In order to be fair, the researcher must identify the respondents and how information about their constructions was obtained. Conflicts and value differences should be displayed. There should also be open negotiation of the recommendations and agenda for future actions. Total inclusion research can be judged to be fair if the varying viewpoints, both for and against (and the conditions under which inclusion would be supported), are included in the report (Keller et al., 1993; Mertens, 1992).

Ontological Authenticity is the degree to which the individual's or group's conscious experience of the world became more informed or sophisticated. This can be determined based on the testimony of the respondents or by means of an audit trail that documents changes in individuals' constructions throughout the process. In the study of increased referrals to a special school, respondents came to understand the discrepancy between policy and practice with regard to referral of students with disabilities to special schools (Mertens, 1990a). The policy said that students with disabilities should be educated as much as possible with general education students and that, as a last resort, before referral to a special school, they should be provided with educational services in a separate, special education classroom in their home school. Local school staff did not support use of the special education classroom because they perceived it as stigmatizing for the student to go to a separate classroom. They preferred to refer a student to the special school when they had exhausted attempts to integrate a student with a disability in a general education classroom.

Catalytic Authenticity is the extent to which action is stimulated by the inquiry process. Techniques for determining this criterion include respondent testimony and examination of actions reported in follow-up studies. Following the completion of the study of referrals at the special school, the state department of education representative asked Mertens (1990a) to assist in implementing the recommendations. For example, personnel from the special school began to serve as consultants to the local schools to assist them in retaining and meeting the needs of the students with disabilities prior to referral to the special school.

QUESTIONS FOR CRITICALLY
ANALYZING QUALITATIVE RESEARCH

1. Did the researcher maintain sufficient involvement at the site to overcome distortions, uncover people's constructions, and understand the context's culture?
2. Did the researcher avoid premature closure?
3. Did the researcher use peer debriefing?
4. Did the researcher use negative case analysis?
5. Did the researcher prepare a statement of beliefs and share those with the peer debriefer?
6. Did the researcher use member checks?
7. Did the researcher use triangulation?
8. Did the researcher provide sufficient thick description?
9. Did the researcher do a dependability audit?
10. Did the researcher do a confirmability audit?
11. Did the researcher display conflicts and value differences?
12. Did the individuals and groups become more informed or sophisticated about their experiences?
13. Did the evaluation stimulate action?

QUESTIONS AND ACTIVITIES
FOR DISCUSSION AND APPLICATION

1. In your opinion, why are qualitative research methods appropriate or not appropriate for special education and under what circumstances?
2. What are the philosophical assumptions of the interpretive/constructivist paradigm, and what are their methodological implications in special education?
3. Explain the main types of qualitative research, that is, ethnography, phenomenology, grounded theory, and case studies. How are they similar and different? Give an example in special education of an application of each of these approaches.
4. Explain the three methods of collecting data that can be used in qualitative research. Give examples of how these could be applied in special education.
5. Given the following research problem, explain what the researchers could do to improve the quality of their study. Structure your answer using the following categories:

(a) credibility
(b) transferability
(c) dependability
(d) confirmability
(e) authenticity

Example: Pull-out programs (e.g., resource rooms or remedial classes) have been criticized for segregating low-achieving students, providing them with a fragmented curriculum, and allowing regular classroom teachers to avoid responsibility for meeting all the students' needs. Pull-in programs have been proposed as one alternative, where the special education or remedial teacher provides instruction in the regular classroom. This study used observations of two pull-in programs to obtain information about implementation, instructional context, and variability among classrooms implementing pull-in. Three pull-out programs taught by the same special and remedial education teachers served as comparison groups (Gelzheiser & Meyers, 1992).

6. Given the following research problem, explain what the researchers could do to improve the quality of their study. Structure your answer using the following categories:

(a) credibility
(b) transferability
(c) dependability
(d) confirmability
(e) authenticity

The researcher observed mainstreaming programs for deaf youths at the elementary, middle, and high school levels operated by the local school district for two years to investigate how deaf and hearing youths were educated together (Higgins, 1992). He observed in self-contained and mainstream classes, in the cafeteria, and on the playground. He talked with the principal, administrators, teachers, other staff, parents, and students, and he read about other programs.

7. Talk with people with disabilities, their parents, and their advocates about the research process.

8. Select a research problem in special education. Describe how you could approach it from both a quantitative and a qualitative perspective. What are the strengths and weaknesses of each approach as applied to your problem area?

9. Identify a qualitative study and examine it specifically to determine to what extent and in what ways the researchers have critiqued their own research methods and what the implications of the identified limitations had on their conclusions.

7

Mixed Methods and Mixed Model Designs

The Early Childhood Research Institute on Inclusion (ECRII) chose mixed methods to investigate the ecological system of inclusion for children with disabilities in preschool programs (Li, Marquart, & Zercher, 2000). They wanted answers to a number of questions such as: What are the goals that families, teachers, program administrators, and policy makers have for inclusion? What are their multiple definitions and ways of implementing inclusion? What are the barriers to and facilitators of inclusion in various settings? The researchers used mixed methods to gain a broader perspective and deeper understanding of different levels of the systems and interactions than they could obtain through a single method of research.

IN THIS CHAPTER

- Mixed methods and mixed models research are defined and their typical characteristics are discussed.
- The importance of mixed methods and mixed models in special education research is explored.
- The philosophical assumptions of this approach are explained, along with the methodological implications of those assumptions.

- Specific approaches to mixed methods and mixed models research are presented, along with examples of these approaches.
- Questions for critically analyzing mixed methods and mixed models research are provided.

DEFINITION AND CHARACTERISTICS

Mixed methods and mixed models designs include both qualitative and quantitative features in the design, data collection, and analysis (Teddlie & Tashakkori, 2002). A mixed method design is one in which both quantitative and qualitative methods are used to answer research questions in a single study, while mixed model designs are those studies that are part of a larger research program and are designed as complementary to provide information related to several research questions, each answered with a different methodological approach. (See Table 7.1 for brief definitions of mixed methods/mixed models terms.) While mixed methods has an intuitive appeal, it also demands that the researcher be expert in both approaches to research or work with a team that has such expertise. There are issues related to the design of studies as well, insuring the quality of a mixed methods approach, that are explored in this chapter.

Qualitative and quantitative data collection can occur in parallel form (in which two types of data are collected and analyzed concurrently) or sequential form (in which one type of data provides a basis for collection of another type of data). The mixed methods can also involve the conversion of qualitative data to a quantitative form or vice versa. Teddlie and Tashakkori (2002) described the following characteristics as those of a truly mixed approach methodology which they called a mixed model design or study: (1) it would incorporate multiple approaches in all stages of the study (i.e., problem identification, data collection, data analysis, and final inference) and (2) it would include a transformation of the data and their analyses through another approach (e.g., content analysis of qualitative data followed by a quantitative analysis of the same data after they had been quantitized). The intent may be to seek a common understanding through triangulating data from multiple methods or to use multiple lenses simultaneously to achieve alternative perspectives that are not reduced to a single understanding.

Greene and Caracelli (2002) suggest that many researchers do not adhere to the full complement of characteristics that define a mixed model design listed by Teddlie and Tashakkori. Rather, social researchers mix methods to a varying degree at various points in their research and still call their work mixed methods research. Researchers can insert multiple mixed options into their work at various points in the research process, including the definition of purpose, overall design, methods, sampling, data recording, analysis, and interpretation.

Table 7.1   The Language and Designs of Mixed Methods

Mixed method research: Uses both qualitative and quantitative methods in a single study or a multiphase study.

Mixed model research: Uses both qualitative and quantitative methods in studies that are part of a larger research program and are designed as complementary to provide information related to several research questions, each answered with a different methodological approach.

Parallel form: Concurrent mixed method/mixed model designs in which two types of data are collected and analyzed.

Sequential form: One type of data provides a basis for collection of another type of data.

Points at which mixed methods can be applied: Problem identification, data collection, data analysis, and/or final inference.

This language is adopted from Tashakkori & Teddlie (2003). This chapter will not discuss multiple methods which is defined as a study that uses more than one method, but stays within one worldview (i.e., uses more than one quantitative method in a study or uses more than one qualitative method in a study).

Importance to Special Education

Mixed methods have particular value when a researcher is trying to solve a problem that is present in a complex educational or social context (Teddlie & Tashakkori, 2002). Because mixed methods designs incorporate techniques from both the quantitative and qualitative research traditions, they can be used to answer questions that could not be answered in any other way. Many researchers have used mixed methods because it seemed intuitively obvious to them that this would enrich their ability to draw conclusions about the problem under study. Morse (2002) describes the advantages to using mixed methods this way:

> By combining and increasing the number of research strategies used within a particular project, we are able to broaden the dimensions and hence the scope of our project. By using more than one method within a research study, we are able to obtain a more complete picture of human behavior and experience. Thus, we are better able to hasten our understanding and achieve our research goals more quickly. (p. 189)

Newman, Ridenour, Newman, and DeMarco (2002) suggest that when the purpose of the research is complex, it is necessary to have multiple questions which frequently necessitate the use of mixed methods. Mixed methods have the potential to contribute to addressing multiple purposes and thus to meeting the needs of multiple audiences for the results.

The Early Childhood Research Institute on Inclusion conducted a multiphase study of the ecological systems of inclusion that used mixed methods (Li, Marquart, & Zercher, 2000). They described the need for and advantages of this approach as follows:

> This study was designed to answer key questions about the goals that families, teachers, program administrators, and policy makers have for inclusion; multiple definitions and ways of implementing inclusion; and barriers to and facilitators of inclusion in various settings. In order to understand the complex nature of the social ecology in inclusive programs, ECRII researchers used a mixed-method design for data collection and analysis. The multiple methods and measures provided a broader perspective and deeper understanding of different levels of the ecological systems and the interactions among different levels than could be achieved by a single-method design. (p. 117)

Feuer, Towne, and Shavelson (2002) support the legislatively mandated randomized field trials described in Chapter 4 of this book, while at the same time, they recognize a need for multiple methods. They wrote:

> When properly applied, quantitative and qualitative research tools can both be employed rigorously and together often can support stronger scientific inferences than when either is employed in isolation. Again, the key to progress lies in the capacity and willingness of investigators from these different perspectives to constructively engage each other's differing perspectives around the common goal of advancing understanding. (p. 8)

Philosophical Assumptions: Pragmatism, Mixing Paradigms, and Transformation

Based on a review of social research that claimed to use mixed methods, Greene and Caracelli (2002) concluded that inquiry decisions are rarely, if ever, consciously rooted in philosophical assumptions or beliefs. Rather, researchers based their choice of mixed methods on the nature of the phenomena being investigated, the contexts in which the study is conducted, or the funding agencies requirements. Nevertheless, they did not conclude that paradigms and their associated philosophical assumptions were irrelevant, merely unexamined. They further suggested that by attending too little to philosophical ideas and traditions that many mixed-method inquirers are insufficiently reflective and their practice insufficiently unproblematized. Examining the philosophical assumptions underlying research, mixed methods or not, can offer a better understanding of the complex social world in which special education operates.

Teddlie and Tashakkori (2002) propose the use of pragmatism as a philosophical orientation to guide mixed methods researchers. Simply put, pragmatists consider the research question to be more important than either the method they use or the worldview that is supposed to underlie the method. These researchers use the criterion "what works" to determine which method to use to answer a specific research question. Thus, the pragmatic orientation rejects the "either/or" mentality suggested by a choice between the postpositive and the constructivist paradigms. Here is how Tashakkori and Teddlie (1998) describe the pragmatic researcher:

> . . . pragmatists decide what they want to research, guided by their personal value systems; that is, they study what they think is important to study. They then study the topic in a way that is congruent with their value system, including variables and units of analysis that they feel are the most appropriate for finding an answer to their research question. They also conduct their studies in anticipation of results that are congruent with their value system. This explanation of the way in which researchers conduct their research seems to describe the way that researchers in the social and behavioral science actually conduct their studies, especially research that has important social consequences. (p. 27)

This pragmatic basis can be contrasted with that of the transformative/emancipatory paradigm in which the emphasis is on the inclusion of values and viewpoints, especially of marginalized groups as the driving force for all aspects of the research. Mertens (2002) and House and Howe (1999) question the notion of the centrality of the researcher's values in the pragmatic paradigm. They raise questions in terms of whose values, which values, and the role of the researcher within the context of values. While Tashakkori and Teddlie (1998) claim that practicality should serve as the value basis for a researcher's choices, researchers within the transformative/emancipatory paradigm would ask: Practical for what? As House and Howe write, "Something could be practical for bad ends. Using practicality as the primary criterion means evaluators (researchers) may serve whatever ends clients or policy makers endorse. Evaluation (research) should be premised on higher social goals than being useful to those in power" (p. 36).

Cresswell, Guttman, & Plano-Clark (2002) and Mertens (2002) noted that a mixed methods design could also fit within a transformative framework if it was designed to reflect, in both perspective and outcomes, a dedication to social change at levels ranging from the personal to the political. Furthermore, they contend that it is possible to conduct almost any mixed methods study with a transformative or advocacy purpose.

Mixed Methods/Mixed Models Design Options

The specific mixed methods/mixed models approaches are defined by the ordering of the application of the quantitative and qualitative methods (simultaneously or sequentially), as well as at what point the mixing of methods occurs. Teddlie and Tashakkori (2002) distinguish between types of designs that used mixed methods to answer the research questions in a single study (they call those mixed method designs) and those that are part of a larger research program with multiple complementary studies and more than one research question, each answered with a different methodological approach (they call those mixed model designs). Cresswell (2003) also talks about the extent to which either the qualitative or quantitative aspect of the study is dominant; thus, he writes about dominant–less dominant designs. Table 7.2 provides a summary of four design options for a mixed methods/mixed models approach.[1]

Types of mixed method and mixed models designs include:

1. Pragmatic Parallel Mixed Method/Model Design. This is a design in which qualitative and quantitative data are collected and analyzed to answer a single study's research questions (Onwuegbuzie & Teddlie, 2002). The final inferences are based on both data analyses results. The two types of data are collected independently at the same time or with a time lag. (If the research is designed with two relatively independent phases, one with qualitative questions and data collection and analysis techniques and the other with quantitative questions and data collection and analysis techniques, then it is called a Parallel Mixed Model Design. The inferences made on the basis of the results of each strand are pulled together to form meta-inferences at the end of the study.)

Example: Li et al. (2000) provide a detailed example of a Pragmatic Parallel Mixed Method Design in their study of preschool inclusion. They planned an ecological systems study that consisted of a case study at each of sixteen inclusion programs to provide an in-depth analysis of inclusion in the programs. They wanted to determine barriers to and facilitators of inclusion, as well as describe idiosyncratic issues. Quantitative and qualitative data were collected and analyzed concurrently.

The quantitative data were collected using six 30-minute observations of each child using an ecobehavioral observational system called the Code for Active Student Participation and Engagement Revised (CASPER II) (Brown, Favazza, & Odom, 1995), a peer rating sociometric assessment (Asher, Singleton, Tinsley, & Hymel, 1979), and the Battelle Developmental Inventory (Newborg, Stock, Wnek, Guidubaldi, & Svinicki, 1988). The qualitative data included participant observations that occurred in each preschool inclusion program two or three times per week for 6 to 16 weeks. The observers wrote field notes that included descriptions of the physical environment, classroom participants, activities, and interactions among participants. Observations lasted between one and five hours. In addition, open-ended interviews were conducted with professionals, administrators, and family members. Teachers and family members also completed a Friendship Survey (Buysse, 1993). Observers who used the CASPER II observation system were asked to write Post-CASPER notes following each session in which they identified the type of interaction that most represented the child's behavior during the 30-minute observation.

Table 7.2   Mixed Method/Mixed Model Design Options and Examples

Temporal Relation	Philosophical Paradigm	
	Pragmatic	*Transformative/Emancipatory*

Parallel	Characteristics:
	  – Both qualitative and quantitative data are collected to answer the research question(s).
	  – Two types of data are collected simultaneously or with a small time lag.
		Characteristics:
		  – Uses mixed methods to promote change at any level, personal to political
		  – Deliberately seeks underrepresented populations
		  – Gives primacy to value-based and action-oriented dimensions

	Example:
	The ecological systems of inclusion in early childhood programs (Li, Marquart, & Zercher, 2000)
	  – 16 case studies; quantitative behavioral observation system; peer rating sociometric assessment; qualitative participant observations, open-ended interviews
		Example:
		Shared Reading Project for deaf children (Delk & Weidekamp, 2001; Mertens, Delk, & Weidekamp, 2003)
		  – Designed to meet the needs of traditionally underserved deaf and hard-of-hearing students: members of diverse ethnocultural groups, those with secondary disabilities, people in rural areas, those that come from homes where English is not the primary language; quantitative surveys; reading logs; qualitative interviews; deaf interviewers conducted interviews of deaf tutors.

Sequential	Characteristics:
	  – One type of data provides a basis for collection of another type of data.
		Characteristics:
		  – Same as Sequential Transformative/ Emancipatory, except

(Continued)

Table 7.2 (Continued)

Temporal Relation	Philosophical Paradigm	
	Pragmatic	Transformative/Emancipatory
	– It answers one type of question by collecting and analyzing two types of data. – Inferences are based on the analysis of both types of data.	– One type of data provides a basis for collection of another type of data.
	Example: Family perception of preschool inclusion (Li et al., 2000) – Face-to-face interviews with families; used the results to develop quantitative data through telephone interviews	Example: Parent experiences with their young deaf or hard-of-hearing child (Meadow-Orlans, Mertens, & Sass-Lehrer, 2003) – National quantitative survey, in-depth telephone interviews with targeted groups; focus groups with ethnic/racial minority families

Each data set was analyzed according to appropriate analytic techniques (e.g., frequency tabulations were used to produce graphs for each child for each category of behavior observed using the CASPER II system). Child case summaries and vignettes were written for each child using thematic coding of the qualitative data. Thus, the results from each data set could be compared to increase the explanatory value of the findings. For example, the peer rating data indicated that one child was very sociable. The observation data provided a vignette describing the nature of her behavior to illustrate how this characteristic was manifested by that child.

2. Pragmatic Sequential Mixed Method/Model Design. This is a design in which one type of data (e.g., quantitative) provides a basis for the collection of another type of data (e.g., qualitative) (Onwuegbuzie & Teddlie, 2002). It answers one type of question by collecting and analyzing two types of data. Inferences are based on the analysis of both types of data. A sequential mixed model design is one in which the conclusions that are made on the basis of the first strand lead to formulation of questions, data collection, and data analysis for the next strand. The final inferences are based on the results of both strands of the study. In some cases, the second strand or phase of the study is used to confirm or disconfirm the inferences of the first strand or to provide further explanation for unexpected findings in the first strand. This approach can be used to generate hypotheses to be explored in more depth, or to develop surveys that use correct language for the population.

Examples: Li et al. (2000) provide an example of a Sequential Mixed Model Design in their study of family perceptions of preschool inclusion. They conducted face-to-face interviews with 112 families as a way of collecting qualitative data without imposing preconceived notions about inclusion. They sampled seven families from each of sixteen programs to interview. This provided them with in-depth information on the families' perspectives. They then used the results of a preliminary analysis of the family interviews to develop a telephone survey that was designed to collect standardized information on a broader and more representative sample of families using the inclusive programs.

The face-to-face interviews used a semistructured protocol that asked about the child, the child's history, the decision-making process about the program, perceptions of the program as well as the child's social relationships, and participation in family and community activities. The telephone survey instrument consisted of precoded closed-ended questions on the child's current program and services, decision making about the program and educational goals, sources of support for the family, the child's social relationships and participation in activities outside the school program, and demographic information.

The data from the interviews and surveys were analyzed using appropriate analytic techniques for the respective qualitative and quantitative methods. These separate tracks were then brought together in a mixed methods analysis at the data comparison and integration stage (see Chapter 10 for further details of analytic methods).

Evaluators at the U.S. General Accounting Office used a similar strategy in a study examining the effectiveness of the Americans with Disabilities Act (USGAO/PEMD, 1993, cited in Chelimsky, 1998). They interviewed people with disabilities before developing the survey of the broader community. They used the responses in constructing both the design and the survey instruments. Based on the comments of the people with disabilities, they realized a need to ask probing questions of business owners and operators, not just about observable barriers. The people with disabilities brought up the need to be aware of invisible barriers as well, such as whether a blind person with a guide dog might be refused entry to a café or restaurant.

3. Transformative Sequential Mixed Methods/Model Design. Creswell et al. (2002) define a transformative mixed methods design as any research project that uses mixed methods with a goal of social change at levels ranging from the personal to the political. The design gives primacy to the value-based and action-oriented dimensions of different inquiry traditions (Greene & Caracelli, 1997).

Example: The Shared Reading Project (SRP) provides an example of a transformative mixed method design that used sequential qualitative and quantitative data collection and analysis strategies (Delk & Weidekamp, 2001; Mertens, Delk, & Weidekamp, 2004). The SRP is designed to provide hearing parents and caregivers with visually-based strategies to read books to their deaf and hard-of-hearing children, from birth through age eight. The SRP was designed to meet the needs of five groups of traditionally underserved deaf and hard-of-hearing students, including members of diverse ethnocultural groups, those who have secondary disabilities, people who live in rural areas, those who come from homes in which a spoken language other than English is used, and/or those who are lower achieving academically. Tutors, most of whom are deaf, visited the families in their homes to teach them signing and reading strategies and answer their questions about the process of teaching their children to read.

The SRP collected both quantitative and qualitative data to address multiple evaluation questions. The quantitative measures included closed-ended surveys and logs that the families kept that indicated such things as the demographic characteristics and the number of times families used the books that the tutors brought them between visits. The qualitative data were collected through in-person, on-site interviews with the families, tutors, and site coordinators. Foreign language interpreters were used in homes where the spoken language was other than English. Deaf interviewers conducted the interviews with the deaf tutors which were video-taped and then transcribed. Participants were asked to describe such things as their role in the project, their emotional experiences during the project, and successes and challenges.

The quantitative and qualitative data were analyzed with a specific attempt to identify the impact of the project on the traditionally underserved groups. Quantitative data indicated that 104 of the 116 children belonged to at least one of the traditionally underserved groups. The quantitative and qualitative data were disaggregated in the analysis in order to provide a picture of the unique successes and challenges faced by members of these groups in teaching their deaf and hard-of-hearing children to read. Because the focus was on traditionally underserved groups, the results were shared with the people in their communities to determine lessons learned and options for additional action. Because of the demonstrable results in terms of improved literacy, several of the sites have moved to institutionalize the SRP, incorporating it into their regular school program. In some sites, the skill of the deaf tutors has been increasingly recognized, and they have been given responsibilities to work in the classrooms as well as at the students' homes. One site has made a decision to expand the program to include Hmong and Latino families of children enrolled in the school.

4. Transformative Sequential Mixed Methods/Models. This approach shares the transformative goal described in option 3 mentioned previously, as well as the characteristics of the sequential option described in option 2.

Meadow-Orlans, Mertens, and Sass-Lehrer (2003) provide an example of a transformative sequential mixed method design in their study of parents' experiences with their young deaf and hard-of-hearing children. The study proceeded in three phases: a quantitative national survey, individual parent interviews, and focus group interviews. The initial phase of the study was designed not only to provide a broad picture of parents' early experiences, but also to investigate differences in experiences based on such characteristics as race/ethnicity, parent hearing status, presence of additional disabilities beyond hearing loss, level of parent education, and socioeconomic status of the family. The National Parent Project survey was designed to obtain information directly from families by eliciting descriptions of their experiences, evaluations of effectiveness of services, and recommendations for improvement. Parents provided important insights throughout the project from the design of the survey and interview protocol to the analyses and implications of the findings.

The quantitative data analysis indicated great diversity in the characteristics of the families and their responses to the survey questions. For example, one-third of the participating parents had children with a disability in addition to a hearing loss, and many of these families encountered difficulties obtaining needed services. Overall families generally expressed satisfaction with the services their children received; however, some families, particularly non-White families, were less satisfied with their services.

These findings led to the qualitative portion of the study which used in-depth telephone interviews and a purposive sampling strategy to investigate in more depth the experiences of families with children with co-occurring disabilities, parents who were deaf or hard-of-hearing, parents of children with cochlear implants, and families of color. In the final phase, three focus groups of parents were conducted in large urban areas with the intention of expanding the number of Hispanic and African American families represented in the sample. Using very open-ended questions, participants provided insights into their experiences, feelings, and concerns during the time of suspicion and confirmation of their child's hearing loss, the people or services that were most helpful, needs that were not addressed by early intervention services, their communication decision-making process, and advice they had for professionals and for other parents.

The data were analyzed and reported within the larger national context, while still preserving the subgroup analyses of traditionally underrepresented groups. Special attention was given to interrogating bodies of knowledge that have become institutionalized as established concepts and practices that were determined by groups that traditionally have power in our society. Banks (2000) suggests that the groups in power (generally professionals) largely determine for those with less power (parents) what are the accepted practices. These "cultural facts" are accepted without challenge until the voices of individuals affected have the opportunity to articulate their experiences and express their perspectives. Thus, the parents' comments served as a basis to give insights not only to other parents who might be starting down the road of life with their deaf or hard-of-hearing child, but also to professionals who serve this population.

CRITICALLY ANALYZING MIXED METHODS RESEARCH

Tashakkori and Teddlie (2002) suggest that there is a unique character to mixed methods that transcends a simplistic combination of methods. Therefore, they suggest the term "inference quality" to refer to issues that would be termed internal validity in quantitative terms or trustworthiness in qualitative terms.

For Newman et al. (2002), the concept of validity is best supported by looking at the consistency between the research purpose, the question, and the methods used. Strong consistency grounds the credibility of research findings and helps assure that audiences have confidence in the findings and the implications of research studies. Therefore, one criterion for increased validity in a research study with multiple purposes and questions would be the use of a mixed methods design.

One approach to critically analyzing a mixed methods study would be to use the criteria that are presented in Chapters 4 and 5 (quantitative methods) for the quantitative portion of the study and those in Chapter 6 (qualitative methods) for the qualitative portion. This is not a bad strategy and could be a useful way to assess the quality of the individual parts of the study. Morse (2002) suggests that researchers begin their critique of the quality of a mixed methods design by looking at the integrity of the methods as they are derived from the assumptions of each paradigm. So, using the questions in Chapters 4, 5, and 6 to critically analyze the methods for particular approaches in a project is appropriate.

However, tensions can arise because conflicting demands can be present when more than one paradigm is operationalized (Morse, 2002). For example, if the researcher is working inductively within the qualitative part of the study, the sample is small and purposively selected and therefore would not meet the criteria for a quantitative sample that needs to be larger and have been randomly selected. Morse contends that if a quantitative component is being sought, then a separate, randomized sample must be added for that portion. Small samples do raise issues of potential bias. Morse (2002) also raised the issue related to the use of a qualitative or quantitative data collection method to supplement the findings from the main study. For example, a quantitative study might include one or two focus groups to add a qualitative dimension to the main study. The researcher in such circumstances needs to acknowledge the limitations of the qualitative data in that they cannot stand alone. They are only intelligible and interpretable when they are linked to the data from the main quantitative part of the study.

When looking at the conclusions of a mixed method design, it is possible that the results from both methods will agree with each other and thus confirm the conclusions reached. It is also possible that they will not agree with each other. Then, the researcher must explore plausible explanations for the disagreement. It may be due to the difference in approach or because of changes in the context over time that could influence performance on the dependent measures.

The selection of different methods in a study may be necessary to accommodate differences based on disability, culture, language, reading or writing levels, gender, class, and race/ethnicity for specific subgroups in a population (Mertens, 2002). Practically, individuals with different types of disabilities may be better able to provide accurate information about themselves if a qualitative or quantitative method is used. For example, in the Delk and Weidekamp (2002) study, telephone surveys were not appropriate for deaf individuals without adequate English writing skills. Other human dimensions such as race/ethnicity also need to be considered in the design of a study. As Stanfield (1999) noted, an atmosphere of distrust has developed between researchers and many members of racial/ethnic minority communities because of historical events such as the Tuskegee experiments in which Black men with syphilis were left untreated so that researchers could study the progress of the disease. Mixed methods may be necessary to provide an opportunity to build a sense of trust between the researcher and the community. A researcher could define the problem to be studied through a qualitative phase of interacting with members of the community, using observation and interviewing. If trust can be developed, then it might be appropriate to introduce a quantitative phase to the project.

These issues and concerns then give rise to the following questions that can be used to critically analyze mixed methods/mixed models research studies:

QUESTIONS FOR CRITICALLY ANALYZING MIXED METHODS/MODELS RESEARCH

1. What are the multiple purposes and questions that justify the use of a mixed method design?

2. Has the researcher matched the purposes and questions to appropriate methods?

3. To what extent has the researcher adhered to the criteria that define quality for the quantitative portion of the study?

4. To what extent has the researcher adhered to the criteria that define quality for the qualitative portion of the study?

5. How has the researcher addressed the tension between potentially conflicting demands of paradigms in the design and implementation of the study?

6. Has the researcher appropriately acknowledged the limitations associated with data that were collected to supplement the main data collection of the study?

7. How has the researcher integrated the results from the mixed methods? If necessary, how has the researcher explained conflicting findings that resulted from different methods?

8. What evidence is there that the researcher developed the design to be responsive to the practical and cultural needs of specific subgroups on the basis of such dimensions as disability, culture, language, reading levels, gender, class, and race/ethnicity?

QUESTIONS AND ACTIVITIES
FOR DISCUSSION AND APPLICATION

1. In your opinion, what are the advantages and disadvantages of using mixed methods/mixed models in special education research?

2. Talk to potential users of research information or think of yourself as a consumer. What are the strengths and weaknesses of a mixed method/mixed model approach?

3. What are the philosophical assumptions that underlie the mixed methods approach? How can you integrate the assumptions of the three major paradigms (postpositivist, interpretive/constructivist, and transformative/emancipatory) to guide your thinking in the use of mixed methods? What are the assumptions of the pragmatic paradigm and their implications for special education research?

4. Explain the main design options for mixed methods/mixed models research. Give an example of how each of these could be applied in special education research.

5. Select a research problem in special education research. Find a research study that uses a mixed methods/mixed model approach. Use the questions for critically analyzing mixed methods research to identify its strengths and weaknesses. What improvements would you suggest for that study?

6. Design a study using a mixed methods design. Explain how your design respects the integrity of the qualitative and quantitative methods. Explain how you would address the criteria implicit in the questions for critically analyzing mixed methods research.

7. Using one or more of the studies from the quantitative or qualitative chapters, rethink the study using mixed methods. How would the study change? What would you gain? What would you lose?

NOTE

1. In Tashakkori and Teddlie, several typologies of mixed methods/mixed models designs are presented in various chapters. They note that the formal field of mixed methods research is in its adolescence and therefore it is to be expected that various typologies would be present in the literature. The main points of definition appear to be the temporal relation between the quantitative and qualitative data collections (parallel vs. sequential), philosophical paradigm underlying the work (e.g., pragmatic or transformative/emancipatory), priority given to either qualitative or quantitative approaches (Creswell had described this as dominant, subdominant relations), and purpose of the research (confirmatory or exploratory). If design options were presented for each possible combination of these dimensions, then there would be 28 possible designs for mixed methods/ mixed models. If each possibility were presented for both mixed methods and mixed models, there would be 56 possible types. If you were to add the dimension of the four possible points at which mixed methods approaches could be applied, the possible types increase to a point that is not very functional. For the sake of parsimony, we have elected to include four possible dimensions to define major types of mixed methods/mixed models designs.

8

Identification and Selection of Research Participants

Women with disabilities experience poorer employment outcomes than women without disabilities and men with and without disabilities (Doren & Benz, 2001).

The meaning of this statement is not clear unless the reader knows something about the sample of individuals from which the data were collected to make this statement. Research results are ambiguous and difficult to interpret if the characteristics of the sample are not clear.

IN THIS CHAPTER

• Conceptual and operational definitions for special education students are described for the categories included in the federal legislation (Individuals with Disabilities Education Act), as well as for several emerging areas.

• Designing and selecting samples are described in terms of three choices available to researchers: probability-based samples, purposeful samples, and volunteer samples.

• Issues specific to special education samples are discussed, such as unique characteristics associated with different disability areas, practical constraints, comparison groups, sample size, sampling error, and sampling bias.

• The topics of generalizability, transferability, external validity, ethics, and confidentiality are also included.

• Questions for critically analyzing sampling designs and procedures are provided.

Much of this chapter explains the various definitions of the categories of disabilities, as well as the research implications of those definitions. Readers who are very familiar with special education categories may be able to skim through the first part of the chapter. For readers with less familiarity with the categories, an appendix of definitions from the federal legislation is provided (see Appendix 1).

The problems associated with the identification and selection of research participants are especially complex in special education research in that definitions of who is and who is not included in a disability category are quite variable. For example, the *23rd Annual Report to Congress on the Implementation of the Individuals with Disabilities Education Act* (U.S. Department of Education, 2001a) indicates that 5,683,707 persons between the ages of 6 and 21 have a disability (see Table 8.1). The definition for persons with disabilities that is used to determine that number includes any child who has:

> . . . mental retardation, a hearing impairment including deafness, a speech or language impairment, a visual impairment including blindness, serious emotional disturbance, (hereafter referred to as emotional disturbance), an orthopedic impairment, autism, traumatic brain injury, other health impairment, a specific learning disability, deaf-blindness, or multiple disabilities, and who, by reason thereof, needs *special education* and *related services*. (34 Code of Federal Regulations §300.7(a)(1))

The 2000 U.S. Census used this definition of disability:

> A long-lasting physical, mental, or emotional condition. This condition can make it difficult for a person to do activities such as walking, climbing stairs, dressing, bathing, learning, or remembering. This condition can also impede a person from being able to go outside the home alone or to work at a job or business.

The number of people with a disability based on that definition between the ages of 5 and 20 in 2000 was 5,214,334. The slight age difference between the two groups or the variation in definitions could account for the difference in numbers from the two sources.

Clarity in describing special education populations is important for understanding the professional literature and communicating research results to others and in the designing of studies (i.e., selecting samples, measures, and so on). Researchers have a responsibility to describe fully and clearly the characteristics of those persons studied and the educational contexts in which services are provided. Although this section of the text focuses primarily on methods for clearly defining characteristics associated with disabilities, researchers in special education should be aware of and report all important characteristics of the sample, including ethnicity and gender. A larger percentage of minorities and males have traditionally been identified as needing special education services (Garland-Thomson, 2001; Losen & Orfield, 2002; Rousso, 2001); therefore, the researcher must be precise about issues regarding ethnicity and gender in discussing the generalizability or transferability of a study's results.

Considerable controversy exists as to the wisdom of using labels for children with disabilities (Gage & Berliner, 1991). Proponents of labeling believe labels help identify children with special needs, help in further diagnosis and treatment, and facilitate communication, legislation, and administration in serving exceptional students. Opponents feel that labels are misleading, allow for misdiagnosis, and encourage stereotyping instead of encouraging accurate assessment and treatment of students' needs. The problem with labels is illustrated by this quote from a parent in one of the author's focus groups: "The school staff see my son as mentally retarded and ask, 'what can mentally retarded kids do?' They never say, 'What can Sam do?'" We feel that categories should be broad, but they should not conceal the range and complexity of the characteristics, needs, and abilities of the students.

POPULATION AND SAMPLE DEFINITION

Types of Definitions: Conceptual and Operational

Research constructs such as special education labels can be defined in two ways: Conceptual definitions are those that use other constructs to explain the meaning, and operational definitions are those that specify how the construct will be measured. For example, special education is conceptually defined in federal legislation (34 Code of Federal Regulations §300.26) as follows:

(1) As used in this part, the term special education means specially designed instruction, at no cost to the parents, to meet the unique needs of a child with a disability, including—
  (i) Instruction conducted in the classroom, in the home, in hospitals and institutions and in other settings; and
  (ii) Instruction in physical education.

(2) The term includes each of the following, if it meets the requirements of paragraph (a)(1) of this section:

(i) Speech-language pathology services, or any other related service, if the service is considered special education rather than a related service under State standards;

(ii) Travel training; and

(iii) Vocational education.

When using a conceptually defined construct, the other constructs used in the definition must be defined as well, such as at no cost, child with disabilities, and physical education. For example:

Travel training means providing instruction, as appropriate, to children with significant cognitive disabilities, and any other children with disabilities who require this instruction, to enable them to—

(i) Develop an awareness of the environment in which they live; and

(ii) Learn the skills necessary to move effectively and safely from place to place within that environment (e.g., in school, in the home, at work, and in the community). (34 Code of Federal Regulations §300.26)

An operational definition of special education might be "services provided in schools by teachers and related service personnel who have special education certification." You could then go to a school and ask the principal to identify students who receive services from teachers and related service personnel who have special education certification. For research purposes, the conceptual definition must be accompanied by an operational definition in order to communicate to the reader what was actually done in the research.

Population Size: How Many Children Have Disabilities?

The U.S. Office of Special Education publishes an annual report to Congress that provides information on the extent to which children and youths with disabilities are receiving special education and related services (U.S. Department of Education, 2001a). The number of students, ages 6 through 21, with disabilities served under Part B of IDEA reached 5,683,707 in 1999-2000, a 2.6% increase over the 1998-1999 school year. The number of children served has increased steadily since 1990-1991, when a total of 4,361,751 students were served. A ten-year comparison between 1990-1991 and 1999-2000 reveals that the total number of students, ages 6 through 21, served had grown by 30.3% (see Table 8.1).

States and outlying areas report data on students served in thirteen disability categories: specific learning disabilities, speech or language impairments, mental retardation, emotional disturbance, multiple disabilities,

Table 8.1   Changes in Number of Students Ages 6 Through 21 Served Under IDEA by Disability Category, 1990-1991 and 1999-2000

	1990-1991	1999-2000	Difference	Change (%)
Specific Learning Disabilities	2,144,017	2,871,966	727,949	34.0
Speech or Language Impairments	987,778	1,089,964	102,186	10.3
Mental Retardation	551,457	614,433	62,976	11.4
Emotional Disturbance	390,764	470,111	79,347	20.3
Multiple Disabilities	97,629	112,993	15,364	15.7
Hearing Impairments	59,211	71,671	12,460	21.0
Orthopedic Impairments	49,340	71,422	22,082	44.8
Other Health Impairments	56,349	254,110	197,761	351.0
Visual Impairments	23,682	26,590	2,908	12.3
Autism	a	65,424		
Deaf-Blindness	1,524	1,845	321	21.1
Traumatic Brain Injury	a	13,874		
Developmental Delay	b	19,304		
All Disabilities	4,361,751	5,683,707	1,321,956	30.3

a. Reporting on autism and traumatic brain injury was first required in 1992-1993.

b. Optional reporting on developmental delay for students ages 3 through 7 was first allowed in the 1997-1998 school year.

Source: U.S. Department of Education, Office of Special Education Programs, Data Analysis System (DANS).

hearing impairments, orthopedic impairments, other health impairments, visual impairments, autism, deaf-blindness, traumatic brain injury, and developmental delay. Developmental delay, the most recently added disability category, is applicable only to children ages 3 through 9, and its use for students ages 6 through 9 is optional for states and local educational agencies (LEAs). In 1999-2000, 22 states used the developmental delay category for children ages 6 through 9.

The relative distribution of students with disabilities across the thirteen disability categories did not change significantly from 1998-1999 to 1999-2000. Specific learning disabilities continued to be the most prevalent disability, representing one-half of the students with disabilities served under IDEA (2,871,966 or 50.5%). Speech or language impairments (1,089,964 or 19.2%), mental retardation (614,433 or 10.8%), and emotional disturbance (470,111 or 8.3%) were the next most used disability categories. Almost 9 out of 10 students, ages 6 through 21, served under IDEA were classified under one of these four disability categories.

Infants and Toddlers, Birth Through Two

Under the 1997 IDEA reauthorization, "infants and toddlers with disabilities are defined as children from birth through age two who need early intervention services because they . . .

> . . . are experiencing developmental delays, as measured by appropriate diagnostic instruments and procedures, in one or more of the following areas:
> cognitive development;
> physical development, including vision and hearing;
> communication development;
> social or emotional development;
> adaptive development; or
> . . . have a diagnosed physical or mental condition that has a high probability of resulting in developmental delay.

The term may also include, if a state chooses, children from birth through age two who are at risk of having substantial developmental delays if early intervention services are not provided." (34 Code of Federal Regulations §303.16)

In 1999-2000, 205,769 children and their families in the United States received early intervention services under Part C of the Individuals with Disabilities Education Act (IDEA). This figure represents 1.8% of the nation's infants and toddlers, according to July 2000 population estimates from the U.S. Census Bureau (U.S. Department of Education, 2001). National Early Intervention Longitudinal Study (NEILS) data indicate that boys made up 61% of the early intervention population and 65% of those with developmental delays. The largest racial/ethnic group in the early intervention population was White (56%), followed by Black (21%), Hispanic (15%), and Asian/Pacific Islander (5%). Most children (64%) were eligible for early intervention because of a developmental delay. Around 40% of the children who began early intervention at 12 months of age or less needed services for reasons related to prenatal/perinatal abnormalities. Among older children, a speech or communication problem was the most frequent reason for receipt of early intervention services.

Children Ages 3 Through 9

Under IDEA, states and local educational agencies (LEAs) are allowed to use the term "developmental delay" with children ages 3 through 9, rather than one of the thirteen disability categories. This means that, if they choose, states and LEAs do not have to say that a child has a specific disability. For children ages 3 through 9, a state and LEA may choose to include as an eligible "child with a disability" a child who is experiencing developmental delays in one or more of the following areas:

physical development,

cognitive development,

communication development,

social or emotional development, or

adaptive development . . . and who, because of the developmental delays, needs special education and related services. (34 Code of Federal Regulations §300.7(b)(1)(2), 300.313(b))

"Developmental delays" are defined by the state and must be measured by appropriate diagnostic instruments and procedures.

For children ages 3 through 5 with disabilities and those 2-year-olds who will turn 3 during the school year, states reported serving 588,300 preschool children with disabilities during the 1999-2000 school year. This number represents approximately 5% of all preschoolers who lived in the United States and its outlying areas during the year. State-reported data for 1999-2000 indicate that 67.3% of preschoolers who received services under IDEA were White (non-Hispanic), 15.7% were Black (non-Hispanic), 13.7% were Hispanic, 2.1% were Asian/Pacific Islander, and 1.2% were American Indian/Alaska Native. U.S. Census Bureau population estimates indicate that 61.8% of children ages 3 through 5 were White (non-Hispanic), 13.7% were Black (non-Hispanic), 19.3% were Hispanic, 4.3% were Asian/Pacific Islander, and 0.9% were American Indian/Alaska Native. Although these percentages are roughly comparable, they do suggest underrepresentation of Hispanic children and overrepresentation of White children in the Part B preschool population. To a lesser extent, Black children appeared to be overrepresented, and Asian/Pacific Islander children appeared to be underrepresented.

Categories of Special Education Populations: Definitions

IDEA includes thirteen categories of special education populations that are eligible for federal funding. (Children are counted by their specific disability only for ages 6 through 21.) For each population, we present the federal conceptual definition in Appendix 1. For newer populations or those not explicitly defined in the federal legislation, Appendix 1 also contains definitions from the *Diagnostic and Statistical Manual of Mental Disorders* (4th ed.) (DSM-IV) (American Psychiatric Association, 1994). This volume provides the most commonly accepted definitions of such disability areas as Attention Deficit Hyperactive Disorder and special forms of autism, such as Asperger's Syndrome. In the next section, we provide an operational definition of each category along with a discussion of characteristics relevant to research design. Finally, we present concerns about two specific populations: infant and toddler special populations and at-risk populations.

Specific Learning Disability

The ambiguity of the definition of learning disabilities in federal legislation and other sources has led to many classification problems. A review of prevalence studies of learning disabilities among the general population revealed that prevalence estimates have ranged from 2% to 30%, depending on the criteria used for identification (Kavale & Forness, 1998).

An operational definition typically found in research studies is to include participants who have already been identified by the school system as having a learning disability. For example, Hall, Peterson, Webster, Bolen and Brown (1999) indicated that their participants were students who had previously been identified as LD. The school system used the North Carolina State Procedures Governing Programs and Services for Special Needs (North Carolina Department of Public Instruction, 1993) as the basis for the diagnosis.

Controversy continues to surround the definition of learning disabilities for three reasons (Bennett & Ragosta, 1988). First, disorders that comprise learning disabilities are poorly conceptualized; for example, minimal brain dysfunction, perceptual disability, and dyslexia all refer to conditions whose etiology, symptoms, prevalence, and treatment are uncertain (Reid & Hresko, 1981). Second, the definition requires an ability-achievement discrepancy not the result of other factors, such as mental retardation, emotional disturbance, economic disadvantage, or sensory or physical impairment. This assumes that you can reliably differentiate causes of school failure. Third, learning disability is built on the idea of under-achievement and thus assumes that potential can be measured. In reality, tests can only predict future achievement, from which potential is inferred. Also, underachievement is not peculiar to children with learning disabilities.

The population with learning disabilities is very heterogeneous. Despite this heterogeneity, certain general characteristics about the learning disabled population have been noted which have implications for research (Gersten, Baker, & Lloyd, 2000; Ysseldyke, 2001). Poor basic skills, particularly in reading, may prevent accurate assessment of higher level abilities as well as impede assessment of other skills that are dependent on text reading.

Speech or Language Impairments

While federal legislation combines these two categories, educators tend to separate speech and language disorders. Speech disorders are those that deviate so far from the speech of other people that they call attention to themselves, interfere with communication, or cause the speaker or listener to be distressed (Gage & Berliner, 1991). For example, speech disorders include problems with articulation (omissions, substitutions, distortions, and additions of sounds), voice (pitch, loudness, and quality), and fluency (stuttering). Language disorders are those that arise in the basic understanding of the symbols we use to convey ideas (e.g., delayed language development and aphasia, that is, difficulty in comprehending or formulating messages).

Marinellie and Johnson (2002) provide an example of an operational definition of language impairment:

> The experimental group was comprised of fifteen participants who qualified for speech-language services because they had language impairments. They were enrolled in Grade 3 (six children), Grade 4 (four children), and Grade 5 (five children) in one elementary school in a primarily working-class community in a small Midwestern city. A certified speech-language pathologist (SLP) had previously diagnosed these children as having a language impairment that was not the result of depressed intellectual functioning, emotional disturbances, hearing loss, or physical defects. Thus, all the participants met the inclusionary and exclusionary criteria for specific language impairment (SLI, as described in Stark and Tallal, 1981). These students were currently enrolled in language intervention at their school. (p. 45)

Mental Retardation

Operational definitions of mental retardation vary by state, but a definition based solely on IQ is not adequate because of the construct of adaptive behavior. The American Association on Mental Retardation (2002) offers the following definition of adaptive behavior:

> Adaptive behavior is the collection of conceptual, social, and practical skills that people have learned so they can function in their everyday lives. Significant limitations in adaptive behavior impact a person's daily life and affect the ability to respond to a particular situation or to the environment.

Limitations in adaptive behavior can be determined by using standardized tests that are normed on the general population including people with disabilities and people without disabilities. On these standardized measures, significant limitations in adaptive behavior are operationally defined as performance that is at least two standard deviations below the mean of either (1) one of the following three types of adaptive behavior: conceptual, social, or practical or (2) an overall score on a standardized measure of conceptual, social, and practical skills.

Thus, adaptive behavior includes sensorimotor, communication, self-help, socialization, daily living, and vocational skills. Adaptive behavior can be assessed by tests such as the Vineland Social Maturity Scale or the Adaptive Behavior Scale. (Note: For sources of additional information about the tests used in special education, the reader is referred to Chapter 9.)

Mental retardation is a disability characterized by significant limitations both in intellectual functioning and in adaptive behavior as expressed in conceptual, social, and practical adaptive skills. This disability originates before the age of eighteen. A complete and accurate understanding of mental retardation involves realizing that mental retardation refers to a particular state of functioning that begins in childhood, has many dimensions, and is affected positively by individualized supports. As a model of functioning, it includes the contexts and environment within which the person functions and interacts and requires a multidimensional and ecological approach that reflects the interaction of the individual with the environment and the outcomes of that interaction with regard to independence, relationships, societal contributions, participation in school and community, and personal well-being (American Association for Mental Retardation, 2002).

The World Health Organization (2002) recognizes four levels of mental retardation, based on IQ: Mild, with a mental age of 8.5 to 11.0 years; Moderate, with a mental age of 6.0 to 8.5 years; Severe, with a mental age of 3.75 to 6.0 years, and Profound, with a mental age of 0 to 3.75 years. Based on acknowledged limitations of IQ testing and the need to integrate abilities related to adaptive behavior, there is an increasing tendency to drop these distinctions. The American Association on Mental Retardation (AAMR) developed a classification system based on the degree of support required for the child with mental retardation to function at his or her highest level (Hallahan & Kaufmann, 2000). These categories include: Intermittent, Limited, Extensive, and Pervasive. (See Table 8.2 for the definitions of these categories according to the AAMR.)

The measurement of deficits in adaptive behavior is subjective and depends on both the standards of the individuals making the judgment and the environment to which the student is expected to adapt (Ysseldyke & Algozzine, 1990). The AAMR definition provides a framework for the determination of the individual's functioning in a variety of environments.

Emotional Disorders

Operational definitions of behavior or emotional disorders may use psychological tests, such as the Rorschach Ink Blot, Minnesota Multiphasic Personality Inventory, or the Vineland Social Maturity Scale, or clinical interviews administered by trained specialists and supplemented by

Table 8.2   Classification of Mental Retardation Based on Levels of Support by AAMR

Classification	Supports Needed
Intermittent	Supports are provided "as needed." The individual may need episodic or short-term support during life span transitions (such as job loss or acute medical crisis). Intermittent supports may be low or high intensity when provided.
Limited	Supports are intense and relatively consistent over time. They are time-limited but not intermittent. They require fewer staff members and cost less than more intense supports. These supports likely will be needed for adaptation to the changes involved in the school-to-adult period.
Extensive	Supports are characterized by regular involvement (e.g., daily) in at least some setting (such as home or work) and are not time-limited (e.g., extensive home-living support).
Pervasive	Supports are constant, very intense, and are provided across settings. They may be of a life-sustaining nature. These supports typically involve more staff members and intrusiveness than the other support categories.

Source: Hallahan & Kaufmann, 2000.

careful observations of the challenging behavior and the conditions under which it occurs.

Multiple Disabilities

The heterogeneity of students who fit under the definition of multiple disabilities makes it especially important for researchers to describe the precise operational definition that is used. Constructing definitions or descriptions is difficult because the types and severity of the disabling conditions must be specified. Gee, Graham, Goetz, Oshima, and Yoshioka (1991) provided the following information about a student with multiple disabilities: blind (no light perception); physical disabilities and point of motor control (severe contractures and profound involvement of all four limbs; control over his head turn to the right (1 inch) when his head is supported; minimal control over his right arm movement away from his body (when assisted to bring his arm down to rest on his wheelchair tray); profound intellectual disability; and complex health care needs (severe seizure disorder, complex neurological and biobehavioral state changes, and digestive/nutritional difficulties).

Hearing Impairments (and Deafness)

Hearing disabilities range from total deafness to mild losses. Many operational definitions of hard-of-hearing and deafness have been developed (Bennett & Ragosta, 1988). Definitions of hearing loss are based on the two qualities of sound: loudness and pitch (Meadow, 1980). Loudness is measured in decibels (dB), from 0 for the softest sound to 120 for extremely loud sounds. Conversation is generally in the 60 to 70 dB range. Pitch or frequency of sounds is measured by hertz (Hz) or cycles per second. The frequencies that are most important for understanding speech are in the range of 500, 1,000, and 2,000 Hz. Paul and Quigley (1990, p. 41) provided the following operational definition of hearing loss based on results from the better unaided ear averaged across the speech frequencies, according to the International Standards Organization:

Degree of Impairment	Description
up to 26 decibels	Normal
27 to 40 decibels	Slight
41 to 55 decibels	Mild
56 to 70 decibels	Moderate
71 to 90 decibels	Severe
91+ decibels	Profound

Individuals in the slight, mild, and moderate categories are considered to be hard-of-hearing. Those in the severe and profound categories are considered to be deaf.

Certain general characteristics of deaf populations that have been reported have implications for conducting research. For example, students with mild losses rely mostly on speech when communicating with teachers and parents, and 85% have intelligible speech (Karchmer, Milone, & Wolk, 1979). More commonly, those with profound losses rely on manual communication, and only about 25% have intelligible speech. The students with severe losses fall between those with mild and profound losses. Deaf children present special challenges for researchers because of their well-documented delays in academic skills, language development, and socioemotional skills (Marschark, 1997). Deaf and hard-of-hearing children leave school with a third grade reading level on the average. (Note: Deaf children who are born to hearing parents often experience a delay in acquiring language, which affects their later abilities to learn to read. Academic performance is generally higher for students whose parents are deaf and who use American Sign Language from birth.)

Orthopedic Impairments

The category of orthopedic impairments includes a wide variety of impairments, some so mild as to be of no concern to the researcher. Some would require modification of the physical environment or additional means of communication or aids to instruction or locomotion. All would require a careful description of the participants' characteristics. Bennett and Ragosta (1988) provide a detailed explanation of the characteristics usually associated with cerebral palsy, poliomyelitis, muscular dystrophy, multiple sclerosis, and impairments caused by physical injury (e.g., amputation of limb or injury to spinal cord). For example, they describe characteristics associated with multiple sclerosis that would be of concern to the researcher, such as impaired sensation, lack of coordination, double vision, slurred speech, memory loss, spasticity, or paralysis of extremities. The disease is progressive and unpredictable, and therefore, it would be important to clearly explain the status of the participants in the study.

Other Health Impairments

This category also includes a wide variety of impairments, some of which would be of no concern to researchers. However, the researcher should be aware of the traditional classifications of such diseases as epilepsy (Barr, 2000). While many diseases can be controlled with medication, the effects of medication on the subject's ability to participate in research must be considered. For example, medication for epilepsy can affect coordination, vision, attention, and memory.

Two categories of children who may be included in the other health impairment group in need of special education include those with attention deficit hyperactivity disorder (ADHD) or attention deficit disorder (ADD). Children with ADHD are hyperactive or disruptive and have trouble paying attention. The problem appears to be an inability to process information quickly enough when presented with too much information. As a result, the child will tune out almost immediately and become either hyperactive (ADHD) or passive and lethargic (ADD). During the 1997 reauthorization hearings of the IDEA, Congress rejected the inclusion of ADD and ADHD as separate categories in the legislation because they took the position that children with these disabilities could meet the eligibility criteria for services in the current categories.

The *Diagnostic and Statistical Manual of Mental Disorders* (4th ed.) (DSM-IV) (American Psychiatric Association, 1994) provides the most commonly accepted definition of attention deficit hyperactivity disorder. The DSM-IV suggests that identification of children with ADD/ADHD be given both a clinical evaluation and an educational evaluation. The clinical evaluation can be based on such rating scales as the Teacher Report Form and Parent Report Form by Achenbach and Edelbrock (1983) or the revised Child

Behavior Profile and Child Behavior Checklist (Achenbach, 1991). Other parent and teacher rating scales can be found in Barkley (1998). The educational evaluation should include classroom observations as well as assessments of the child's productivity. Hall et al. (1999) used the DSM-IV guidelines to identify the ADHD students in their study. They indicated that the school system and psychologists obtained data on ADHD students with respect to behavior ratings in comparison to same age peers, parent and teacher ratings, and observation data in more than one setting.

Visual Impairment Including Blindness

Blindness and low vision are defined in the *International Classification of Diseases* (10th ed.) (ICD10) (World Health Organization, 2002):

- Blindness is defined as visual acuity of less than 3/60 or corresponding visual field loss in the better eye with best possible correction.

- Low vision corresponds to visual acuity of less than 6/18, but equal to or better than 3/60 in the better eye with best possible correction.

Visual impairments cover a wide range, from those with no vision whatsoever to those who can have 20/20 vision with corrective lenses. A more important distinction is based on the functional abilities of visually impaired individuals (Bennett & Ragosta, 1988). Most partially sighted and many legally blind individuals differ from totally blind individuals because they can use vision for participating in research, for example, reading large-type materials, holding pages close, and using magnification devices. Totally blind individuals depend on their tactual or auditory senses, thus using readers, Braille books, audiotapes, raised-line drawings, three-dimensional models, talking calculators, or Braille computers.

Deaf-Blindness

An operational definition of persons with deaf-blindness would combine the measurement of deafness described with the measurement of blindness discussed in the section on visual impairments. Students categorized as deaf-blind must also be described in terms of the presence of other disabling conditions. Researchers interested in working with the deaf-blind population should be aware that this group is also quite heterogeneous. Heterogeneity can be introduced through a number of variables, such as (1) variation in the range of hearing and vision loss, (2) presence of additional disabilities (it is estimated that about 60% of students with dual-sensory impairments also are severely to profoundly retarded [Paul & Quigley, 1990]), or (3) cause of the disabilities (e.g., Usher's syndrome involves progressive sensory impairment).

The *Annual Survey of Deaf and Hard of Hearing Children and Youth* revealed that about 2% of the hearing impaired sample are legally blind, and another 4% have uncorrected visual problems (Gallaudet Research Institute, 2001). The high incidence of deaf-blindness and additional disabling conditions has led to the placement of many students in programs for multiple disabilities, rather than in programs that specialize in deaf-blindness (Paul, 2001). Implications for researchers include: (1) care must be taken in reporting the characteristics of this heterogeneous group and (2) access to participants may be through programs for students with multiple disabilities, rather than deaf-blindness programs.

In one study that included a person with deaf-blindness, the authors described him as follows: some light perception in the left eye; functional hearing loss; physical disabilities and point of motor control (profound involvement in all four limbs, control over his right hand movement over and to the right, control of head turning when his head is down, holds head up for 5 seconds); profound intellectual disability; and complex health care needs (gastrointestinal degenerative disorder and severe seizure disorder) (Gee et al., 1991).

Autism

The *Diagnostic and Statistical Manual of Mental Disorders* (DSM-IV) (1994) is the guidebook that many professionals use to define autism. In this latest revision, five disorders are identified under the category of Pervasive Developmental Disorders: (1) Autistic Disorder, (2) Rett's Disorder, (3) Childhood Disintegrative Disorder, (4) Asperger's Disorder, and (5) Pervasive Developmental Disorder Not Otherwise Specified or PDDNOS (National Information Center for Children and Youth with Disabilities, 2003). These definitions are presented in Appendix 1.

Doctors are divided on the use of the term Pervasive Developmental Disorder (PDD). Many professionals use the term PDD as a short way of saying PDDNOS. Some doctors, however, are hesitant to diagnose very young children with a specific type of PDD, such as Autistic Disorder, and therefore only use the general category label of PDD. This approach contributes to the confusion about the term because the term PDD actually refers to a category of disorders and is not a diagnostic label. The appropriate diagnostic label to be used is PDDNOS—Pervasive Developmental Disorder Not Otherwise Specified—not PDD. PDD refers to the overall category of Pervasive Developmental Disorders, and the term PDDNOS refers to the specific disorder Pervasive Developmental Disorder Not Otherwise Specified. All of the disorders that fall under the category of PDD share, to some extent, similar characteristics. All types of PDD are neurological disorders that are usually evident by age three. In general, children who have a type of PDD have difficulty in talking, playing with other children, and relating to others, including their family.

The Confusion of Diagnostic Labels. The intent behind the DSM-IV is that the diagnostic criteria not be used as a checklist, but rather as guidelines for diagnosing pervasive developmental disorders. There are no clearly established guidelines for measuring the severity of a person's symptoms. Therefore, the line between autism and PDDNOS is blurry (Boyle, 1995).

As discussed earlier, there is still some disagreement among professionals concerning the PDDNOS label. Some professionals consider Autistic Disorder appropriate only for those who show extreme symptoms in every one of several developmental areas related to autism. Other professionals are more comfortable with the term Autistic Disorder and use it to cover a broad range of symptoms connected with language and social dysfunction. Therefore, an individual may be diagnosed by one practitioner as having Autistic Disorder and by another practitioner as having PDDNOS (or PDD, if the practitioner is abbreviating for PDDNOS).

Generally, an individual is diagnosed as having PDDNOS if he or she has some behaviors that are seen in autism but does not meet the full DSM-IV criteria for having Autistic Disorder. Despite the DSM-IV concept of Autistic Disorder and PDDNOS being two distinct types of PDD, there is clinical evidence suggesting that Autistic Disorder and PDDNOS are on a continuum (i.e., an individual with Autistic Disorder can improve and be rediagnosed as having PDDNOS, or a young child can begin with PDDNOS, develop more autistic features, and be rediagnosed as having Autistic Disorder). To add to the list of labels that parents, teachers, and others may encounter, a new classification system was recently developed by ZERO TO THREE: National Center for Infants, Toddlers, and Families (1994). Under this system, called the *Diagnostic Classification of Mental Health and Developmental Disorders of Infancy and Early Childhood*, the term Multisystem Developmental Disorder or MSDD is used to describe pervasive developmental disorders.

In one study, autism was operationally defined on the basis of a diagnosis from an outside agency and the confirmation of that diagnosis by an experienced clinical psychologist (Harris, Handleman, Gordon, Kristoff, & Fuentes, 1991). They also used the Childhood Autism Rating Scale to measure autistic behavior.

No Specific Test Available. Currently, no objective biological test, such as a blood test or an X-ray examination, can confirm a child's PDDNOS diagnosis. Diagnosing PDDNOS is complicated and much like putting together a jigsaw puzzle that does not have a clear border and picture. Therefore, it is reasonable to say that when a PDDNOS diagnosis is made that it reflects the clinician's best guess. Obtaining an accurate diagnosis requires an assessment conducted by a well-trained professional who specializes in developmental disorders, usually a child psychiatrist, developmental pediatrician, pediatric neurologist, developmental pediatrician, child psychologist, developmental psychologist, or neuropsychologist. Suggested assessments include a medical evaluation; interviews with parents, child, and child's teacher; behavior rating scales; direct behavioral observations; and psychological, educational, communication, and occupational assessments.

Traumatic Brain Injury

Towne and Entwisle (1993) operationally defined traumatic brain injury by describing the amount of time that had passed since the injury in months, the duration of the coma following injury, the duration of post-traumatic amnesia, and the level of cognitive functioning as measured by the Level of Cognitive Functioning Scale (Hagen, Malkmus, Durham, & Bowman, 1979). Russell (1993) recommended inclusion of similar types of information in her paper on educational consideration in traumatic brain injury.

Developmental Delay

Developmental delay is the newest category of disability added in the 1997 legislation. It is a term that states may use to report children ages 3 through 9. Conditions that are associated with developmental delay include Down's syndrome and other chromosomal abnormalities; sensory impairments, including vision and hearing; inborn errors of metabolism; microcephaly; severe attachment disorders, including failure to thrive; seizure disorders; and fetal alcohol syndrome.

Researchers should explain the meaning of developmental delay following the parameters set forth in the federal regulations, that is, specifying the areas of developmental delay, level of functioning, and criteria and procedures that were used to determine the child's status. For example, one study included 124 children, ages 3 through 6 years, with mild and moderate disabilities (Cole, Mills, Dale, & Jenkins, 1991). The researchers clarified the meaning of developmentally delayed with the following information:

> . . . includes children with deficits of at least 1.5 standard deviations below the mean in two or more of the areas of cognitive, language, social, gross motor, and fine motor development, or 2 standard deviations below the mean in any one area. Regarding specific diagnostic categories, approximately 80% of the participants were delayed in language, 50% were cognitively delayed, 65% exhibited fine motor deficits, 60% demonstrated delays in gross motor deficits, and 60% exhibited social-emotional delays. (p. 37)

DESIGNING AND SELECTING SAMPLES

Rarely is it possible or even necessary to collect data on all the individuals in a group (e.g., there are almost three million students who are considered to be learning disabled). The target population is defined as all the members of a group of people to whom we wish to generalize the results of our research. For example, the target population in the study of the employment experiences of females with disabilities (as compared to males) is the U.S. population of students in special education in the 1985-1986 school year who were in grades 7 through 12 or at least 13 years old (Wagner, 1992). Those individuals from whom data are actually collected are called a sample. The sample Wagner used included more than 8,000 youths, ages 13 to 21, and special education students in secondary schools in the 1985-1986 school year. Researchers need to be aware that there is a difference between the group to whom you wish to infer the results (the target population) and the accessible population (the group from which the sample is actually drawn). The confidence of inference is stronger to the accessible population than to the target population.

A researcher has three main options for the selection of the sample: probability-based sampling, purposeful sampling, or volunteer sampling. Each of these options will be discussed briefly in the following section. For more detailed explanations, the reader is referred to Gall, Gall, and Borg (2003), Creswell (2003), Patton (2002), and Mertens (1998).

Probability-Based Sampling

The basic rationale for choosing probability-based sampling strategies is to lessen the effects of bias in the results by using some form of random selection. Random selection means that each person has an equal or known probability of being selected from the population. (This is different from random assignment discussed in Chapter 4 in which individuals from a known sample are randomly assigned to the experimental or control groups.)

In order to use probability-based sampling, it is usually necessary to have a sampling frame, that is, a list of all the individuals or programs from which you plan to select your study participants. For example, you might use the Council for Exceptional Children's published membership list as your sampling frame. The quality of the chosen sample is dependent on the accuracy and completeness of the list. If there is a large turnover in membership or if some distinct subset of an eligible group does not join the organization, then there would be systematic bias in the sample from that perspective.

Simple Random Sampling. Simple random sampling means that each individual in the defined population has an equal and independent chance of being selected as a member of the sample. Independent means that the selection of one individual does not affect the selection of anyone else. Simple random sampling techniques yield research data that can be generalized to a larger population, within margins of error that can be determined statistically, and it allows the use of inferential statistics (explained in Chapter 9) for group comparisons. Simple random samples can be generated in a number of ways, for example, by computer generation of random numbers; putting all the names of the individuals in the population into a hat and drawing them out "at random"; or using a table of random numbers, randomly selecting a row or column in the table and then taking all the numbers in that row or column until enough participants have been selected.

Systematic Sampling. This technique can be used if all the names of the defined population are on a list which is not in some systematic order that would create a bias in the sample. It involves choosing every nth name from the list. For example, if you need to select 100 participants from a list of 1,000 individuals, divide the needed sample size by the number of individuals on the list (1,000/100 = 10). Then pick a random number less than 10 as a place to start on the list and choose every 10th name.

Stratified Sampling. In many situations, the researcher will want to do subgroup analyses with the data (e.g., comparing hard-of-hearing students with deaf students or African Americans with Caucasians). In these circumstances, stratified sampling is needed in order to have proportionate samples for the subgroup analyses. The desired strata (i.e., categories to be used for comparison) are defined, and individuals are randomly sampled within those strata (Henry, 1990; Lipsey, 1990).

This is the type of sampling that Wagner (1992) used to study gender differences. The list of students in the target population was stratified into three age groups (13 to 15, 16 to 18, and over 18) for each of the federal special education disability categories, and youths were randomly selected from each age/disability group so that approximately 800 to 1,000 students were selected in each disability category (with the exception of deaf-blind, for which fewer than 100 students were served in the districts and schools included in the sample). If the researcher expects to have small samples in subgroups, Lipsey (1990) explains how to over-sample certain groups and adjust for small cell sizes.

Cluster Sampling. The researcher may find it easier to get a list of all the schools with more than twenty visually impaired students than to get a list of all visually impaired students. Therefore, the researcher can start with a list of the schools and randomly select schools from the list. Then, data can be collected from all individuals at those schools, or a random sample of the students within those schools can be obtained for multistage cluster sampling.

Purposeful Sampling

Patton (2002) identified the following types of purposeful sampling:

Sampling extreme or deviant cases. Particularly unusual cases are selected in order to shed light on a specific problem, for example, the most and least successful students in the program.

Sampling typical cases. Individuals are chosen because they represent typical cases in a program (i.e., not extreme or deviant cases).

Maximum variation sampling. Cases are selected that represent a range on some dimension, for example, students who are mainstreamed for varying amounts of time during the school day.

Sampling critical cases. Cases are selected that are particularly important, based on some criteria of special significance to the researcher or the intended user of the research data, for example, including all students who had speech therapy prior to starting elementary school.

Sampling politically important or sensitive cases. This is a variation of the critical cases sampling strategy in which the researcher samples (or avoids sampling) politically important or sensitive cases, for example, a board member's child.

Convenience sampling. The researcher takes the sample that is easiest to come by.

Snowball sampling. The researcher proceeds by using initially selected participants to recommend other participants.

In qualitative research, sampling is relatively flexible. The researcher includes participants according to relevant criteria, based on an analysis of the data being collected and the emerging research questions. Many researchers who write from the transformative paradigm reject the term subject as dehumanizing (Reinharz, 1992). They prefer to use a term such as participant, thus recognizing the active exchange of information that occurs between the researcher and those who are asked to provide information in the study.

Volunteer Samples

For practical, ethical, and legal reasons, a researcher may not be able to use either random or purposeful sampling. Because consent forms must be signed in most research studies with human participants, nearly all educational research must be conducted with volunteer samples. Research on volunteer samples indicates that they tend to be better educated, from higher social-class status, and more intelligent (Gall, Gall, & Borg, 2003). Therefore, research conducted with volunteer participants generally tends to yield an optimistic picture of a treatment's effects.

Special Education Sampling Issues

In all research that involves students, there are concerns about privacy and revealing personally identifiable information. Because of this, researchers in special education often must collaborate with school officials to identify and select subjects, including families.

The heterogeneity, as well as the inconsistency in classification, of special education groups was mentioned in the section on definition of populations. In addition to those problems, other issues related to sampling are specific to research in special education.

Unique Factors Specific to Special Education Populations

For each special education group, several variables are uniquely associated with an accurate depiction of the nature of the individuals selected. For example, Mertens (1990b, 1991b) identified the following unique variables associated with deaf populations:

1. Family background characteristics: hearing status of parents and communication mode used in the home.

2. Student background characteristics: age at which loss occurred, degree and cause of loss, communication skills, degree of loss, hearing aid usage, presence of additional disabilities, and intelligibility of speech.

3. School or school district conditions: size of deaf student enrollment, support services, and expenditures.

4. Within-school conditions: deaf student-teacher ratio.

5. Instructional personnel characteristics: signing ability and training and experience working with deaf students.

6. Student attitudes: impulsivity and internal/external control.

7. Student placement: residential, mainstreamed, or self-contained classrooms.

8. Instructional personnel, including teachers and interpreters: communication mode used in the classroom and home.

Given the heterogeneity found within the special education populations, researchers must include an explanation of the characteristics that are unique to that population.

The variation within individuals with disabilities suggests a need for special caution in studies that attempt to match students in experimental and control groups. You have to be very careful that the disability is really the same and that the participants are similar on other key characteristics. It is all about interpretation and use, as well as external validity and variability of results by population studied. (See Chapter 9.)

Practical Considerations

The number and distribution of special education students impacts the sample design (i.e., the steps and procedures the researcher uses in planning and taking a sample. For example, in Florida, almost all of the districts with full-time programs for students with visual impairments have fewer than twenty students in the entire district. With potential participants scattered among many schools, the difficulty of identifying a sample and the variability of contextual factors increase. In particular with low-incidence populations, the expense of travel increases and complicates obtaining the necessary informed consents (Gersten, Baker & Lloyd, 2000).

The changing patterns in educational settings are exemplified by the area of deafness, where enrollment in residential schools decreased between 1978 and 1988 by 38%, with fewer than 10,000 of the 46,000 deaf students enrolled in residential schools (Schildroth, 1989). During that ten-year period, the number of individual schools serving deaf students increased substantially, growing from 4,789 in 1978 to 8,310 in 1988. Approximately one-half (4,096 of the 8,310) of the programs had only one deaf student enrolled in 1988. Currently, the majority of deaf children receive their education in mainstream settings (Siegel, 2001). Eleven years after the passage of IDEA, of those schools with deaf and hard-of-hearing children, 52% had one deaf or hard-of-hearing child while 24% had 2 or 3 deaf or hard-of-hearing children.

Comparison Group

You may recall the discussion in Chapter 4 of nonequivalent control groups in that you may have students with learning disabilities in each group, but they may differ widely on several other important variables that could affect the outcome of the study. In many research designs, the students' performance or characteristics are compared with those of another sample that varies on some specified characteristic (the comparison group). DeStefano and Wagner (1991) discussed options and problems associated with selecting an appropriate comparison group. They described four common comparison groups.

The general population can be used as a comparison. Often extant data are available for such a comparison from such databases as High School and Beyond and National Longitudinal Survey of Youth. But students with disabilities differ from nondisabled peers in important ways. As a part of the National Longitudinal Transition Study, Marder and Cox (1990) reported that the disabled population contained more males, Blacks, urban dwellers, people with lower incomes (<$25,000), household heads without high school diplomas, and single-parent households. Also, other mediating factors differentiate the general education population from the disabled population, such as participation in special school programs, decreased options for interaction with nondisabled peers, and social stigma.

Comparisons across disability categories are an option. It is important to disaggregate data by disability groups because of the heterogeneity that has been discussed previously. There is also heterogeneity within categories that must be addressed, such as variations in IQ levels in the learning disabled category.

Cross-unit comparisons involve the comparison of students with disabilities in one school or school district with students in another school or school district. In such comparisons, the researcher must be sensitive to demographic differences and differences in the educational philosophies, policies, and practices.

Longitudinal studies that examine changes over time for the same students or similar groups of students allow comparison with one group at two or more points in time. The researcher must again be sensitive to historical influences, such as changes in demographic conditions, policy (e.g., changes in graduation requirements), or economic conditions in the community.

Sample Size

Insufficient sample size can be a problem because of the practical considerations discussed previously, but also because of the need to disaggregate the data or because of attrition (DeStefano & Wagner, 1991). Many factors go into decisions concerning sample size: size of the population, expected strength of the treatment variable, degree of variability on the characteristics of interest between or among the groups, specific research approach, desired degree of statistical significance in the findings, and logistics. Very rough rules of thumb for sample sizes for different research approaches are presented in Table 8.3.

When it is necessary to disaggregate the sample by disability areas, race, gender, or other variables, the sample cell sizes may become too small for meaningful interpretation. For example, in a study of reclassification trends in special education, the researchers were interested in the impact of a change in service district on the reclassification rate (Mertens, Harper, Haigh, & Hayden, 1992). However, only 4% of the sample changed service districts during the three-year period of the study. Therefore, sample sizes disaggregated by disability condition and age would have been too small to make meaningful interpretations. Henry (1990) describes strategies for weighting in subpopulation analyses, and Lipsey (1990) describes ways to design research that will be sufficiently sensitive to detect the intended effects.

Attrition is a second reason for small sample sizes (DeStefano & Wagner, 1991). In the National Longitudinal Transition Study, researchers experienced a 2% per year loss for youths who were in the first wave of the survey in 1987, with higher attrition rates for older youths and those who were no longer in secondary school. They recommended that the initial

Table 8.3   Rough Rules of Thumb for Sample Sizes

Type of Research	Recommended Sample Size
Correlational	About 30 observations
Multiple regression	At least 15 observations per variable
Survey research	100 observations for each major subgroup; 20 to 50 for minor subgroups
Causal comparative, experimental, or quasi-experimental	About 15 observations per group
Ethnography	About 30 to 50 interviews
Case studies	Can be only one case or can be multiple cases
Phenomenology	Approximately 6 participants
Grounded theory	About 30 to 50 interviews
Participative inquiry	Small "working team"; whole communities for meetings; samples for surveys
Focus groups	7 to 10 people per group; 4 groups for each major audience

Adapted from Mertens (1998)

sample size be increased by an appropriate percentage so that the desired sample size would still be available at the end of the study.

Sampling Error and Sampling Bias

Sampling error is the difference between characteristics of the sample and the population and can be estimated with random samples (DeStefano & Wagner, 1991). The sampling error is a function of sample size; smaller samples have larger errors associated with them. When probability sampling is used, the researcher should report estimates of sampling error (Mertens, 1998).

Sampling bias affects the generalizability of the study. The researcher must explore potential bias and present potential bias to the reader. To assess bias, the researcher must determine the comparability of the population that the sample purports to represent and the samples of participants for which data are available.

Henry (1990) identified a number of factors that affect bias. Two of these include response rate and the extent to which students who were included differ from those the sample is purported to represent. Sample bias increases as response rate decreases because of the heterogeneity of a small sample. Therefore, with survey research in particular, follow-up of nonrespondents and comparison of nonrespondents with respondents is essential.

GENERALIZABILITY, EXTERNAL VALIDITY, AND TRANSFERABILITY

In the positivist paradigm, external validity is the extent to which the findings of a study can be applied to people and settings outside the research study (Gall, Gall, & Borg, 2003). Population validity is one source of external validity that concerns the extent to which the results of an experiment can be generalized from the specific sample that was studied to a larger group of participants. In the empiricist tradition, the question is asked: To what extent can I generalize from the study sample to a defined population?

In the constructivist paradigm, Guba and Lincoln (2000) suggest that the criterion of transferability should be used to answer the question: How can we determine the degree to which the findings of a particular inquiry may have applicability in other contexts or with other respondents? The two strategies they suggest for dealing with this issue are thick description and use of purposeful sampling. Thick description means that the narrative is developed in such a way that judgments about the degree of fit or similarity may be made by others who may wish to apply all or part of the findings elsewhere. Purposeful sampling was previously discussed in the section on designing and selecting samples.

ETHICS AND CONFIDENTIALITY

Researchers in special education must follow appropriate ethical principles to ensure that the rights of participants in the study are protected, such as those developed by the American Psychological Association for conducting research with human participants (American Psychological Association, 2002).

Sieber (1992) offered a logical ethical framework to guide researchers and those responsible for the ethical review of research based on the federal regulations that require protection of human participants. This includes the use of an Institutional Review Board (IRB) to safeguard the participants' rights and to ensure that proper procedures are followed with reference to participants' consent to participate in research. She recommended the following principles for researchers to follow:

1. The study should be designed to minimize risk to the participants in the research.

2. Researchers should only attempt to undertake research in areas in which they are competent to do so, thereby decreasing threats to the welfare of the participants.

3. Participants should be fully informed as to the potential consequences of the research, both risks and benefits.

4. When research participants are people with disabilities, they are considered to have a higher degree of vulnerability. Special precautions must be taken to protect them from risk. Recommended strategies include consulting with experts and members of the vulnerable community to determine appropriate strategies.

5. Researchers must obtain informed consent from adults and informed assent from minors. Consent is usually needed from the parent or guardian for minors and from school officials if the research is carried out in the school.

6. Researchers should prevent harm from coming to the participants. However, they should also be prepared to offer suitable compensation if an unforeseen harm does occur.

Special education has had a strong ethical component since its inception because it developed largely from a commitment to the ethical requirement that all individuals be provided with access to a decent public education, regardless of how they might differ from the general population with respect to various skills, abilities, and powers that affect school performance (Howe & Miramontes, 1991). The Council for Exceptional Children (CEC) developed a formal ethical code that addressed the specific ethics of conducting research with special education populations (Council for Exceptional Children, 1997). The CEC's code of ethics states that special education professionals are required to protect the rights and welfare of participants, interpret and publish research results with accuracy and a high quality of scholarship, support a cessation of the use of any research procedure that may result in undesirable consequences for the participants, and exercise all possible precautions to prevent misapplication or misuse of a research effort. Special education researchers, like practitioners, must be alert to the implicit value commitments and consequences that attend categorizing individuals as learning disabled, mentally retarded, and so on. The researcher must grapple with the problem of trying to balance general principles that apply to special education populations with the values and interests that characterize individual cases.

In line with the ethical principles that have been discussed previously, researchers must also be aware of the need for current and long-term protection for their participants. It must not be possible to identify participants at the time of the study and report, and also it should not be possible some time down the road to identify them, either using the original database or if additional data becomes available that when combined with facts reported in the study could identify the original participants or participant. This is more often the case in qualitative research when a person is in a situation or place that could reveal his or her identification later, when new data are available. This also happens when seemingly unidentifiable quotes are used.

Access to information can be complicated when there are several agencies involved, for example, school and mental health. The researcher must determine who the gatekeepers are and what the proper procedures are for accessing information in each of the agencies.

The view of ethics as written about by feminists and minorities has parallel (though not exact) applicability to persons with disabilities (Mertens, 1998). For example, in Cook and Fonow's (1990) discussion of the feminist perspective of ethics in research, they note the use of language as a means of subordination, such as the use of masculine pronouns, application of offensive adjectives to women's experiences, and the subsumption of women under male categories. Parallels exist in the writings of minorities about race research, such as defining single motherhood as a moral or social problem (e.g., broken home) when it applies to minority women, but as an alternative family structure when it applies to White women. Stanfield (1993b) notes that how elites talk and write has a profound role in reproducing the racial order of things. Social science discourse involves an elite way of talking and writing that in race-centered societies creates a public image of the dominant and of the oppressed that appears to be objective and value-free. Oppressive use of language persists in the identification of persons with disabilities. Even the word disability is negative, defined in terms of what cannot be done. In the area of deafness, deaf people prefer to be thought of as a cultural group that uses visual-gestural communication, not as a group who cannot hear.

QUESTIONS FOR CRITICALLY ANALYZING SAMPLE DESIGN AND IMPLEMENTATION

1. What is the population of interest? How was the sample chosen? Probability? Purposeful? Volunteer?

2. What are the characteristics of the sample? To whom can you generalize the results? Is adequate information given about the characteristics of the sample?

3. How large is the population? How large is the sample? What is the effect of the sample size on the interpretation of the results?

4. Is the sample selected related to the target population?

5. Who dropped out during the research? Were they different from those who completed the study?

6. In qualitative research, was thick description used in the description of the sample?

7. In qualitative research, what is the effect of using purposeful sampling on the transferability to other situations?

8. Are female participants excluded, even when the research question affects both sexes? Are male participants excluded, even when the research question affects both sexes?

9. Does the researcher report the sample composition by gender and other background characteristics, such as race/ethnicity and class?

10. Have all proprietal concerns been addressed using IRB guidelines for setting in which the research is being conducted?

QUESTIONS AND ACTIVITIES FOR DISCUSSION AND APPLICATION

1. Why is it important for the researcher to provide specific explanations of the methods used to identify and select the sample?

2. Where do you stand on the labeling controversy? Should labels be abandoned as misleading or retained as functional?

3. What is the difference between a conceptual and an operational definition? Give an example of each.

4. Choose one conceptual definition of a disability area. Brainstorm as many ways as you can to operationally define that area. What are the strengths and weaknesses of the different operational definitions you generated?

5. What are the differences between the three types of sampling strategies: probability-based, purposeful, and volunteer/convenience? Describe a situation in which you might use each type of sampling strategy. What are the advantages and disadvantages of each?

6. How do factors that are unique to each disability area influence sampling and the interpretation of research findings?

7. What problems are encountered in trying to select an appropriate comparison group?

8. What do generalizability and external validity mean? How can they be enhanced in a research study?

9. Using the questions for critical analysis (1 through 5, 8, 9, and 10), critique the following description of a sample and suggest alternatives to improve the study:

In a study of intellectual functioning of children with autism, children from two classes in a developmental disabilities center participated (Harris et al., 1991). One class (the segregated class) served only children with autism, while the other was an integrated class that included normally developing children. Because they did not have enough peers from the integrated class to provide a comparison group, they used an additional four children from a university day care facility. The sample for the study of intellectual functioning included nine children with autism and nine normally developing children. There was one girl in each group.

10. Using the questions for critical analysis (1 through 10), critique the following description of a sample and suggest alternatives to improve the study:

Sue, Andrew, and John attended an early intervention preschool for hearing-impaired children that focused on supporting the children's acquisition of language, be it spoken or signed, as a prerequisite to literacy learning. The preschool was divided into three levels, Preschool I, Preschool II, and Kindergarten, and children were placed according to age and mode of communication, that is, either oral/aural English or total communication. Sue (age 3.11), Andrew (age 5.0), and John (age 5.10) were chosen to participate as case studies because they each had profound hearing losses, they had hearing parents, there was some difference in their socioeconomic status, and their verbal language worlds reflected the multiplicity, diversity, and variability typically experienced by profoundly deaf children (Williams, Kantor, & Pinnell, 1992, p. 5).

9

Information Collection

Did students with mental retardation increase their ability to use socially acceptable interaction skills as a result of the new intervention? Were they able to effectively use the skills in the classroom? Did the learning transfer to other settings, including the home? What was the cost of the intervention? Did the experimenters use learning strategies appropriate for learners with mental retardation? Did the students have the necessary entry level skills to be able to benefit from the social skills training?

The common theme to all of these questions is the need for information. Researchers acquire information about people, products, programs, organizations, and environments through the process of data collection in order to answer research questions and defend conclusions and recommendations, based on the findings from the research. The goal of this chapter is to explore the issues and processes for data collection from persons with disabilities.

IN THIS CHAPTER

- The purpose of information collection in relation to the needs of the research is presented.
- Accommodations necessary for collection of data from persons with disabilities are discussed.
- The basic types of information sources available to the researcher are set forth.

- Criteria for judging the technical adequacy of data collection instruments are described.
- Suggestions for selecting and using data collection instruments are discussed.
- Questions for critically analyzing information collection in research are provided.

THE PURPOSE OF INFORMATION COLLECTION

The purpose of information collection is to learn something about people or things as directed by the research questions or hypotheses. The focus is on a particular attribute or quality of the person or thing being measured. For example, MacMillan, Widaman, Balow, Hemsley, and Little (1992) were interested in how students with learning disabilities felt about school. The attribute that they were measuring was attitude toward school. In addition to collecting information about the dependent variable, in many research projects it is also important to collect information about the research participants, the intervention, and the context in which the research was conducted. This is particularly true for impact research where the researcher plans to make claims not only about what happened to participants – how they changed or did not change–but also about why these results were observed. In order to make a convincing argument, the researcher will require information from a variety of sources.

Researchers face two challenges when developing the information collection strategies for the proposed research: (1) the attribute(s) to be measured must be identified and (2) a decision must be made about how to measure the attribute(s). The process of determining how to measure the attribute is referred to as operationalizing. For example, MacMillan et al. (1992) operationalized the concept of attitudes toward school by selecting the Survey of School Attitudes (SSA) (Hogan, 1975) as their dependent measure.

An essential step in the process of collecting information is developing an information collection plan. Without a plan, the researcher is likely to encounter several false starts at this phase of the research. The research questions are used to guide the development of the data collection plan (see Chapter 3 for strategies for developing your research questions). Most research will be aimed at answering a number of research questions. For each question, the researcher needs to set forth a plan to collect information to answer the question. The plan should identify the source(s) of information, special considerations to be made in the collection process (see accommodations discussion following), who will be collecting the information and when, and at what point the data are needed for analysis, interpretation, and reporting. Finally, and perhaps most important, the plan should include a timeframe and process for field testing the data collection process and instruments – things rarely work out as planned.

As noted in Chapter 2, the research questions or hypotheses guide the researchers' response to these two challenges. A major resource is the literature review, but it is also suggested that the researcher discuss the proposed research with other professionals interested in the same research topic. The purpose is to identify what others have considered relative to the targeted attributes and their measurement. When collecting data from persons with disabilities, modifications in strategies and materials of those described for the nondisabled populations are often required.

Types of Accommodations

Thurlow, Ysseldyke, and Silverstein (1993) summarized the status regarding knowledge about accommodations in testing students with disabilities as follows: "There does not currently exist a set of guidelines about acceptable accommodations that is based on comprehensive, empirical research" (p. 3). Since 1993, there has been an intensive study of accommodations of assessments and assessment conditions. In fact, a recent review of the topic by Pitoniak and Royer (2001) references nearly 100 articles on the subject.

Pitoniak and Royer (2001) present a very informative treatment of salient issues related to test accommodations including legal and legislative considerations as well as research on the effects of the accommodations on test score interpretation. One of the major concerns that remain is the validity of the test under the accommodation conditions – Does the score accurately reflect the student's understanding of the construct being measured, rather than the influence of his or her disability?

Pitoniak and Royer cite important resources that should be consulted by the special education researcher or evaluator who plans to make accommodations in the test or testing conditions:

- *The Standards for Educational and Psychological Testing* (American Educational Research Association, American Psychological Association, and National Council on Measurement in Education, 1999) (hereafter called the 1999 Standards). According to Pitoniak and Royer, the 1999 Standards include six strategies for test accommodation: (1) modification of presentation format, including the use of Braille or large-print booklets for visually impaired examinees or the use of written or signed test directions for hearing-impaired examinees; (2) modification of response format, including providing a scribe to mark answers or allowing the use of a computer to record responses; (3) modification of timing, including extended testing time or frequent breaks; (4) modification of test setting, including individual administration and altering lighting or other physical test setting conditions; (5) using only parts of a test, which is more relevant to clinical settings; and (6) using alternate assessments. The 1999 Standards also include twelve standards specifically applicable when testing individuals with disabilities.

- The Assessment Accommodation Checklist developed by Elliott, Kratochwill, and Gilbertson (1998) provides a categorization of accommodations that might be used depending on the individuals being assessed and the assessment conditions. The checklist categories cited in Pitoniak and Royer are: (1) motivational instructions designed to produce optimal effort, (2) provision of assistance prior to testing, (3) flexible scheduling of tests, (4) changes in test setting, (5) assistance in understanding test directions, (6) assistance during assessment, (7) provision of aids such as adaptive technology, and (8) changes in test format or content (as might be required, e.g., with visually impaired students).

Dynamic Assessment of Testing Accommodations created by Fuchs and Fuchs (1999) is based on the assumption that the accommodations should produce a significant test performance gain for the students for whom the accommodation is made and requires the administration of tests under both accommodation and nonaccommodation circumstances to determine if there is an accommodation gain. If there is an accommodation gain, then the accommodation would be used.

Pitoniak and Royer cite the work of Thurlow, House, Boys, Scott, and Ysseldyke (2000) who have developed a categorization system for assessing the impact of the accommodation. Three categories are suggested where the impact on test interpretation (validity) that the proposed accommodation will have ranges from none to potential to probable. The three categories developed by Thurlow et al. are:

- Category 1, accommodations that are not expected to influence test score interpretation because they are unrelated to the construct being measured;
- Category 2, accommodations that could pose a threat to test score interpretation depending on what is being measured; and
- Category 3, accommodations involving a change in the construct being measured and resulting scores to be interpreted cautiously. For example, allowing an examinee with a disability to use a calculator on a mathematics test could change the nature of what the test is measuring.

The 1999 Standards cite examples when test accommodations may be inappropriate. The test-taker's disability may be directly relevant to the characteristic being measured in the assessment. For example, if the assessment was aimed at identifying a particular set of skills relevant to succeeding on an employment task, it would be inappropriate to mask the interaction of disability and task competence through modifications. A second and perhaps obvious challenge to the appropriateness of modification occurs when the purpose of the assessment is to identify a specific disability. Finally, the 1999 Standards caution that, as noted by Fuchs and Fuchs (1999), there are occasions when the test does not need to be modified – no gain would be observed.

Collecting Information from "Hard to Reach" Participants

Research and evaluation studies addressing issues related to special education often are confronted with the challenge of collecting information from participants who for various reasons cannot respond to typical assessment processes. These include persons whose disability prevents them from responding. For example, a person with a visual impairment or individuals with limited English or low literacy skills may not be able to take a written assessment. In addition, the age of the participant may preclude his or her involvement in the traditional assessment process. For example, researchers working with young children may have to engage the assistance of the child's parents. A very helpful resource for adapting research and evaluation strategies for hard to reach participants may be found at http://ag.arizona.edu/fcr/fs/evaluation/adapeval.htm.

Sources of Information

Hedrick, Bickman, and Rog (1993) identified two types of information sources available to researchers: primary and secondary. Primary information sources include people (program participants), observations of events (classroom instruction), physical documents (products/projects), and assessments (achievement tests). Secondary sources include administrative records (placement records), prior research studies (data collected by other researchers), national databases (the National Assessment of Educational Progress ([NAEP]), and various forms of documentary evidence (evaluation reports).

Primary Information Sources

Collection of data to address research questions can be accomplished through a variety of techniques. Surveys, interviews, and observations are discussed in Chapters 5 and 6 and will not be discussed in this chapter.

Alternative Assessment and Portfolios

Performance assessment is a process for collecting information through systematic observation in order to make decisions about an individual. Performance assessment relies on the use of multiple types of assessments, not a single test or measurement device, and assessment occurs across time. The primary vehicle for assessment is the direct observation of performance in the form of behavior and products. Performance assessment is an essential element of alternative assessment, and the portfolio is the vehicle through which performance assessment information is stored.

Performance assessment or curriculum-based assessment is typically designed to collect information on the instructional needs and/or progress of students through the continuous, direct observation of student performance (Fuchs & Deno, 1991). The assessment is keyed to the existing curriculum content and is based on enroute and terminal instructional objectives. The information collected reflects both the student's approach to the learning task and the products developed. This type of assessment is especially valuable as an alternative to standardized assessments in which students with disabilities may not be able to participate. These types of assessments are best used to measure the progress of individual students rather than to compare the performance of one student to another.

The information contained in the portfolios may serve as measures of the dependent variable in a research study and include collections of participant work representing a selection of the participant's performance, such as written assignments, videotapes, or solutions to mathematics problems. Many states and school divisions use portfolios as an alternative to standardized assessment. Thompson, Quenemoen, Thurlow, and Ysseldyke (2001) provide an excellent overview of alternative assessment as a tool to measure the progress of students with disabilities. Another excellent resource on portfolios is found at http://transition.alaska.edu/www/Portfolios/bookmarks.html.

There are challenges to using portfolios in research and evaluation studies because of the subjective nature of the collection and scoring of the information found in the portfolio. Salvia and Ysseldyke (2001), cited in Thompson et al., suggested that the following issues need to be considered:

- How the content will be selected for inclusion in the portfolio
- What quality of work will be included – best versus typical
- Whether students should participate in selecting the work that will be included
- How much information is required to get a true score
- How reliability and validity of the information will be determined

One method for scoring the information in portfolios is the rubric. According to Solomon (2002), a rubric is an assessment tool for verbally describing and scaling levels of student achievement as represented, for example, by products found in a portfolio. The rubric presents a gradation of performance from poor to excellent or above standard, at standard, or below standard, and a scale value for each gradation (1 for poor, 5 for excellent) represents the score.

While there are several types of rubrics, the developmental rubric is the most useful because the score provides a gauge for where the participant is on a continuum and allows the researcher to make comparisons that are

Table 9.1   Tips on Developing Rubrics

Decide whether the rubric addresses the most important aspects of student performance.

- Decide whether or not the rubric addresses the instructional outcome(s) to be measured.
- Decide whether the rubric includes anything extraneous. If so, change the rubric or use a different one.
- Don't pay too much attention to the rubric's stated grade level. It may be usable at other grades with little or no modification.
- See if a rubric from a different subject area can be adapted to fit your needs. Reading rubrics can often be used to assess listening, writing rubrics may be adapted to assess speaking, and fine arts rubrics can sometimes be applied to several different art forms.
- Make sure the rubric is clear.
- Try the rubric out on some actual samples of student work.
- See if you and your colleagues can usually arrive at consensus about what scores to assign a piece of student work.
- Feel free to combine or modify rubrics to make them work better.

Adapted from http://www.rubrics4teachers.com/

both criterion referenced – where the participant is with respect to his or her performance – and normative – where the participant is relative to other participants. Two excerpts from a rubric for evaluating a lesson plan are set forth in Table 9.1. Column one of the rubric gives the first of eight components of an effective lesson. The last four columns, with numbers 1, 2, 3, or 4, offer progressive descriptors for continuous improvement of a lesson. The lesson being evaluated could be given an individual score for each component or the average of the eight components could be presented. Table 9.1 contains tips on developing rubrics, and two sample rubrics are found in Table 9.2 and at this Web site: http://www.rubrics/4teachers.com/.

Tests

Tests are used extensively in research to collect information about student performance. To make the researcher's selection of the appropriate measurement device easier, it is helpful to categorize the numerous types of measures. Several classes of measurement devices are briefly reviewed in the following section. The reader should note that much of the accommodation discussion is aimed at students with disabilities taking tests like those described as follows. For a more in-depth discussion of these topics, the reader should go to Kubiszyn and Borich (2003) and Murphy and Davidshofer (1998).

Table 9.2   Sample Rubric[1]

Geography Mural	Novice	Apprentice	Veteran	Master
Accurate Detail and Depth	Incorrect or little facts, hardly any details (1-3 pts.)	Some facts are accurate, some detail (4-6 pts.)	Substantial amount of facts, good amount of detail (7-9 pts.)	Exceptional amount of facts, vivid descriptions (10-12 pts.)
Clear Focus	Vague and unclear (1-2 pts.)	Some focus, but not organized enough (3-4 pts.)	Well organized and clearly presented (5-6 pts.)	Highly organized and easy to follow (7-8 pts.)
Design	Little to no layout and design (1-3 pts.)	Simple design, but layout could be more organized (4-6 pts.)	Attractive and invites the viewer (7-9 pts.)	Exceptional design and outstanding visual appeal (10-12 pts.)

Sample Rubric for Evaluating a Lesson Plan[2]

Components	1 No evidence	2 Some evidence	3 Evidence	4 Strong evidence
Concepts/ Concept Statement	• No evidence of concept statement(s) • Concept statement(s) do not relate to Ohio Proficiency Test (OPT) outcomes and/or the Ohio Competency Based Model (OCBM)	• Concept statement(s) demonstrates relationship to OPT outcomes and/or the OCBM	• Concept statement(s) clearly defines the focus of the lesson plan and the relation to OPT outcomes and/or the OCBM	• Concept statement(s) clearly defines the focus of the lesson plan and shows the interrelation-ship among concepts and relation to OPT outcomes and/or the OCBM

1. Stix, Andi. (1997). *Creating rubrics through negotiable contracting and assessment.* Washington, DC: U.S. Department of Education. (ERIC Document Reproduction No. ED411274)

2. http://www.uc.edu/certitest/rubric/rubric.htm.

Standardized and Nonstandardized Tests.   We begin with a comparison of standardized and nonstandardized tests. When compared to the non-standardized test, the most distinguishing characteristic of the standard-ized test is its uniformity in directions for administering and scoring the instrument, as well as the developmental cycle that it goes through. The nonstandardized test is usually not developed through a rigorous process and has a limited purpose and application, such as the teacher-made test or that developed by a researcher for a specific study.

With standardized tests, there is a reference group of people who participated in the standardization of the test, to which researchers can compare the performance of their subjects. This reference group is referred to as the norm group. Its raw scores on the test are compiled into norm tables, often in the form of percentile ranks, which furnish the percentage of students in the norm group who received the same score or lower.

Researchers who choose to use standardized measures are faced with the challenge of locating an instrument that was developed with a norm group that matches the research sample. If the research sample is com-posed of students with learning disabilities, then the researcher would have to check the test manual to identify the characteristics of the norm group to determine if students with learning disabilities were in the norm group and if there was a norm table specifically for this group. Unfortunately, tests that are standardized are usually globally referenced to the general population. Thus, most standardized tests do not contain information about the performance of persons with specific disabilities, and persons with more severe disabilities are most frequently omitted. This does not mean that the test could not be used in research directed at this population. Rather, it would be inappropriate to use the norms for interpretations or generalizations. As noted in Chapter 3, the researcher should review the literature to see how other researchers have dealt with this problem in using the proposed measurement device.

Norm Referenced versus Criterion Referenced.   Norm referenced and crite-rion or domain referenced measurement devices represent other types of measurement. Most standardized achievement tests are norm referenced. The purpose of the norm referenced test is to enable the researcher to com-pare the performance of an individual to the performance of like individ-uals in a well-defined, previously tested group. On the other hand, the criterion referenced or domain referenced test addresses the content or domain of the attribute being measured. The intent is to identify how much of the attribute, as defined by the domain, has been acquired or learned by the student, rather than comparing the performance to other subjects, as in the norm referenced test. The concept of criterion is applied when the researcher identifies a particular level of performance that subjects should reach as a result of being exposed to a particular intervention.

Because of the differences in the intended purposes of these two types of tests (comparison with other people as opposed to comparison with a set criterion of performance), the two types of tests are developed using very different methods. The effect of using the tests is also quite different because of the way they are developed. Remember, norm referenced tests are specifically designed to separate people into groups based on performance. All children cannot be above average on norm referenced tests as they are designed to yield a spread of scores over a normal distribution. Items that do not contribute to this spread are deleted from the tests. However, the picture is quite different with criterion referenced tests. The test developer establishes a set criterion, such as able to identify the 26 letters of the alphabet. If all children can accomplish that task, then all have met the criterion. This distinction is especially critical in light of the NCLB requirements that all children be tested regularly and no children will be left behind. By definition, norm referenced tests must leave at least 50% of the children behind. Criterion referenced tests can be passed by all children who have had the opportunity to learn the material and have done so successfully. Success on criterion referenced tests is not determined by comparison with how others do on the test (as is the case for norm referenced tests). It is determined by the exposure to the content and opportunity and ability to learn the knowledge and skills being tested.

Computers and Assessment

In the last ten years tremendous advances have been made in the application of technology to enhance educational opportunities for students with disabilities. Hasselbring and Williams (2000) present a comprehensive overview of the various uses of computer-based technologies to promote the successful integration of students with disabilities in the regular classroom. The authors set forth innovative practices that have been tested with various types of disability. The advances in technology-based assessment have been slower to materialize. Most of the early work has been in the area of computerized administration of standardized tests. For example, Goldberg and Pedulla (2002) studied the differences in performance on the Graduate Record Examination (GRE) according to mode of administration (paper and pencil vs. computerized administration). In addition, they examined the influence of computer familiarity on performance. The results were mixed, but it was interesting to note that familiarity did interact with the outcome. The authors recommended evaluating time constraints when converting examinations from paper-and-pencil to computer-delivery mode.

There have been other advances in the use of technology in data collection. For example, Loeding and Crittenden (1994) examined the use of interactive video technology to enhance the validity and reliability of data collection and scoring and the reduction in the time of administration of the Self-Help InterPersonal Skills (SHIPS) assessment for youth who use sign language. Greenwood et al. (1994) developed and validated the Ecobehavioral Assessment Systems Software (EBASS), a computer-assisted observational system for school practitioners.

Salpeter (2000) recognized the need for more frequent testing, quicker feedback in a form that is useful for students, teachers, and administrators. She provides references to a number of technology-based alternatives, including on-line testing that researchers and educators can use to meet these demands. In time, technology will become a valuable asset to researchers and practitioners for the collection, storage, and reporting of participant performance. While the tools hold great promise for collecting a more accurate assessment of that performance, users are still cautioned to assess the interaction of the mode of assessment and the outcome.

Secondary Sources

Several of the secondary sources, such as administrative records and prior research studies, have been discussed in previous chapters. There are a number of national databases that can serve as a resource for researchers and policy makers who want to compare the performance of their research participants/constituents to national norm groups. The National Assessment of Educational Progress (NAEP), also widely known as the *Nation's Report Card*, reports information for the nation and specific geographic regions of the country. It includes students drawn from both public and nonpublic schools and reports results for student achievement at grades 4, 8, and 12. States may opt to participate in the NAEP so that the state performance and jurisdictions within the state can be compared to the national sample. A list of databases available through the USDOE is found in Appendix 2. In addition to these databases, most states maintain databases that contain the results of assessments conducted with participants in state programs. As noted following, one caution in using these databases is that they may not include students with disabilities or may only include a small subset, thus making the source potentially unrepresentative of the researcher's sample.

Researchers should be aware that there is a considerable information base available for special education research. For example, the federal government requires schools to collect and report data associated with the delivery of services to students with disabilities. These data include information not only on students served, but also on their placement and those who serve them. However, as Maruyama and Deno (1992) note, using extant data sets has its drawbacks. Often, the information is collected to inform policy, not theory development, and is collected at a level that does not allow disaggregation. Further, some national databases actually exclude certain categories of persons. For example, NAEP excludes educable mentally retarded students and those with functional disabilities (unless they can respond to the tasks) (NASDSE, 1988). The exclusion decision is the responsibility of the local school division. Thus, the researcher cannot be sure who is included in the data set. Another data set that researchers and evaluators, as well as policy makers, might want to use is the data set provided through the evaluation of the Upward Bound program, a federally funded program designed to assist disadvantaged students to enter and succeed in higher education (Myers & Schirm, 1999). However, as the authors note, there may be two problems with the database. First, there may be several students who qualified for Upward Bound who chose not to participate or dropped out after entering the program, and second, the program did not always select students who had very low aspirations for going to college or who had very low academic performance. Thus, it is important for the user of the Upward Bound evaluation to know who participated in the study.

Variations in the criteria for inclusion and in the implementation of modifications to testing procedures represent challenges for the use of existing databases in special education research. The basis for inclusion of students with disabilities and the types of acceptable modifications across states in minimum competency programs are quite variable (McGrew, Thurlow, & Spiegel, 1993; Thurlow et al., 1993). In addition, McGrew et al. (1993) reported exclusion rates on the NAEP for students with disabilities that ranged from 33% to 87% across states. The variability in inclusion criteria and accommodations yields test results that are not easily interpretable across groups.

As noted in Chapter 1, most states currently have some type of standards-based assessment that enables schools to identify the performance of students with respect to what they should know and be able to do. These databases are typically available on the Web for descriptive, correlational, and causal comparative research, but they suffer the same exclusionary concerns addressed previously.

Data Collection Strategies

There are a variety of data collection methods available to the researcher. While this text cannot cover these in-depth, it is helpful to provide a thumbnail sketch of the possible options. McNamara (1998) developed such a resource presented in Table 9.3. The general purpose of the methods is presented as well as advantages and disadvantages encountered by the user. In most research, more than one method will be used, as noted in our methods chapters. For example, we often use focus group interviews before designing a survey or questionnaire to determine language, formatting, and response preferences. See Chapters 5 and 6 for additional information on these strategies.

Table 9.3   Overview of Methods to Collect Information

Method	Overall Purpose	Advantages	Challenges
Questionnaires, surveys, and checklists	To quickly and/or easily get a lot of information from people in a nonthreatening way	– can complete anonymously – inexpensive to administer – easy to compare and analyze – administer to many people – can get a lot of data – many sample questionnaires already exist	– might not get careful feedback – wording can bias client's responses – are impersonal – in surveys, may need sampling expert – does not get full story
Interviews	To fully understand someone's impressions or experiences or learn more about their answers to questionnaires	– get full range and depth of information – develops relationship with client – can be flexible with client	– can take much time – can be hard to analyze and compare – can be costly – interviewer can bias client's responses
Documentation review	To get an impression of how program operates without interrupting the program; from review of applications, finances, memos, minutes, and so forth	– get comprehensive and historical information – does not interrupt program or client's routine in program – information already exists – few biases about information	– often takes much time – information may be incomplete – need to be quite clear about what you are looking for – not a flexible means to get data; data restricted to what already exists
Observation	To gather accurate information about how a program actually	– view operations of a program as they are actually occurring	– can be difficult to interpret seen behaviors

(Continued)

Table 9.3 (Continued)

Method	Overall Purpose	Advantages	Challenges
	operates, particularly about processes	– can adapt to events as they occur	– can be complex to categorize observations – can influence behaviors of program participants – can be expensive
Focus groups	To explore a topic in depth through group discussion, for example, about reactions to an experience or suggestion, understanding common complaints, and so forth; useful in evaluation and marketing	– quickly and reliably get common impressions – can be an efficient way to get much range and depth of information in a short time – can convey key information about programs	– can be hard to analyze responses – need a good facilitator for safety and closure – difficult to schedule 6 to 8 people together
Case studies	To fully understand or depict client's experiences in a program and conduct a comprehensive examination through cross comparison of cases	– fully depicts client's experience in program input, process, and results – powerful means to portray program to outsiders	– usually quite time-consuming to collect, organize, and describe – represents depth of information, rather than breadth

McNamara, Carter. (1998). Basics of developing questionnaires, the management assistance program for nonprofits. Retrieved from www.mapfornonprofits.org.

TECHNICAL ADEQUACY OF DATA COLLECTION INSTRUMENTS

The degree of confidence the researcher and those who intend to use the research findings can place on the research depends in large part on the quality of the measurement procedures. The three methods typically employed to assess the quality of measurement in the positivist, quantitative tradition are reliability, validity, and objectivity. Parallel criteria for qualitative approaches are discussed in Chapter 6.

Reliability

In order to be useful, measurement instruments must be consistent. *The Standards for Educational and Psychological Testing* (American Educational Research Association, American Psychological Association, & National Council on Measurement in Education, 1999) defines reliability as follows: "Reliability refers to the consistency of such measurements when the testing procedure is repeated on a population of individuals or groups" (p. 25). When researchers measure a particular attribute, they are concerned about the accurate estimate of the target attribute. If you were to test your students' ability to solve word problems one day and, without additional instruction in mathematics, give them the same test the next time they came to class, you would expect that their scores on the word problem test would be about the same. Ability to solve word problems, like most attributes, does not vary across time without some intervention. In the previous example, if your students' scores changed, then their performance might have been influenced by something other than their ability to solve mathematics word problems. These other influences cause error; the extent to which measurement instruments are free from error indicates their reliability. The more reliable the measurement instrument, the closer the researcher can arrive at a true estimate of the attribute addressed by the measure.

The purpose of measurement is to get an accurate or error-free estimate of a particular attribute. There are two types of error that can influence performance on a measurement instrument: systematic and unsystematic. Systematic errors inflate or deflate performance in a fixed way and thus do not affect a measure's reliability. In the previous example, additional mathematics instruction could be thought of as a systematic influence on performance. The effect of a systematic error on performance is constant and therefore can be predicted.

It is the unsystematic errors that concern researchers. These vary at random from situation to situation and therefore cannot be predicted. Unsystematic errors are produced by factors that fall into three categories: those within the person being measured, the conditions of the administration of the measurement, and changes in the measurement instrument or tasks.

Examples of factors within the individual that could randomly influence behavior are motivation and alertness. Students with attention deficit disorders might have difficulty maintaining concentration across a number of research tasks. Unsystematic changes (those that are not done for the students) in the administration that might influence performance include providing different instructions, changing the environment, or allowing more time. When the items on the instrument or the behaviors being sampled are changed, fluctuations in performance also may arise.

The reliability of a measurement instrument is typically established by comparing performance of the same individuals across time and is expressed in the form of a coefficient of correlation ranging from .00 to 1.00, with 1.00 indicating perfect reliability, which is rarely accomplished for any measure. The closer to 1.00, the more reliable the instrument. Most reliability coefficients range from .75 to .95. The important thing to remember is that anything less than 1.00 indicates the presence of error. The researcher's task is to identify the potential sources of such error and make them public.

How is reliability determined? There are several approaches that researchers can use to determine the reliability of a particular measurement device. The most common are described in the following. For a more thorough review, the reader should consult a text on measurement, such as Kubiszyn and Borich (2003) and Murphy and Davidshofer (1998).

Test-Retest. Test-retest reliability is established by administering the same test to the same individuals on two separate occasions. The second administration can occur either immediately or after a time lapse. Scores from both administrations are correlated to determine the consistency of response. One of the drawbacks of this approach is the potential for practice effect or remembering items across administrations of the test. For example, the test-retest reliability of the WISC Verbal Scale for blind students was reported to be .91, which is generally comparable to those reported for the WISC standardization sample (Tillman, 1973).

Parallel Tests. If practice effects are a concern, then an equivalent (parallel) form of the test can be used in the second administration. Of course, the major concern with the parallel form's reliability check is the degree to which the two tests are equivalent. For example, Schunk and Rice (1992) studied the influence of comprehension strategies on reading achievement in remedial readers. Because they believed the passage familiarity might confound measurement of performance on the dependent variable in a posttest administration, they developed a parallel form that had a .87 correlation with the first form of the test.

Internal Consistency. For estimating internal stability or consistency, the researcher can either use a statistical method such as Cronbach's Coefficient Alpha or the Kuder-Richardson approaches (Gall, Gall, & Borg, 2003) or the split-half method in which the two scores for the test are derived by summing the odd and then the even responses. The assumption here is that breaking the test according to odd and even items will result in two equivalent forms of the test. For example, in the MacMillan et al. (1992) investigation of attitudes toward school held by students with learning disabilities, the authors cited split-half and alpha reliability coefficients ranging from .77 to .99 on the Survey of School Attitudes (SSA) (Hogan, 1975) as evidence to support their selection.

Validity

In determining the appropriateness of a measure for a proposed research study, the researcher needs to be concerned with not only reliability, but also with validity. The conventional definition of the validity of a test is the extent to which it measures what it was constructed to measure. In practice, however, the validity of an instrument is assessed in relation to the extent to which evidence and theory support the interpretations of test scores entailed by the proposed uses of the test. The *Standards for Educational and Psychological Testing* (American Educational Research Association, American Psychological Association, & National Council on Measurement in Education, 1999) views validity as a unitary concept that measures the degree to which all the accumulated evidence supports the intended interpretation of test scores for the proposed purpose. Therefore, it is critical to determine the stated purposes of the test or assessment instruments and align those purposes with the intended use in the research study.

An overarching concern in the study of validity is the extent to which the test measures the attributes it was intended to measure and not bias due to gender, race/ethnicity, class, or disability. To be valid, testing must be nondiscriminatory, that is, tests and procedures used to evaluate a child's special needs must be free of bias based on gender, race, ethnicity, class, disability, or other cultural factors in both the way they are administered and the content of the items on the test. Suran and Rizzo (1983) interpreted the nondiscrimination policy set forth in the special education legislation to mean that tests must be presented in the primary language or mode of communication of the child and no one test or procedure can be used as the sole determinant of a child's education program.

The Educational Testing Service (ETS) recognized the need to fully consider the unique characteristics of special populations at every stage of an assessment program: design and development, administration, interpretation, and reporting results (Mounty & Anderson, 1993). ETS established a Special Population Group to ensure that issues of access, equity, opportunity, and/or outcomes/consequences are addressed. They are studying equal opportunity for female, minority, and disabled students to have access to information, resources, state-of-the-art curricula, and educational technology pertinent to successful performance on standardized tests and large-scale assessment. All types of validity are enhanced by studying differential performance, fairness in testing practices for improved equity, the equalization of access to educational opportunities for successful outcomes, and the use of assessment information.

How can the researcher determine the validity of proposed measurement procedures? Four specific sources of evidence can be used to establish validity (content, concurrent, predictive, and construct validity):

1. **Content Validity.** If the purpose of the test is to measure the effect of a specific teaching strategy or curriculum, then the researcher can establish

content validity by determining if the knowledge, skill, or attitude measured by the test matches the information included in the lessons actually taught. A specifications matrix, which crosses the items of the measurement device and the objectives of the lesson or curriculum, can be helpful in establishing content validity. The higher the degree of overlap, the more the measure can be said to have content validity.

Use of minimum competency tests with students with disabilities provides one example of problems with content validity in special education. Minimum competency tests are used to measure attainment of mastery of skills and competencies, usually for the purpose of determining promotion to the next grade or awarding a high school diploma. In a case heard before the Federal District Court in the state of Georgia, it was found that children with mental retardation were not instructed on the skills tested on a diploma sanction test (*Anderson v. Banks*, 1981, cited in Thurlow et al., 1993). Thus, the test did not have content validity for these students. Some students can succeed with the same content but need modifications in the testing process. Others may have different instructional goals, often focusing on lower levels of skill development. The content validity of the tests should be checked against the student's instructional goals on the IEP. An alternative to minimum competency testing is to examine accomplishment of goals as specified on the IEP (Thurlow et al., 1993). This results in data that is quite complex and variable, and thus interpretation would be difficult across subjects or groups.

2. **Concurrent Validity.** Tests are sometimes used in place of ratings of demonstrations of skills or knowledge in an educational or work environment. A test is said to have concurrent validity if it yields results similar to those obtained from assessment of the actual performance of the skill or task. Certification and licensure tests are used to determine whether individuals have the needed skills and knowledge to assume a professional role. Thurlow et al. (1993) summarized the modifications that ETS has made in the National Teachers Exam to accommodate persons with disabilities.

3. **Predictive Validity.** Often the researcher wants to use the information derived from the administration of an instrument to predict a subject's performance at some future point in time. For example, the research project might be designed to develop an instrument to predict the level of success students with disabilities will have in postsecondary training experiences. Although time-consuming, the typical approach to establishing the predictive validity of a measurement technique is to administer the test, wait until the predicted behavior occurs, and correlate measures of this behavior with the student's performance on the original test.

A study by the American College Testing (ACT) Program (Laing & Farmer, 1984) compared the predictive validity of the ACT for five groups of examinees: students with and without disabilities who took the examination in a standard administration and students with visual impairments, hearing impairments, or motor disabilities (defined as physical and learning disabilities) who took a nonstandard administration. The ability of the examination to predict first-year college grades (the criterion measure) was about the same for examinees with and without disabilities when both groups took the examination under standard testing conditions. Similar results were also reported by ETS on the Scholastic Aptitude Test and the Graduate Record Exam (Willingham, Ragosta, Bennett, Braun, Rock, & Powers, 1988). However, test scores substantially underpredicted college grades for students with hearing impairments who enrolled in colleges that provided them with special services.

4. **Construct Validity.** Finally, the researcher who wants to measure some attribute, such as intelligence or anxiety, must establish construct validity, that is, provide evidence that the test actually measures the intended construct and not some other characteristic, such as lack of access to information because of bias based on gender, ethnicity, class, or disability.

Two other forms of validity that are relevant to research and evaluation in special education should be presented. Storey and Horner (1991) examined **social validation** research methods which focus on the value of having persons with disabilities evaluate research conducted on issues of central import to them—the services they receive, the policies and organizational structures that drive service delivery, as well as their own behaviors, skills, and values. Persons with disabilities were asked to judge the social value and significance of the research. Storey and Horner reviewed the current practice of social validation research, discussing the social validation methods, methodological issues, and conclusions. As a result of their integrated review, they were able to confirm the importance of social validation and provide insightful suggestions to researchers and practitioners who would use the method.

A related validity concern is **consequential validity** that emerged from concerns related to societal ramifications of assessments. Thus, consequential validity is that type of validity evidence that addresses the intended and unintended consequences of test interpretation and use (Messick, 1989; 1995).

Examples of harmful and unintended consequences that relate to the need to determine the consequential validity of an instrument include:

- High stakes testing may negatively impact present and future educational and employment opportunities when a single test score is used to make a decision.
- Lower pass rates may occur on tests by individuals of certain subgroups, such as people with disabilities or racial/ethnic minorities, because of unequal opportunities or inappropriate demands of the testing situation in terms of written or spoken language.
- A less diverse work force may result because of employment tests that increase reluctance to seek employment or complete the required assessments.

- Teachers may narrow the curriculum to teach only what will be on the test.

Messick (1995) suggests that researchers distinguish between adverse consequences that stem from valid descriptions of individual and group differences and adverse consequences that derive from sources of test invalidity such as construct underrepresentation and construct irrelevant variance. If differences are related to the latter, then test invalidity presents a measurement problem that needs to be investigated in the validation process. However, if the differences are the result of valid group differences, then the adverse consequences represent problems of social policy. It is the researcher's responsibility to insure that low scores do not occur because the assessment is missing something relevant to that construct that, if it were present, would have permitted the affected persons to display their competence. In addition, causes of low scores because of irrelevant demands in the testing process can prevent an individual from demonstrating their competence.

The *Standards for Educational and Psychological Testing* also emphasizes the need to distinguish between those aspects of consequences of test use that relate to the construct validity of a test and issues of social policy. Standard 1.24 addresses the issue of consequential validity:

> When unintended consequences result from test use, an attempt should be made to investigate whether such consequences arise from the test's sensitivity to characteristics other than those it is intended to assess or to the test's failure fully to represent the intended construct. (p. 23)

Group differences do not in themselves call into question the validity of a proposed interpretation; however, they do increase the need to investigate rival hypotheses that may be related to problems with the validity of the measurement.

Objectivity

In some research situations, the measurement instrument is a person who serves as an interviewer, observer, or reviewer of documents. When the instrument is a human, users of the research findings are likely to challenge the results by asking: Are these data independent of the person doing the observations? Would another person come to the same conclusions? Would the observer have seen things the same way at a later date? All these concerns relate to fluctuations in the measurement resulting from the subjectivity of the task of observation.

In response to these concerns, the researcher must first establish that the tasks the observer is required to do are valid for the purposes of the research. For example, if the research was intended to describe the social skills of students with learning disabilities, then the researcher would have to present evidence that the observer was looking for essential indicators of social skills. Next, the researcher would gather evidence that the observation task was objective, that more than one observer could look at the same behaviors and reach the same interpretation. The researcher might train two or more observers on the observation scheme and compare their observations. This is usually referred to as interrater reliability, because the purpose is to check the consistency of ratings across observers. Correlations of ratings or percent of agreement are two methods for establishing interrater reliability.

Finally, the researcher should check for fluctuations in rating across time because raters may change as they become more involved with the rating task. They may get better, or they may get tired or bored. Regardless of the reason, their ratings change and result in different interpretations of the same data. In this case, it is important to conduct intrarater reliability studies. Again, percent of agreement within individual rater and correlations of observations across time are two methods for determining intrarater reliability. McIntosh, Vaughn, Hager, and Okhee (1993) trained observers to study the integration of students with learning disabilities in general education classrooms. They used random checks of observers throughout the data collection to ensure interrater and intrarater reliability.

Test Modifications and Technical Adequacy

When tests or testing procedures are modified, questions are raised about the technical adequacy (reliability/validity) of the modified tests (Thurlow et al., 1993). Tests and other evaluation materials are only valid and reliable when used with the same population on which they were developed, for the specific purpose for which they were developed, and when following the same procedures used in development. The 1999 Standard (10.7) that addresses this issue most directly states:

> When sample sizes permit, the validity of inferences made from test scores and the reliability of scores on tests administered to individuals with various disabilities should be investigated and reported by the agency or publisher that makes the modification. Such investigations should examine the effects of modifications made for people with various disabilities on resulting scores, as well as the effects of administering standard unmodified tests to them. (p. 107)

In addition, test developers should include information about evidence of validity for a given inference if it has been established for individuals with specific disabilities. If the data are not available, then the developers should include cautionary statements in manuals regarding the limitations of interpretations with such test scores.

SELECTING AND USING A MEASUREMENT DEVICE

The researcher has two choices with regard to the identification of measurement procedures. Measures may be selected from those that are currently available commercially or those that have been developed by other researchers. If the appropriate measure cannot be found, then the researcher must adapt an existing instrument or build a new one to meet the needs of the proposed research. Development of measurement tools is beyond the scope of this text; the interested reader is referred to such sources as the American Educational Research Association, American Psychological Association, and the National Council on Measurement in Education (1999), Gall, Gall, and Borg (2003), Kubiszyn and Borich (2003), and Murphy and Davidshofer (1998).

The researcher must remember that regardless of the direction of the decision to select, modify, or develop a measurement procedure, the quality of information generated by the use of the device is essential. According to Bennett (1983), there are three basic requirements to consider: (1) special qualifications for the persons administering the instrument, (2) the technical adequacy of the instrument for assessing the desired attributes, and (3) the extent to which the measurement is free from bias based on gender, ethnicity, class, or disability. These features of the measure have been discussed elsewhere. They are presented here as broad guidelines for the researcher who is searching for the appropriate tools. Deficiencies in any of the three areas will affect the quality of information available to answer the research questions. Unfortunately, as Bennett noted, information about these features is not likely to be readily available, particularly for assessments used with persons with disabilities.

The first step in identifying a measurement device for your research is to obtain an information base of all possible existing measures that might be appropriate for your study. There are numerous resources to support this search. As noted in Chapter 2, the current literature is a good starting place. The researcher can locate and review similar research to gain an understanding of which measurement procedures worked well in other related research. In addition to reviewing specific research, the search can be extended to test bibliographic resources such as the *Mental Measurements Yearbooks* (MMY). The MMY describes and critiques over 2,000 commercially available standardized English-language tests, measurements, and assessment tools. Updated semiannually, the MMY is available on-line at http://www.unl.edu/buros/. The companion to MMY, *Tests in Print* is also available at that Web site. The difference is that *Tests in Print* does not include reviews of the tests, but rather is cross-referenced to MMY. Perhaps the most useful Web-based resource for searching for assessment instruments is the ERIC/AE Test Locator (http://ericae.net/testcol.htm). This resource enables the researcher to review over 15,000 tests and research instruments. Thousands of tests are reviewed in these bibliographies. Reviews include not only general test information, but also critiques of the measurement device by experts in the field. Reliability and validity studies also are likely to be cited. Most university libraries contain numerous test bibliographies in print format.

Other sources include:

1.   New York State Teacher Resource and Computer Training Centers: Evaluation Library

The 2-page *Program Evaluation Funnel* was created by Dr. Seth Aldrich. It shows a wide variety of assessment approaches that can be used to collect information about programs, the various qualities of these different assessment approaches, and the corresponding types of evaluation questions (from low to high stakes) that each assessment can address. (See http://www.programevaluation.org/libpg.shtml.)

2.   The Aspen Institute Roundtable on Comprehensive Community Initiatives has developed a database of measures of community-level outcomes in several domains including education, health and human services, youth development, housing, economic development, employment, crime prevention, and community building. We see this Web site as a repository of qualitative and quantitative measurement instruments that is accessible to evaluators and community stakeholders at no cost to the end user. The URL is http://www.aspenroundtable.org (and then click "Measures for Community Research").

Selecting an instrument is guided by one broad criterion: relevance. The relevance question has two parts. First, to what extent is the test under consideration appropriate for the information needs of the proposed research? Of course this is a validity question, and the answer will be found in validity studies for the test being considered. The essential concern for the researcher is the degree of match between the information that will be provided through the administration and the research question being addressed in the research.

The second aspect of the relevance question focuses on the subjects of the intended research. Earlier, we noted that researchers who are reviewing potential standardized tests must be careful to note whether the test was standardized on a norm group that included persons with disabilities like those targeted in the proposed research. If not, then the norms for the test should not be used. Of greater importance, though, is the appropriateness of the tasks or items in the measurement device for the subjects in the proposed study.

We also indicated previously that a critical concern of measurement is acquiring an accurate representation of the attribute being measured.

When information is collected from persons with disabilities, we must be certain that the person's disability does not mask the individual's actual level or amount of the attribute. For example, if we were attempting to measure the aptitude of persons with visual impairments, then we would need to use tasks or items that did not depend on vision. Not doing so would yield an inaccurate measure of aptitude. What we would get is a measure of visual skill as well as aptitude. The importance of taking the characteristics of the administration and content of the measurement device is discussed again in the section of this chapter centering on the use of measurement procedures in research.

Other selection criteria that should be considered include the test format and time for administration. To what extent do the features of the intended test promote or restrict accuracy of assessment of the subjects in the proposed research? Phillips (1994), cited by Pitoniak and Royer (2001), identified five questions that researchers and test administrators should consider when considering an accommodation decision. If any are answered in the affirmative, then the accommodation should not be made.

1. Will format changes or alterations in testing conditions change the skill being measured?

2. Will the scores of examinees tested under standard conditions have a different meaning than scores for examinees tested with the requested accommodation?

3. Would examinees without disabilities benefit if allowed the same accommodation?

4. Does the disabled examinee have the capability for adapting to standard test administration conditions?

5. Is the disability evidence or testing accommodation policy based on procedures with doubtful validity and reliability?

If modifications are made, they should be assessed from the standpoint of the degree to which they violate previous assumptions about the measurement. Field tests of the instrument provide an opportunity to make such judgments. The researcher should then identify the ways in which previous assumptions about the procedures were affected.

When selecting a measurement device for your research, the relevance of the instrument for your intended information needs, as well as the subjects in the study, must be determined. We recommend constructing a specifications matrix which lists all the relevant criteria (both informational and subject-oriented) in the right-hand column and then the potential instruments across the top. At the intersect of each test and criterion, the test is rated for its appropriateness. For most commercially available tests, the researcher can obtain a specimen set, which will contain copies of the test and a test manual that describes administration and scoring procedures. Often the manual will contain discussions of validity and reliability as well as considerations for using the instrument for diverse groups, including persons with disabilities. Useful procedures for selecting a measurement device appropriate to the needs of the researcher are presented in Kubiszyn and Borich (2003) and Murphy and Davidshofer (1998).

Tests do not work the same for all populations and in all test circumstances. Therefore, we recommend that at minimum, researchers gather reliability information for the specific persons studied in the research. Further, to increase the validity of the information, we recommend that multiple measures be used. Thus, if achievement is the focus of the research, the investigator might collect not only paper-and-pencil test data but also work samples, as well as performance in other settings. If researchers are attempting to determine social skill development in students with learning disabilities, they could use direct observation, personal interviews with the subject, peers, and significant others, and reviews of performance reports. Using more than one measurement procedure for gathering evidence in a study increases the dependability of the findings, conclusions, and recommendations.

QUESTIONS FOR CRITICALLY ANALYZING INFORMATION COLLECTION STRATEGIES AND INSTRUMENTS

1. What reliability, validity, and, if appropriate, objectivity indices are available to support the use of the proposed measurement process?

2. Are the procedures used by test developers to establish reliability, validity, and objectivity appropriate for the intended use of the proposed measurement technique? Was the research instrument developed and validated with representatives of both sexes and diverse ethnic and disability groups?

3. Is the proposed measurement tool appropriate for the subjects and conditions of the proposed research?

4. What measurements are required to collect information on the research process?

5. When and from whom is it best to collect information, given the research questions of the proposed research?

6. Does the instrument contain language that is biased, based on gender, ethnicity, class, or disability?

QUESTIONS AND ACTIVITIES FOR DISCUSSION AND APPLICATION

1. Discuss the purpose of information collection in research settings.

2. Locate a commercially developed measure and review the manual to determine how the developers have treated the concepts of reliability, validity, objectivity, and bias based on gender, ethnicity, class, and disability.

3. Review the same test to determine the extent to which it is relevant for specific populations of persons with disabilities (e.g., different types of disabilities, males and females, and diverse ethnic groups).

4. Identify and review several journals in which research on persons with disabilities is reported. Read the instructions to potential authors to see what the journal editors require in the way of evidence of measurement reliability, validity, objectivity, and lack of bias based on gender, ethnicity, and disability.

5. In the same journals, review several articles to determine the ways in which the authors provide evidence of the reliability, validity, objectivity, and lack of bias for their measures. Identify the methods the authors used to ensure that their measures were not biased in that the person's disability could mask true measurement of the intended attributes.

6. Discuss the relative merits of using commercially developed measures and those developed specifically for the purposes of the proposed research.

7. Identify attributes of persons with disabilities that might be the focus of research and determine several different ways in which each attribute might be measured.

8. Identify the alternative sources from which existing information could be collected about students with disabilities that could have a bearing on a particular research initiative.

9. Identify an attribute that might be measured in a research setting. Develop a draft measurement procedure, using the steps outlined in this chapter.

10. Select a commercial instrument or one developed by another researcher and discuss modifications that may be needed for students with disabilities. Which would invalidate the technical adequacy of the test and which would not?

10

Data Analysis, Interpretation, and Use

Will training general education teachers, who have kindergartners with disabilities in mainstream classrooms, to use phonological awareness (PA) (the capacity to blend, segment, rhyme, or in other ways manipulate the sounds of the spoken words) result in improved student achievement (Fuchs, Fuchs, & Thompson, 2002)? What would be the impact of such training if it also included a beginning decoding component? Pretreatment and posttreatment data were analyzed and indicated that the group of students with special needs participating in PA training with beginning decoding instruction did better than the other two groups. Nevertheless, the authors do note that many children, including many of those in the most effective treatment group, did not improve their reading skills.

What can we learn from teachers who have a learning disability (Ferri, Keefe, & Gregg, 2001)? How would their past experiences as a student with a learning disability influence their current practice as special education teachers? Several themes emerged, including their views on strategies for service delivery, the importance of teacher expectations, and the value of conceiving of a learning disability as a tool rather than a deficit. One teacher commented, "I don't want [my students] to go through what I went through — the frustration. And I don't want them to have teachers that have low expectations of them. I want them to have someone that really knows that they can succeed if they have the right tools" (p. 27).

IN THIS CHAPTER

- Basic statistical strategies and challenges in data analysis and interpretation for quantitative research studies are described.
- Analysis and interpretation strategies and issues for qualitative research studies are discussed.
- Issues related to use of the results are discussed in terms of reporting, application to program change and policy formation, and identification of areas in need of additional research.
- Questions for critically analyzing data analysis and interpretation in research studies are provided.

Data analysis procedures are tools we use to interpret the data collected as part of the research process. Before you start, we have provided some tips you might want to review in Table 10.1. Statistics are tools for information reduction that summarize characteristics or performance data in a quantitative way to ease interpretation of the results. Codes, categories, and theoretical models are ways of summarizing and interpreting qualitative data. We now look at data analysis, interpretation, and use in the special education context.

QUANTITATIVE DATA ANALYSIS

It is not possible to either define all the statistical terms or explain all the complexity of formula derivation and use of statistics in such a chapter as this. It is not even possible to introduce all the different kinds of statistics

Table 10.1 Tips on Data Analysis: Look this over before you start

- Develop an initial plan.
- Take at least as much time for analysis as you took to collect the data.
- Analysts and those using the analysis need to have some training in methods.
- Analysis occurs throughout the cycle, not just at the end.
- Analysis procedures depend on the level of data (nominal, ordinal, etc.) and the type of questions.
  - Descriptive
  - Correlation
  - Comparison
- Analysis is best done collaboratively (ask participants, their advocates, and other relevant parties to help with interpretation).
- Creative insights about the findings are the key.
- Field test the analyses before running them – for example, build some tables using dummy data. Show these to stakeholders and ask, "What would you think if we got these data and presented them in these ways?"

or to make it clear when it is appropriate to use which one. The reader is referred to general statistics books for more specific information on this topic (see Abelson, 1995; Heiman, 2001; Salkind, 2000). Definitions for common statistical terms are included in Appendix 3 along with a chart that summarizes when each statistic should be used.

This chapter focuses on the challenges special educators face in data analysis and interpretation. A study of integrating students with disabilities into mainstream classrooms is used to illustrate these challenges (and ways to meet those challenges) for the interpretation of quantitative data (see Table 10.2).

Table 10.2 Sample Research Study for Statistical Analysis Applications

Fuchs, Fuchs, and Thompson (2002) conducted a year-long study of the effectiveness of two beginning-reading programs for kindergartners. The first program provided Phonological Awareness training (PA); the second combined PA with Peer-Assisted Learning Strategies (PA + PALS). PALS is a beginning decoding program that is peer-mediated. A control group did not receive either PA or PA + PALS. Twenty-five of the 400 children in the study had a disability; the majority of the children were certified as disabled because of speech or language impairments. The frequencies of the children with disabilities in each group were 9 in PA + PALS, 6 in PA, and 10 in the control group. There were no statistically significant differences among the study groups on the number of hours per week teachers reported devoting to language arts, the class size, years of teaching experience, or the teacher's age, gender, highest degree earned, or race. There were no statistically significant differences between groups on student demographic or school-related variables. Observations and teacher logs were used to document the implementation of the treatments.

Preliminary analysis revealed that one student in the PA + PALS group scored comparatively much higher than any of the other students in the study; therefore, this student's data were dropped from further analysis (reducing the sample size to 24). They conducted a 1-way ANOVA, using study group as the factor, on pre- to posttreatment growth for five dependent measures. Two statistically significant differences were reported: (1) A statistically significant difference was found for Rapid Letter Sound (RLS) (Levy & Lysunchuk, 1997), a test that assesses the number of letter sounds a student identifies in one minute $(F(2,21) = 3.12, p = .06)$. (2) A statistically significant difference was found on Word Attack Subtest of the Woodcock Reading Mastery Test, Revised, Form G (Woodcock, 1987) $(F(2,21) = 3.59, p < .05)$. (The Word Attack Subtest measures the student's ability to pronounce nonsense words.) Fisher LSD post hoc procedures indicated: on the RLS, the growth of the PA + PALS student reliably exceeded that of PA students, but no other difference was statistically significant. On Word Attack, PA + PALS students' progress was reliably greater than that of PA and control students, whose gains were comparable to each other.

In Table 10.2, a large number of different statistical techniques are included. Descriptive statistics tell you how many children were in the study overall and by different subgroups. The researchers also used inferential statistics (ANOVA) and nonparametric statistics (chi-square analyses) to test for background differences in the teachers and students before the intervention was instituted. The ANOVA was used to compare the class size and years of teaching experience for the eighteen teachers in the study. Chi-square was used for comparisons that were based on categorical data, such as gender, highest degree earned, and race. Because these variables were not statistically different among the groups, the researchers were able to eliminate these as competing explanations for the final results. As you will recall from the chapters on group comparisons earlier in this book, these researchers were following the recommended procedure of checking for group equivalency on variables they thought were important in making interpretations through comparative analysis.

The researchers also looked at preliminary analysis of means, standard deviations, and the distribution of individual scores among the groups. In this way, they were able to identify and subsequently eliminate one outlier – the student whose scores were much higher than all the others at the beginning of the study. They again used ANOVA to test for group differences on pretreatment to posttreatment growth on their dependent measures. The results $F(2,21) = 3.12$, $p = .06$ could be interpreted as F is the statistic that is calculated by the ANOVA test. There are 2 and 21 degrees of freedom. These are the degrees of freedom for between group and within group comparisons (3 groups – one test = 2 degrees of freedom; 24 students – 3 groups = 21 degrees of freedom), and p (the really important part of the report) indicates that the probability is greater than 6% on any one test of the null hypothesis that the groups differ from one another. If you had set your criterion to be equal to or less than $p = .06$, then you would conclude that there is a statistically significant difference between the three sets of scores (which is what Fuchs et al. [2002] did).

Then, you might say that there are three groups, but how do you know where the differences are? That is what the Fisher LSD test allows you to discover. It is a post hoc (meaning it is done after the other tests are finished) test which identifies where in the morass of scores the real differences reside. That is why Fuchs et al. (2002) were able to say that the PA + PALS group was much different from the PA group, and that at least on the Word Attack, PA and control students made comparable progress.

Well, that is the simplified road map through the results section of one study. The next section gets into the complexity of examining the results and interpreting them.

CHALLENGES IN ANALYSIS AND INTERPRETATION

Randomization and sample size are two factors that present challenges to special education researchers who plan to use statistical procedures for data analysis. Following a discussion of these two factors, we present options for researchers to deal with these challenges.

Randomization

Randomization is a necessary condition for the use of typical tests of parametric statistics, for example, t test, ANOVA (Shaver, 1992). Randomization can be achieved by either random sampling (Chapter 8) or random assignment to conditions (Chapter 4). You will recall that random sampling is a critical concern with regard to inferences to the target population. Random sampling is a very difficult condition to meet in most education analyses, and random assignment is not always possible or legal. For example, Fuchs et al. (2002) randomly assigned teachers to study groups; they were not able to randomly assign the individual students to these groups. They did additional subgroup analyses based on a division of the children into low achievers (LA), average achievers (AA), and high achievers (HA) based on their pretest performance on the RLS. They obviously could not assign students to achievement groups because that was an extant condition. They were not able to randomly select their subjects from a larger population; therefore, there are limitations in terms of generalizability as well.

Sample Size

Sample size is a basic influence on statistical significance (Thompson, 1992). Virtually any study can have statistically significant results if a large enough sample size is used. For example, with a standard deviation of 10 and a sample size of 20, a difference of 9.4 between two independent means is necessary for statistical significance at the .05 level in a nondirectional test; with a sample size of 100, a difference of only 4.0 is required; and with a sample size of 1,000, a difference of only 1.2 is required (Shaver, 1992). In simpler terms, this means that a difference between means of 9.4, 4.0, or 1.2 is needed for statistical significance, depending on your sample size. An overly large sample size was not a problem in the Fuchs et al. (1992) study; however, it could be a problem in special education research (see Allen, 1992). More commonly, a very small sample size might prevent the researcher from obtaining statistically significant results.

In the Fuchs et al. (2002) study, they had a total of 24 students with disabilities included in their final analyses, only 8 of whom received the most effective experimental treatment. This small sample size may limit the generalizability of the results. They did address the small sample size by examining the preliminary trends in the data prior to starting the group comparisons. It was by this means that they identified the one student whose scores exceeded those of the other students to the extent that inclusion of his scores would have inappropriately skewed the results to favor the treatment group. This is why they dropped that student from further analyses.

It is often appropriate to report results in a disaggregated mode, for example, to report results by gender, race/ethnicity, or type of disability. In such cases, the researcher must have selected a large enough sample to make the disaggregation meaningful. In the Fuchs et al. (2002) study, 7 of the 8 PA + PALS students, 5 of the 6 PA students, and 5 of the 10 controls were in the low achievers subgroup. The PA + PALS group's more positive outcomes were termed all the more impressive because 87% of them were in the low achievers (LA) group, whereas only 50% of the control group students were in the LA group. A considerably larger portion of the PA children were in the LA group than in the control group. Thus, the poorer performance of PA versus control students could be explained by their lower starting scores.

RESPONSES TO ANALYSIS AND INTERPRETATION CHALLENGES

Suggestions for dealing with these challenges include: (1) choose a different statistic (e.g., effect size or nonparametric statistics), (2) change the design to include plans for replication, and (3) discuss competing explanations and limitations of the study in the report.

Choice of a Statistic

Effect Size (ES). Shaver (1992) and Carver (1992) recommend that researchers report their effect sizes in addition to the level of statistical significance. An effect size is a common metric that allows comparison across different measures; it is also a quantitative expression of the difference between the scores of the experimental and control groups (Gall, Gall, & Borg, 2003). For studies that use means to compare experimental and control groups, the effect size is defined as the difference between the means of the experimental and control groups divided by the average standard deviation for the two groups. An effect size is interpreted by looking at the percentile associated with the effect size. For example, an effect size of .55 means that the average score earned by the experimental group is slightly above the mean of the control group. Calculations with an effect size of .55 reveal that the experimental group's mean is at the 71st percentile of the distribution of scores earned by the control group. An effect size of .00 means that there is no difference between the experimental and control groups. This is a way of describing how well the average student who received the treatment performed, relative to the average student who did not receive the treatment.

Fuchs et al. (2002) did calculate effect sizes in their study, partly to compensate for the small sample size. They obtained ESs between .08 and .69 for the PA + PALS group versus controls on all measures except one related to the number of letters a student could identify in a minute. They had larger ESs for PA + PALS versus PA comparisons on all measures (.19 to 2.76). The control versus PA comparison favored the controls (ESs between .40 and 1.62 on 6 of 8 measures). This is how they interpreted the results: "The ESs on all outcome measures, except RLN [remembering letter names], indicated small-to-moderate differences favoring the PA + PALS children over the PA children" (p. 304).

Snyder and Lawson (1992) warn against a blind interpretation of effect size based on magnitude and suggest that the judgment of significance rests with the researcher's, user's, and reviewer's personal value systems; the research questions posed; societal concerns; and the design of a particular study. For more detailed information on effect size, the reader is referred to Lipsey (1990) or Gall, Gall, & Borg (2003).

Nonparametric Statistics. Nonparametric statistics provide an alternative for researchers when their data do not meet the basic assumption of normality, they have small samples, or they use data of an ordinal or nominal nature (Salkind, 2000).

Design Considerations: Replication

Carver (1992) recommends the replication of studies' results as the best replacement for statistical significance. Building replication into research helps eliminate chance or sampling error as a threat to the internal validity of the results. This also emphasizes the importance of the literature review, as discussed in Chapter 3. Because the Fuchs et al. (2002) results were based on 24 students who were in mainstream classes, it would strengthen their claims to see the study replicated. There are two types of replication open to the researcher: systematic and constructive. Systematic replications call for drawing a sample of participants exactly as in the first study. Constructive replication allows for drawing a sample that is different on an important variable. For example, the research might find that students with learning disabilities from grades 3 to 5 benefited from the intervention. The next study might look at the effects in middle school students. Both types of replication enhance generalizability.

Competing Explanations

As discussed in the chapters on quantitative research methods, the researcher needs to consider competing explanations (threats to internal and external validity). Such competing explanations become critical when it is time to interpret the results. For example, Fuchs et al. (2002) described efforts they made to determine whether initial differences existed between the groups. They concluded that the groups did not differ initially on a number of possible characteristics. They did describe the disabilities of the majority of the students as speech and language impaired, but there was no additional insight into the other disability conditions or their possible impact on the results.

Fuchs et al. (2002) did conduct what they called an idiographic analysis which provided considerable insights that added in the interpretation of their findings. They examined the individual cases of the children in each group to determine the patterns of performance within and across the groups. This analysis revealed that a handful of students with disabilities in the PA + PALS group made very strong pretreatment to posttreatment gains. However, an equal number of children with special needs showed little or no growth on these measures. For example, on Word Attack, 4 of the 9 students' progress was greater than the mean gain of average achievers in the same group, but the remaining 5 students demonstrated no gain whatsoever.

Recognizing Limitations

As should be clear by now, it is not possible to design and conduct the perfect research study in educational settings, particularly in special education. Therefore, it is incumbent upon the researcher to recognize and discuss the limitations of the study. As you will recall, in the chapter on literature review (see Chapter 3), we suggested that you use the research literature to examine inconsistencies and variations from the predicted results. For example, Fuchs et al. (2002) recognized several limitations to their study.

They collected data on the fidelity with which teachers implemented PA or PA + PALS, but they did not obtain fidelity information on the use of PALS by students with special needs. Thus, they cannot say with certainty whether PALS contributed to the observed achievement gain in that condition.

1. They recognized that 21 of the 24 students were certified as speech-impaired or language-impaired, thus limiting the generalizability of their findings.

2. The PALS treatment combined two interventions. It was both peer-mediated and designed to teach decoding activities. Because PA is a teacher-directed intervention, it would be a more rigorous comparison as the PALS was implemented solely as a decoding activity, rather than as the combined intervention with peer-mediation as a confounding factor.

Table 10.3 Comparative Techniques for Interpreting Data

Most performance indicators should be constructed to enable one or more comparisons to other indicators to enhance interpretability and confidence in claims.

- Compare against a prior or recognized general standard.
- Compare to performance in the previous period.
- Compare data among like programs; similar organizational units or geographical areas.
- Look for changes across time within the same program.
- Compare across diverse program models.
- Compare to targets established at the beginning of the performance period.
- Use statistical modeling to predict expected results.

Adapted from the Guide for Developing Performance Indicators, National Academy on Public Administration and Hatry, H. (1999), Performance measurement: Getting results. Urban Institute.

Tips on Interpreting Data

Interpretation of data is a thoughtful exercise, requiring much more effort than simply checking levels of statistical significance in the results. Table 10.3 contains some helpful hints to guide you in the interpretation of data. (Note: These tips can have applicability to both quantitative and qualitative data.)

Fuchs et al. (2002) demonstrate the thoughtfulness needed in interpreting a complex pattern in results. They do conclude that their data indicate that PA + PALS is effective in strengthening the early reading skills of a sizable portion of children with disabilities in mainstream kindergartens without teachers making major modifications in the procedures or seeking the assistance of specialists. However, they do not forget that too many children did not seem to profit from the treatment at all. They conclude:

> . . . teachers and researchers do not know how to make mainstream instruction sufficiently clear, compelling, differentiated, iterative, data-driven, and supportive so that all children will learn. (p. 306)

Their ideas for the need for additional research are discussed later in this chapter.

QUALITATIVE DATA ANALYSIS AND INTERPRETATION

Data analysis in most qualitative studies occurs throughout the study (Bogdan & Biklen, 2003). Findings are generated and systematically built as successive pieces of data are gathered.

The actual mechanics of qualitative data analysis are beyond the scope of this text. The reader is referred to Miles and Huberman (1994) for a logical positivist approach to qualitative data analysis that results in data displays such as graphs, charts, matrices, and networks. Many texts are available that describe the interpretive/constructivist approach to data analysis (Bogdan & Biklen, 2003; Denzin & Lincoln, 2000; Patton, 2002; Tesch, 1990). Weitzman (2000) provides a description of computerized analysis of qualitative data.

While data analysis and interpretation is an ongoing process in qualitative studies, the researcher does move through various stages of these activities during the course of the study. In addition, the special education researcher should be aware of the following principles and practices in qualitative data analysis:

1. Bogdan and Biklen (2003) and many other authors emphasize the point that analysis occurs throughout the data collection process. Initially, while the researcher is in the field, he or she reflects on impressions, relationships, patterns, commonalities, and the like.

Keeping an open mind in the beginning of the study allows you to make decisions about what to focus on in the study and the best approach for achieving the understanding you seek. For this reason (and for many others), it is a good idea to do a pilot study in the setting or in a similar setting in which you intend to conduct your study. Early experiences should lead to a focus that is more meaningful. You can share your initial impressions with people on-site to be sure you are not missing something important or misinterpreting things you see. The pilot study or early stages of the study should be used to modify the next steps and sources and types of data you choose. For example, during a study of special education training in Egypt, Mertens (1993) shared the results of her initial impressions with participants who were deaf, blind, or nondisabled on a daily basis. This allowed the participants to be informed of any hypotheses that the researcher was formulating and to add their own interpretations to the data.

For both quantitative and qualitative analyses, there is a two-step process involved: First, we conduct the analyses, and second, we interpret the data to develop findings. The analyses are mechanistic; the interpretation is a human process that should engage the researchers and participants, as well as other relevant groups.

2. The researcher should conduct a more detailed (yet still preliminary) analysis periodically throughout the data collection period. Organize your notes and look over the data that you have. This second level of analysis occurs when the researcher sits down to organize and develop the variety of data collected in the field to develop detailed notes. The researcher analyzes the logic and the correspondence of data to initial impressions in the field. Periodically throughout the study, the researcher carefully and thoroughly studies all the data, seeking similarities, differences, correspondence,

categories, themes, concepts and ideas, and analyzes the logic of previous analytic outcomes, categories, and weaknesses or gaps in the data.

3. Data analysis is a reflective activity that requires that you, as the researcher, maintain a set of notes that record the analytic process, thus providing accountability.

You should keep another set of notes as well. Qualitative researchers are encouraged to engage in the process called progressive subjectivity (mentioned previously in Chapter 6). Some researchers choose to keep a journal, while others use side notes or memos to themselves to record their thoughts, feelings, hunches, and so forth as they progress through the study. This is good data to use for reflection, as well as discussion with your peer debriefer to help uncover any hidden biases or roads that have not yet been taken, but that might be considered. Keller (1993) used peer debriefing in his case study of a girl with Down's syndrome by exposing his research findings to an uninvolved peer. Outside referees can also be asked to review the data analysis procedures and results.

4. There are some mechanics of data analysis that you need to attend to as well. These include the transcription of data from field notes or audiotapes or videotapes to text form and the decision to use computer-based software for analysis or not (Patton, 2002). The decision of whether or not to use computer-based software for analysis should be made before the transcribing is done if possible, because certain packages require different formatting. It is easier to type the transcript in the proper format on the first try instead of modifying it later. Table 10.4 presents two Web sites that have excellent lists of computer-based software for qualitative analysis. As these programs tend to change over the years, it is best to check Web sites such as these to see what is newest. If these Web sites fail, then quick searches of www.google.com with the search terms "qualitative analysis software" would yield up-to-date information. David Fetterman has some resources at *owner-empowerment-evaluation97@lists.Stanford.EDU* that you might want to check out.

Transcription takes a lot of time. Plan at least four hours for transcribing one hour of interview data. There are good arguments for paying someone else to transcribe your data (time being number one). However, there are good arguments for you to do it yourself, especially if this is your first study of this type. Two of these reasons include: accuracy of the transcription and taking advantage of the opportunity to immerse yourself in the data. While transcription might seem like a straightforward task, there are decisions to make – especially if the tapes are hard to understand, have multiple people talking at once, or the interviewee does not use clearly articulated, grammatically perfect English. You, as the researcher, are in the best position to make those initial decisions. If it is possible, it is a good practice to show passages that you are uncertain of to the interviewee again for accuracy. Other issues sometimes arise with regard to exact transcription versus what the interviewee meant to communicate in the passage.

Table 10.4 Web Sites for Qualitative Research: Data Analysis Resources

- Computer Assisted Qualitative Data Analysis Software
  (http://caqdas.soc. surrey.ac.uk/)

The CAQDAS Project is funded by the UK Economic and Social Research Council. It does not have commercial links to any software developer or supplier. It aims to provide practical support, training, and information in the use of a range of software programs which have been designed to assist qualitative data analysis. It also provides a platform for debate concerning the methodological and epistemological issues arising from the use of such software packages.

- Judy Norris maintains a Web site at the University of Alberta, Canada
  (http://www.ualberta.ca/~jrnorris/qual.html)

Norris' Web site contains links to pages with many resources for qualitative data analysis, including most of the commercially available packages. It also provides resources on a broad range of qualitative topics, including philosophical and methodological issues. Links are provided to many useful qualitative resources, such as online journals that publish qualitative research studies.

Goodley (1998) provides a poignant example of research with young people in England who had learning difficulties. He wrote up the transcriptions trying to keep them as accurate in a word-to-word manner as possible. This meant the text appeared as the informant spoke, using phrases like "I says" and "Yer knows," as well as representing her accent so that the word "something" was spelled "sommat." When Goodley showed the transcript to the informant, she was not happy with it because it did not read well and portrayed her in what she considered a disrespectful way. He rewrote it using proper grammar and showed it to her again. She was still quite unhappy and decided to write her own version of her experiences. In the end, the informant agreed that her own story told in her own way and the researcher's edited version could both be used in his report.

5. Take a break. Some methodologists recommend that the researcher wait for up to one month before conducting the final analysis of the data in order to gain a fresh perspective on the nature of the data and the problems (Bogdan & Biklen, 2003).

6. The formal (final) analysis process begins with reading all the data at once and then dividing the data into smaller, more meaningful units. Bogdan and Biklen (2003) recommend using such category types as setting, context, processes, activities, strategies, relationships, and theoretical concepts. Remember, the categories are flexible and are modified as further data analysis occurs. For example, a researcher might start with a

category called "finances" and find later that it is more functional to divide that category into "current finances" and "future financial needs." It is a very good idea to review your literature review and perhaps to update it as new themes emerge. For example, in Mertens' (1992) study of contextual factors that influence the success of total inclusion program planning, she identified such categories as the state's Least Restrictive Environment policy, quality of existing services, strength of advocacy groups, process of communicating information to parents and staff, and number and characteristics of the students involved.

7. The data segments are organized into a system that is predominantly derived from the data, that is, the data analysis process is inductive. Some guiding research questions can be formulated at the beginning of the process; however, additional categories or themes are allowed to emerge from the data. In the total inclusion study, Mertens (1992) used a semistructured interview guide, based on previous research on factors that influence the success of total inclusion programs. However, the participants were first asked an open-ended question about advice they would give to others who might want to implement a total inclusion program.

8. The main analytic process is comparison, that is, the researcher uses comparison to build and refine categories, define conceptual similarities, find negative evidence, and discover patterns. Bogdan and Biklen (2003) recommend using visual displays of the data and formulating metaphors to help with this phase of the analysis. Mertens (1992) discovered that a top-down approach to implementing a total inclusion program created more negative feelings than a shared governance approach. Other problems were common to all the schools studied, such as the need for additional training and support staff; however, the feelings expressed by students, parents, and staff were more negative in the top-down schools.

9. Qualitative data analysis is neither scientific nor mechanistic. The basis for judging the quality of analysis in a qualitative study rests on corroboration, to be sure that the research findings reflect people's perceptions (Stainback & Stainback, 1988). Several of the criteria for judging the quality of qualitative studies in general, presented in Chapter 6, have relevance for the quality of the data analysis in particular. Specifically, triangulation requires the convergence of multiple data sources from a variety of participants under a variety of conditions. It should be noted that all people and sources may not agree, and this difference in opinion should be made explicit in the report.

10. The result of an analysis is some type of higher-order synthesis in the form of a descriptive picture, patterns, or themes or emerging or substantive theory. The results of the study of total inclusion planning processes consisted of a framework for decisions related to implementing a program to bring students with disabilities into their neighborhood schools (Mertens, 1992). Factors that were identified fit in the following

broad categories: planning and contextual factors, parental involvement, training, logistics, curriculum issues, and spillover effects.

11. How do you know when you are finished with the analysis? Unlike quantitative statistical analysis, there is no test of statistical significance to tell the researcher that the data analysis is at an end. Lincoln and Guba (1985) recommend that the data analysis be stopped with the emergence of regularities, that is, no new information is emerging with additional data analysis. Grounded theory researchers have termed this a state of saturation, that is, new data fit into the categories already devised (Morse, 1995). Charmaz (2000) warns the researcher to not be lulled into a false sense of closure too soon. She suggests that we query ourselves with these questions: Is the handle we gain the best or most complete one? Does it encourage us to look deeply enough? Additionally, she indicates that researchers who have based their findings on sustained field research will be more able to approach a point of saturation without accepting an overly simplistic picture of their results. Analytic work may continue in different forms for many years after the initial reports are written as the researcher reaches deeper levels of understanding of the data.

REPORTING RESEARCH

Researchers have a wide range of options available to them for reporting their research, such as memos, presentations at professional meetings, briefings, journal articles, and technical reports. Typically, a research report includes an introduction (with a literature review), method, results, and discussion. The exact structure differs depending on the type of research (quantitative/qualitative/mixed), audience, and purpose of the report. Research reports can have multiple uses for different audiences; thus, alternative reporting formats should be considered for dissemination. Table 10.5 has some tips to think about when it is time to write the report.

In both quantitative and qualitative studies, the researcher should tie the results back to the purpose for the study and to the literature in the discussion section of the report. Further, findings should be based on data, and caution should be exercised in recommendations for practice.

Quantitative reports typically report results using tables and graphs. They also tend to use a detached style, avoiding the use of the first person and employing the passive voice. While qualitative reports can use tables and graphs (Miles & Huberman, 1994), they typically present results in a more narrative style and include more personal revelations about the author (Van Maanen, 1988).

In qualitative reports, Patton (2002) recommends highlighting one of the strengths associated with qualitative methods: thick description. The reader will look for a deep and valid description and well-grounded hypotheses and theories that emerge from a wide variety of data gathered

Table 10.5 Tips for Displaying and Reporting Research

- Effective data presentation fits the audience and intended uses.
- Whenever possible, field test/practice the presentation/report using a stakeholder group.
- Accurate data presentation fits the nature of the underlying data and assumptions.
- Target multiple audiences. Find opportunities to present your research.
- Simplify. Pare ruthlessly to key points.
- Tailor to audience. Use examples.
- Stay focused on the bottom line – possible actions.
- Report in many different ways (written, briefing, video . . .).
- Use powerful graphics, not just means and standard deviations.
- Make helpful recommendations.

Adapted from M. Hendricks in Handbook of Practical Evaluation.

over an extended period of time. The researcher should also seek contextual meaning, that is, attempt to understand the social and cultural context of the situation in which the statements are made and the behaviors exhibited. This includes a description of relevant contextual variables such as home, community, history, educational background, physical arrangements, emotional climate, and rules.

In qualitative reporting, the researcher can choose to report individual case studies, integrate the findings across cases, or do both. Wolcott (2001) has written an excellent book on writing up the results of qualitative research that presents different options for organizing the information.

In conclusion, with regard to ethics and writing, if the research has been completed in a fairly small community, then it is very important that the write-up not contain information presented in such a way that individuals can be identified. This might mean that information (e.g., school attended, age, and professional position) that would be nice to know but could be associated with a specific person might have to be excluded. It might mean that a synthesis of results be provided to a greater extent than quotations from individuals in which they could be recognized.

BEYOND REPORTING: USING RESEARCH RESULTS

Research results can be used for many different purposes, including developing or revising policy, making program changes, informing stakeholder groups, and identifying areas in need of additional research. Chapter 1 included listings of potential research questions related to the

Table 10.6 Areas in Need of Additional Research in Special Education

- Standards based reform
- Personnel development
- Over-identification
- Family involvement
- School climate, discipline, and Positive Behavior Systems
- Inclusion (e.g., attitudinal factors, variation in ability levels in classrooms, structural properties)
- Demographic shifts and diversity
- Low-incidence populations
- Uses of technology
- Early intervention strategies
- Newer and emerging specific disability groups (e.g., ADD, ADHD, Traumatic Brain Injury, Asperger's Syndrome, children with cochlear implants)
- Impact of state block funding
- Transition programming
- Test and classroom accommodations
- Evidence-based instruction
- Scientifically based research on reading

trends and issues that are affecting special education. Table 10.6 provides a review of these areas, along with other topics that are in need of additional research.

The majority of research articles end with a section on ideas for additional research. This is not self-serving in order to keep researchers employed. Researchers start their studies by examining what is known about a problem and what needs to be known. No research study can answer all the questions of importance on a topic. It is incumbent upon researchers to reflect on where their study has taken us and what the next steps are to fully understand the problems in interpretation.

Two examples of researchers who leave us with thoughts regarding need for additional research follow:

1. Fuchs et al. (2002) provided an excellent example at the end of their study on early literacy for children with mild disabilities. After examining the patterns in the data, they concluded that additional research was needed. They suggested the following areas in need of further research:

   - What are the effective systems needed to deliver services to all students?
   - How can generalists and specialists in mainstream classrooms work more effectively to this end?

- If schools must rely on expert instruction outside the general classroom to affect successful outcomes for all students, then how can teachers and researchers integrate what professionals do across different settings more effectively than they have in the past?

2. Kolb and Hanley-Maxwell (2003) conducted a qualitative research study that explored parental views about critical social skills for adolescents with high-incidence disabilities (learning disabilities, mild cognitive disabilities, and emotional or behavioral disabilities). They discovered that parents of these students believed that students who are truly successful in later life need not only academic knowledge, but also the social skills of empathy, discernment, and intuition. They suggested the following areas as future research topics:
   - What are the components of the skills of intuition, discernment, and empathy?
   - How can these skills be taught to students with disabilities, when should they be taught, and how do these skills relate to each other and other identified skills?
   - How will the new educational standards and academic skills assessments that are required by federal legislation impact a school's ability or willingness to address topics related to character education, emotional intelligence, and social skills training?

Researchers and research students interested in a topic area can often look at the last few paragraphs of a research article or report to identify areas in need of future research. In addition, major research centers in special education typically maintain Web sites that are rich resources in terms of the available research and areas that are identified as being in need of more research. For example, see:

- The National Center to Improve the Tools of Educators (http:// idea. uoregon.edu/~ncite/), developed by Doug Carnine and Ed Kameenui at the University of Oregon, includes comprehensive reviews of literature on mathematics and reading instruction for students with disabilities.
- The National Center for Educational Outcomes (http://education. umn.edu/nceo/), directed by Martha Thurlow at the University of Minnesota, provides national leadership in the participation of students with disabilities in national and state assessments, standards-setting efforts, and graduation requirements. The site also provides access to an on-line bibliography on accommodations that allows you to search for empirical research studies on the effects of various testing accommodations for students with disabilities.
- The National Center for Low-Incidence Disabilities (http://www. nclid.unco.edu/) at the University of Northern Colorado provides

access to information about services for infants, children, and youth who are deaf or hard-of-hearing, blind or visually impaired, or have severe disabilities. Students and researchers can find links to research studies on many topics that affect these populations.

- The Council for Exceptional Children (http://www.cec.sped.org/) maintains a Web site that is fully searchable and can provide information on specific disability populations, as well as policy and legislative initiatives nationally and internationally.
- Web sites related to specific disability groups can be searched to explore research needs. For example:
- American Association of the Deaf-Blind http://www.tr.wou.edu/dblink/aadb.htm
- American Association on Mental Retardation http://www.aamr.org
- The Association for Educators of the Deaf and Hard of Hearing's Preparing Tomorrow's Teachers for Technology http://www.deafed.net
- The International Dyslexia Association http://www.interdys.org
- National Information Center for Children and Youth with Disabilities http://www.nichcy.org
- Muscular Dystrophy Association http://www.mdausa.org
- National Association for the Mentally Ill http://www.nami.org
- National Attention Deficit Disorder Association http://www.add.org
- National Center for Learning Disabilities http://www.ncld.org
- National Federation of the Blind http://www.nfb.org

Paradigms and Methods: A Shifting Balance?

While some researchers claim that a shift in paradigms is occurring and is necessary (Guba & Lincoln, 1989; Peck & Furman, 1992), others are calling for a more balanced approach in which educational issues can be addressed from both a positivist and a constructivist framework (Gaylord-Ross, 1990-1992; Levitan, 1992). Gaylord-Ross (1990-1992) wrote:

> While these research methods [experimental, positivist research] have led to advances in the field, the question still remains whether a research model endemic to special education will emerge. It may be asking too much to expect an applied field to generate a new model for research. Yet if the quality and contributions of an applied science are to increase, one might hope for a unique research methodology to emerge. (p. xiii)

Gaylord-Ross did not see the emergence of a new research methodology in the near future. He felt that researchers could benefit by new treatments of cumulative databases and the presenting of information from multiple studies. It is the authors' hope that, by synthesizing the issues and methodological challenges that are either unique to or highly salient for special education, this volume will lead to an improvement of the quality of research and the lives of persons with disabilities.

QUESTIONS FOR CRITICALLY ANALYZING DATA ANALYSIS AND INTERPRETATION

Quantitative Research

Note: The reader is referred to the general statistical texts referenced at the beginning of this chapter for an explanation of the statistical terms and concepts used in these questions.

1. What types of statistical analyses were used? Were they appropriate to the level of measurement, hypotheses, and the design of the study? What alpha level was used to determine statistical significance?

2. Is there statistical significance? What was the effect size?

3. Does the researcher interpret significance tests correctly (i.e., avoid saying the results were highly significant or approached significance)?

4. When the sample size is small and the effect size is large, are the results underinterpreted? If the sample size is large and effect size is modest, are the results overinterpreted?

5. Are many univariate tests of significance used when a multivariate test would be more appropriate?

6. Are basic assumptions for parametric, inferential statistics met (i.e., normal distribution, level of measurement, and randomization)?

(Note: Criteria 3 through 6 were adapted from Thompson, 1988.)

Qualitative Research

1. Did regularities emerge from the data such that addition of new information would not change the results?

2. Was there corroboration between the reported results and people's perceptions? Was triangulation used? Were differences of opinions made explicit?

3. Was an audit used to determine the fairness of the research process and the accuracy of the product in terms of internal coherence and support by data?

4. Was peer debriefing used? Were outside referees used? Was negative case analysis used? Were member checks used?

5. Is the report long and rambling, thus making the findings unclear to the reader?

6. Was the correct conclusion missed by premature closure, resulting in superficial or wrong interpretations?

7. Did the researcher provide sufficient description?

Interpretation Issues

1. How do you account for the results? What are the competing explanations, and how did the authors deal with them? What competing explanations can you think of, other than those the author discussed?

2. How would the results be influenced if applied to different subjects (e.g., rural or urban)?

3. What were the processes that caused the outcomes?

4. What conclusions and/or interpretations are made? Are they appropriate to the sample, type of study, duration of the study, and findings? Does the author overgeneralize or undergeneralize the results?

5. Is enough information given so that an independent researcher could replicate the study?

6. Does the researcher relate the results to the hypotheses, objectives, and other literature?

7. Does the researcher overconclude? Are the conclusions supported by the results?

8. What extraneous variables might have affected the outcomes of this study? Does the author mention them? What were the controls? Were the controls sufficient?

9. Did the author acknowledge the limitations of the study?

QUESTIONS AND ACTIVITIES
FOR DISCUSSION AND APPLICATION

1. How can sample size influence statistical significance? Why is this particularly important in special education research?

2. Why is randomization important in choice of statistical test? Why is this particularly important for special education research?

3. What can a researcher do when the basic assumptions for parametric inferential statistics are not met?

4. Answer the questions for critical analysis of data analysis and interpretation in quantitative research and for interpretation issues for the following study:

   Example: The National Longitudinal Transition Study (NLTS) of Special Education Students findings demonstrated that young women with disabilities had a pattern of experience in early years after secondary school that differed significantly from that of men (Wagner, 1992). Females were significantly less involved in employment and other productive activities outside the home and also had less social involvement. The data indicate that females in secondary special education were more seriously impaired than their male peers. The authors explored a number of competing explanations. For example, do disabilities occur more frequently among males? Are learning disabilities more frequently ignored in females? Also, females were significantly less likely to have taken occupationally specific vocational training. Finally, females with disabilities were more likely to become mothers (and particularly single mothers) in the early years after leaving school.

5. What is the basis for judging the quality of data analysis and interpretation in qualitative research?

6. Answer the questions for critically analyzing data analysis and interpretation in qualitative research and for interpretation issues for the following study:

   Example: This case study examined the integration of autistic students in a high school setting (Ferguson, 1992). The researcher gathered data over a 4-month period. Initially, the observations lasted between 1 and 2 hours and occurred once or twice per week across a variety of settings and time. Gradually, the visits became less frequent and were interspersed with interviews of teachers, administrators, support staff, and students. The autistic students spend most of their time apart from typical students, in a self-contained classroom. Only two of the students go out for any classes. Integration in the shop class and home economics class works because the special education teacher accompanies the students and adapts the materials for them. The students are nonverbal and thus are not actively disruptive.

7. Find a friend and both of you read the same article. Compare your interpretations of the results. Do you agree or disagree? What is the basis for your conclusions?

Appendix 1

Federal Definitions for Individuals with Disabilities

The following definitions of thirteen categories of federally recognized disabilities and others are from the Code of Federal Regulations and the *Diagnostic and Statistical Manual of Mental Disorders* (4th ed.) (DSM-IV) (American Psychiatric Association, 1994).

SPECIFIC LEARNING DISABILITY

The federal regulations provide the following conceptual definition of learning disability:

> . . . a disorder in one or more of the basic psychological processes involved in understanding or in using language, spoken or written, that may manifest itself in an imperfect ability to listen, think, speak, read, write, spell, or to do mathematical calculations, including conditions such as perceptual disabilities, brain injury, minimal brain dysfunction, dyslexia, and developmental aphasia. . . . The term does not include learning problems that are primarily the result of visual, hearing, or motor disabilities, of mental retardation, of emotional disturbance, or of environmental,

cultural, or economic disadvantage. (34 Code of Federal Regulations §300.7(c)(10))

Speech and Language Impairments

The federal regulations provide the following conceptual definition of speech or language impairments:

> "Speech or language impairments" means a communication disorder, such as stuttering, impaired articulation, a language impairment, or a voice impairment, that adversely affects a child's educational performance. (34 Code of Federal Regulations §300.7(c)(11))

Mental Retardation

The conceptual definition of mental retardation provided in the federal regulations states:

> "Mental retardation" means significantly subaverage general intellectual functioning existing concurrently with deficits in adaptive behavior and manifested during the developmental period that adversely affects a child's educational performance. (34 Code of Federal Regulations §300.7(c)(6))

Emotional Disturbances

The conceptual definition of serious emotional disturbance presented in the federal regulations is:

> (i) The term means a condition exhibiting one or more of the following characteristics over a long period of time and to a marked degree that adversely affects a child's educational performance:
>   (A) An inability to learn that cannot be explained by intellectual, sensory, or health factors.
>   (B) An inability to build or maintain satisfactory interpersonal relationships with peers and teachers.
>   (C) Inappropriate types of behavior or feelings under normal circumstances.
>   (D) A general pervasive mood of unhappiness or depression.
>   (E) A tendency to develop physical symptoms or fears associated with personal or school problems.
>
> (ii) The term includes schizophrenia. The term does not apply to children who are socially maladjusted, unless it is determined

that they have an emotional disturbance. (34 Code of Federal Regulations §300.7(c)(4))

Multiple Disabilities

A conceptual definition of multiple disabilities provided in the federal regulations states:

... concomitant impairments (such as mental retardation-blindness, mental retardation-orthopedic impairment, etc.), the combination of which causes such severe educational needs that they cannot be accommodated in special education programs solely for one of the impairments. The term does not include deaf-blindness. (34 Code of Federal Regulations §300.7(c)(7))

Hearing Impairments (and Deafness)

The conceptual definition of hearing impairments provided in the federal regulations states:

"Hearing impairments" means ... an impairment in hearing, whether permanent or fluctuating, that adversely affects a child's educational performance but that is not included under the definition of deafness in this section. (34 Code of Federal Regulations §300.7(c)(5))

Deafness is defined as:

... a hearing impairment that is so severe that the child is impaired in processing linguistic information through hearing, with or without amplification, that adversely affects a child's educational performance. (34 Code of Federal Regulations §300.7(c)(3))

Orthopedic Impairments

A conceptual definition of orthopedic impairments provided in the federal regulations states:

"Orthopedic impairments" means ... a severe orthopedic impairment that adversely affects a child's educational performance. The term includes impairments caused by congenital anomaly (e.g., clubfoot, absence of some member, etc.), impairments caused by disease (e.g., poliomyelitis, bone tuberculosis, etc.), and impairments from other causes (e.g., cerebral palsy, amputations, and fractures or burns that cause contractures). 34 Code of Federal Regulations §300.7(c)(8))

Other Health Impairments

The conceptual definition for other health impairments is presented in the federal regulations as follows:

> Other health impairment means having limited strength, vitality or alertness, including a heightened alertness to environmental stimuli, that results in limited alertness with respect to the educational environment, that—
>
> (i) Is due to chronic or acute health problems such as asthma, attention deficit disorder or attention deficit hyperactivity disorder, diabetes, epilepsy, a heart condition, hemophilia, lead poisoning, leukemia, nephritis, rheumatic fever, and sickle cell anemia; and
>
> (ii) Adversely affects a child's educational performance. (34 Code of Federal Regulations §300.7(c)(9))

Visual Impairment Including Blindness

The federal regulations provide the following conceptual definition of visual impairments:

> ... an impairment in vision that, even with correction, adversely affects a child's educational performance. The term includes both partial sight and blindness. (34 Code of Federal Regulations §300.7(c)(13))

Deaf-Blindness

The conceptual definition of deaf-blindness provided in the federal regulations states:

> ... concomitant hearing and visual impairments, the combination of which causes such severe communication and other developmental and educational needs that they cannot be accommodated in special education programs solely for children with deafness or children with blindness. (34 Code of Federal Regulations §300.7(c)(2))

Autism

The federal regulations conceptual definition of autism is as follows:

> ... a developmental disability significantly affecting verbal and nonverbal communication and social interaction, generally evident before age 3, that adversely affects a child's educational performance.

Other characteristics often associated with autism are engagement in repetitive activities and stereotyped movements, resistance to environmental change or change in daily routines, and unusual responses to sensory experiences. The term does not apply if a child's educational performance is adversely affected primarily because the child has an emotional disturbance, as defined in paragraph (b)(4) of this section. (34 Code of Federal Regulations §300.7(c)(1)(i))

The Diagnostic and Statistical Manual of Mental Disorders (DSM-IV) (1994) is the guidebook that many professionals use to define autism. In this latest revision, five disorders are identified under the category of Pervasive Developmental Disorders: (1) Autistic Disorder, (2) Rett's Disorder, (3) Childhood Disintegrative Disorder, (4) Asperger's Disorder, and (5) Pervasive Developmental Disorder Not Otherwise Specified or PDDNOS (National Information Center for Children and Youth with Disabilities, 1998).

Definition of the PDD Category

All types of PDD are neurological disorders that are usually evident by age three. In general, children who have a type of PDD have difficulty in talking, playing with other children, and relating to others, including their family. According to the definition set forth in the DSM-IV (American Psychiatric Association, 1994), Pervasive Developmental Disorders are characterized by severe and pervasive impairment in several areas of development:

- social interaction skills;
- communication skills; or
- the presence of stereotyped behavior, interests, and activities. (p. 65)

Definitions of the Five Types of PDD

(1) ***Autistic Disorder.*** Autistic Disorder, sometimes referred to as early infantile autism or childhood autism, is four times more common in boys than in girls. Children with Autistic Disorder have a moderate to severe range of communication, socialization, and behavior problems. Many children with autism also have mental retardation. The DSM-IV criteria by which Autistic Disorder is diagnosed are presented in the following.

Diagnostic Criteria for Autistic Disorder

A. A total of six (or more) items from (1), (2), and (3), with at least two from (1), and one each from (2) and (3):

(1) qualitative impairment in social interaction, as manifested by at least two of the following:

   (a) marked impairment in the use of multiple nonverbal behaviors such as eye-to-eye gaze, facial expression, body postures, and gestures to regulate social interaction

   (b) failure to develop peer relationships appropriate to developmental level

   (c) a lack of spontaneous seeking to share enjoyment, interests, or achievements with other people (e.g., by a lack of showing, bringing, or pointing out objects of interest)

   (d) lack of social or emotional reciprocity

(2) qualitative impairments in communication as manifested by at least one of the following:

   (a) delay in, or total lack of, the development of spoken language (not accompanied by an attempt to compensate through alternative modes of communication such as gesture or mime)

   (b) in individuals with adequate speech, marked impairment in the ability to initiate or sustain a conversation with others

   (c) stereotyped and repetitive use of language or idiosyncratic language

   (d) lack of varied, spontaneous make-believe play or social imitative play appropriate to developmental level

(3) restricted repetitive and stereotyped patterns of behavior, interests, and activities, as manifested by at least one of the following:

   (a) encompassing preoccupation with one or more stereotyped and restricted patterns of interest that is abnormal either in intensity or focus

   (b) apparently inflexible adherence to specific, nonfunctional routines or rituals

   (c) stereotyped and repetitive motor mannerisms (e.g., hand or finger flapping or twisting, or complex whole-body movements)

   (d) persistent preoccupation with parts of objects

B. Delays or abnormal functioning in at least one of the following areas, with onset prior to age 3 years: (1) social interaction, (2) language as used in social communication, or (3) symbolic or imaginative play.

C. The disturbance is not better accounted for by Rett's Disorder or Childhood Disintegrative Disorder. (APA, 1994, pp. 70-71)

   (Reprinted with permission from the *Diagnostic and Statistical Manual of Mental Disorders*, Fourth Edition. Copyright 1994 American Psychiatric Association.)

(2) **Rett's Disorder**. Rett's Disorder, also known as Rett Syndrome, is diagnosed primarily in females. In children with Rett's Disorder, development proceeds in an apparently normal fashion over the first 6 to 18 months at which point parents notice a change in their child's behavior and some regression or loss of abilities, especially in gross motor skills such as walking and moving. This is followed by an obvious loss in abilities such as speech, reasoning, and hand use. The repetition of certain meaningless gestures or movements is an important clue to diagnosing Rett's Disorder; these gestures typically consist of constant hand-wringing or hand-washing (Moeschler, Gibbs, & Graham, 1990). The diagnostic criteria for Rett's Disorder as set forth in the DSM-IV appear in the following.

Diagnostic Criteria for Rett's Disorder

A. *All of the following:*
   (1) apparently normal prenatal and perinatal development
   (2) apparently normal psychomotor development through the first 5 months after birth
   (3) normal head circumference at birth

B. Onset of all of the following after the period of normal development
   (1) deceleration of head growth between ages 5 and 48 months
   (2) loss of previously acquired purposeful hand skills between ages 5 and 30 months with the subsequent development of stereotyped hand movements (e.g., hand-wringing or hand-washing)
   (3) loss of social engagement early in the course (although often social interaction develops later)
   (4) appearance of poorly coordinated gait or trunk movements
   (5) severely impaired expressive and receptive language development with severe psychomotor retardation. (APA, 1994, pp. 72-73)
   (Reprinted with permission from the *Diagnostic and Statistical Manual of Mental Disorders*, Fourth Edition. Copyright 1994 American Psychiatric Association.)

(3) *Childhood Disintegrative Disorder*. Childhood Disintegrative Disorder, an extremely rare disorder, is a clearly apparent regression in multiple areas of functioning (such as the ability to move, bladder and bowel control, and social and language skills) following a period of at least 2 years of apparently normal development. By definition, Childhood Disintegrative Disorder can only be diagnosed if the symptoms are preceded by at least 2 years of normal development and the onset of decline is prior to age 10 (American

Psychiatric Association, 1994). DSM-IV criteria are presented in the following.

Diagnostic Criteria for Childhood Disintegrative Disorder

A. Apparently normal development for at least the first 2 years after birth as manifested by the presence of age-appropriate verbal and nonverbal communication, social relationships, play, and adaptive behavior.

B. Clinically significant loss of previously acquired skills (before age 10 years) in at least two of the following areas:
   (1) expressive or receptive language
   (2) social skills or adaptive behavior
   (3) bowel or bladder control
   (4) play
   (5) motor skills

C. Abnormalities of functioning in at least two of the following areas:
   (1) qualitative impairment in social interaction (e.g., impairment in nonverbal behaviors, failure to develop peer relationships, lack of social or emotional reciprocity)
   (2) qualitative impairments in communication (e.g., delay or lack of spoken language, inability to initiate or sustain a conversation, stereotyped and repetitive use of language, lack of varied make-believe play)
   (3) restricted, repetitive, and stereotyped patterns of behavior, interests, and activities, including motor stereotypes and mannerisms

D. The disturbance is not better accounted for by another specific Pervasive Developmental Disorder or by Schizophrenia. (APA, 1994, pp. 74-75)

   (Reprinted with permission from the *Diagnostic and Statistical Manual of Mental Disorders*, Fourth Edition. Copyright 1994 American Psychiatric Association.)

   (4) **Asperger's Disorder**. Asperger's Disorder, also referred to as Asperger's or Asperger's Syndrome, is a developmental disorder characterized by a lack of social skills; difficulty with social relationships; poor coordination and poor concentration; and a restricted range of interests, but normal intelligence and adequate language skills in the areas of vocabulary and grammar. Asperger's Disorder appears to have a somewhat later onset than Autistic Disorder or at least is recognized later. An individual with Asperger's Disorder does not possess a significant delay in language development; however, he or she may have difficulty understanding the subtleties

used in conversation, such as irony and humor. Also, while many individuals with autism have mental retardation, a person with Asperger's possesses an average to above average intelligence (Autism Society of America, 1995). Asperger's is sometimes incorrectly referred to as "high-functioning autism." The diagnostic criteria for Asperger's Disorder as set forth in the DSM-IV are presented in the following.

Diagnostic Criteria for Asperger's Disorder

A. Qualitative impairment in social interaction, as manifested by at least two of the following:
    (1) marked impairment in the use of multiple nonverbal behaviors such as eye-to-eye gaze, facial expression, body postures, and gestures to regulate social interaction
    (2) failure to develop peer relationships appropriate to developmental level
    (3) a lack of spontaneous seeking to share enjoyment, interests, or achievements with other people (e.g., by a lack of showing, bringing, or pointing out objects of interest)
    (4) lack of social or emotional reciprocity

B. Restricted repetitive and stereotyped patterns of behavior, interests, and activities, as manifested by at least one of the following:
    (1) encompassing preoccupation with one or more stereotyped and restricted patterns of interest that is abnormal either in intensity or focus
    (2) apparently inflexible adherence to specific, nonfunctional routines or rituals
    (3) stereotyped and repetitive motor mannerisms (e.g., hand or finger flapping or twisting, or complex whole-body movements)
    (4) persistent preoccupation with parts of objects

C. The disturbance causes clinically significant impairment in social, occupational, or other important areas of functioning.

D. There is no clinically significant general delay in language (e.g., single word used by age 2 years, communicative phrases used by age 3 years).

E. There is no clinically significant delay in cognitive development or in the development of age-appropriate self-help skills, adaptive behavior (other than in social interaction), and curiosity about the environment in childhood.

F. Criteria are not met for another specific Pervasive Developmental Disorder or Schizophrenia. (APA, 1994, p. 77)

(Reprinted with permission from the *Diagnostic and Statistical Manual of Mental Disorders*, Fourth Edition. Copyright 1994 American Psychiatric Association.)

(5) ***Pervasive Developmental Disorder Not Otherwise Specified.*** Children with PDDNOS either (a) do not fully meet the criteria of symptoms clinicians use to diagnose any of the four specific types of PDD previously mentioned and/or (b) do not have the degree of impairment described in any of the previously mentioned four PDD specific types.

According to the DSM-IV, this category should be used "when there is a severe and pervasive impairment in the development of social interaction or verbal and nonverbal communication skills, or when stereotyped behavior, interests, and activities are present, but the criteria are not met for a specific Pervasive Developmental Disorder, Schizophrenia, Schizotypal Personality Disorder, or Avoidant Personality Disorder" (American Psychiatric Association, 1994, pp. 77-78).

Traumatic Brain Injury

The federal regulations conceptually define traumatic brain injury as follows:

"Traumatic brain injury" means . . . an acquired injury to the brain caused by an external physical force, resulting in total or partial functional disability or psychosocial impairment, or both, that adversely affects a child's educational performance. The term applies to open or closed head injuries resulting in impairments in one or more areas, such as cognition; language; memory; attention; reasoning; abstract thinking; judgment; problem-solving; sensory, perceptual, and motor abilities; psychosocial behavior; physical functions; information processing; and speech. The term does not apply to brain injuries that are congenital or degenerative, or to brain injuries induced by birth trauma. (34 Code of Federal Regulations §300.7(c)(12))

Developmental Delay

Developmental delay is the newest category of disability added in the 1997 legislation. It is a term that states may use to report children ages 3 through 9. The category includes a child:

(1) who is experiencing developmental delays, as defined by the State and as measured by appropriate diagnostic instruments

and procedures, in one or more of the following areas: physical development, cognitive development, communication development, social or emotional development, or adaptive development; and

(2)who, by reason thereof, needs special education and related services. (34 Code of Federal Regulations §300.7(b)(1)(2))

A State using the term "developmental delay":

(b)   determines whether it applies to children aged 3 through 9, or to a subset of that age range (e.g., ages 3 through 5).
(2)   A State may not require an LEA to adopt and use the term developmental delay for any children within its jurisdiction.
(3)   If an LEA uses the term developmental delay for children described in §300.7(b), the LEA must conform to both the State's definition of that term and to the age range that has been adopted by the State.
(4)   If a State does not adopt the term developmental delay, an LEA may not independently use that term as a basis for establishing a child's eligibility under this part. (34 Code of Federal Regulations §300.313(b))

Conditions that are associated with developmental delay include Down's syndrome and other chromosomal abnormalities; sensory impairments including vision and hearing; inborn errors of metabolism; microcephaly; severe attachment disorders, including failure to thrive; seizure disorders; and fetal alcohol syndrome.

Appendix 2

Data Available Through Extant Data Bases

EARLY CHILDHOOD

Early Childhood Longitudinal Studies

The ECLS is sponsored primarily by NCES in collaboration with other federal agencies and organizations. It provides detailed information on children's health, early care, and early school experiences through two cohorts, the Kindergarten Cohort and the Birth Cohort. This is one of the first nationally representative studies to capture a picture of early childhood development and educational experiences. The main study (Kindergarten Cohort) began in fall 1998 with a nationally representative sample of approximately 23,000 kindergartners from approximately 1,000 kindergarten programs. These children will be followed longitudinally through the fifth grade. The sampled kindergartners will come from a wide variety of public and private kindergarten programs and from diverse racial/ethnic and socioeconomic backgrounds. The Birth Cohort includes a nationally representative sample of approximately 15,000 children born in the calendar year 2000 who will be followed longitudinally from birth through the end of first grade. The sampled children will come from diverse racial/ethnic and socioeconomic backgrounds.

ELEMENTARY/SECONDARY

Common Core of Data (CCD)

The CCD is the Department of Education's primary database on public elementary and secondary education in the United States. CCD is a comprehensive, annual, national statistical database of information concerning all public elementary and secondary schools (approximately 91,000) and school districts (approximately 16,000), which contains data that are designed to be comparable across all states. The CCD consists of five surveys completed annually by state education departments from their administrative records. Information includes a general description of schools and school districts, including name, address, and telephone number; data on students and staff, including demographics; and fiscal data, including revenues and current expenditures.

Current Population Survey, October - CPS

The CPS is a monthly survey designed to collect data on labor force participation of the civilian noninstitutional population. (It excludes military personnel and inmates of institutions.) In October of each year, questions on school enrollment by grade and other school characteristics are asked about each member of the household.

Education Finance Statistics Center - EDFIN

The EDFIN is designed to conduct research to improve the collection and reporting of education finance information. EDFIN projects explore definitional, measurement, collection, reporting, and analysis issues related to education finance for elementary/secondary or postsecondary public or private education.

Fast Response Survey System - FRSS

The FRSS was established in 1975 to collect issue-oriented data quickly and with minimum response burden. FRSS was designed to meet the data needs of U.S. Department of Education analysts, planners, and decision makers when information could not be collected quickly through traditional NCES surveys. The data collected through FRSS are representative at the national level, drawing from a universe that is appropriate for each study.

HIGH SCHOOL AND BEYOND - HS&B

The HS&B describes the activities of seniors and sophomores as they progressed through high school, postsecondary education, and into the workplace. The data span 1980 through 1992 and include parents, teachers, high school transcripts, student financial aid records, and postsecondary transcripts in addition to student questionnaires and interviews.

High School Transcript (HST) Studies

These studies provide the U.S. Department of Education and other educational policy makers with information regarding current course offerings and students' course-taking patterns in the nation's secondary schools.

National Education
Longitudinal Study of 1988 - NELS:88

The NELS:88, which began with an eighth grade cohort in 1988, provides trend data about critical transitions experienced by young people as they develop, attend school, and embark on their careers. Data were collected from students and their parents, teachers, and high school principals and from existing school records such as high school transcripts. Cognitive tests (mathematics, science, reading, and history) were administered during the base year (1988), first follow-up (1990), and second follow-up (1992). Third follow-up data were collected in 1994. All dropouts, who could be located, were retained in the study. A fourth follow-up was completed in 2000.

National Household Education Survey - NHES

The National Household Education Surveys Program (NHES) is a household-based data collection system designed to address a wide range of education-related issues. The NHES collects timely data about the educational activities of the U.S. population. NHES surveys have been conducted in 1991, 1993, 1995, 1996, 1999, and 2001. Most NHES surveys have been conducted on a repeating basis to measure the same phenomena at different points in time. The NHES includes surveys on adult education, parent and family involvement in education, before-school and after-school programs and activities, civic involvement, early childhood program participation, household library use, school readiness, and school safety and discipline.

National Longitudinal Study
of the H.S. Class of 1972 - NLS-72

The NLS-72 describes the transition of young adults from high school through postsecondary education and the workplace. The data span 1972 through 1986 and include postsecondary transcripts.

Private School Survey - PSS

The purposes of Private School Survey (PSS) data collection activities are to build an accurate and complete list of private schools to serve as a sampling frame for NCES sample surveys of private schools and to report data on the total number of private schools, teachers, and students in the survey universe. The PSS is conducted every two years with the first collection during the 1989-1990 school year and again in 1991-1992, 1993-1994, 1995-1996, 1997-1998, 1999-2000, and 2001-2002, which is currently being edited, and then every two years thereafter.

School District Demographics - SDDS

The School District Demographics Web site provides access to school district geographic and demographic data useful for describing and analyzing characteristics of school districts, children, and K-12 education.

School Survey on Crime and Safety - SSOCS

The School Survey on Crime and Safety (SSOCS) will collect information on crime and safety from school principals in U.S. public schools. SSOCS will be administered in spring 2000. After that initial survey, NCES plans to conduct SSOCS every two years in order to provide continued updates on crime and safety in U.S. schools. SSOCS:2000 is a nationally representative cross-sectional survey of 3,000 public elementary and secondary schools. Data are collected on such topics as frequency and types of crimes at school, frequency and types of disciplinary actions at school, perceptions of other disciplinary problems, and descriptions of school policies and programs concerning crime and safety.

Schools and Staffing Survey - SASS

The Schools and Staffing Survey (SASS) collects extensive data on American public and private elementary and secondary schools. Teachers, principals, schools, school districts, and library media centers are components of the SASS survey system. SASS provides data on characteristics and qualifications of teachers and principals, teacher hiring practices, professional development, class size, and other conditions in schools. SASS data are designed to allow comparisons of public and private schools and staff and permit the analysis of trend data. In addition, SASS data are state-representative for the public sector and affiliation-representative for the private sector. Public schools are also linked to their respective districts. Public charter schools and their teachers and principals were included in the 1999-2000 administration of the SASS. The next SASS administration is planned for the 2003-2004 school year.

National Assessment of Educational Progress (NAEP)

The National Assessment of Educational Progress (NAEP), also known as "the Nation's Report Card," is the only nationally representative and continuing assessment of what America's students know and can do in various subject areas. Since 1969, assessments have been conducted periodically in reading, mathematics, science, writing, U.S. history, civics, geography, and the arts.

National Assessments of Adult Literacy - NAAL

The National Assessments of Adult Literacy (NAAL) provides nationally representative and a continuing assessment of English language literacy skills of American adults. NAAL seeks to describe the status of adult literacy in the United States, report on national trends, and identify relationships between literacy and selected characteristics of adults. NCES has conducted adult literacy assessments since 1985. A nationally representative sample of adults will be assessed again in 2002, providing an indication of the nation's progress in adult literacy since 1992.

BASICS OF DEVELOPING QUESTIONNAIRES

Written by Carter McNamara, Ph.D. Applies to nonprofits and for-profits unless noted.

Whether developing questions for questionnaires or interviews or focus groups, there are certain guidelines that help to ensure that respondents provide information that is useful and can later be analyzed.

Categories of Information

Key Preparation

Directions to Respondents

Content of the Questions

Wording of the Questions

Order of the Questions

Related Library Links

On-Line Discussion Groups

(For information about the use of questions and types of questions, see Types and Formats of Questions.)

KEY PREPARATION

Before you start to design your questions, clearly articulate what problem or need is to be addressed using the information to be gathered by the questions. Review why you are doing the evaluation and what you hope to accomplish by it. This provides focus on what information you need and, ultimately, on what questions should be used. (See Planning Your Program Evaluation.)

Directions to Respondents

1. Include a brief explanation of the purpose of the questionnaire.

2. Include a clear explanation of how to complete the questionnaire.

3. Include directions about where to provide the completed questionnaire.

4. Note conditions of confidentiality, for example, who will have access to the information, if you are going to attempt to keep their answers private and only accessed by yourself and/or someone who will collate answers. (Note that you cannot guarantee confidentiality about their answers. If a court sued to see answers, you would not likely be able to stop access to this information. However, you can assure that you will make every reasonable attempt to protect access to their answers. You should consider using an informed consent form, as well.)

Content of Questions

1. Ask about what you need to know, that is, get information in regard to the goals or ultimate questions you want to address by the evaluation.

2. Will the respondent be able to answer your question, that is, does he or she know the answer?

3. Will the respondent want to answer the question, that is, is it too private or silly?

Wording of Questions

1. Will the respondent understand the wording, that is, are you using any slang, cultural-specific, or technical words?

2. Are any words so strong that they might influence the respondent to answer a certain way? Attempt to avoid use of strong adjectives with nouns in the questions, for example, "highly effective government," "prompt and reliable," and so forth.

3. To ensure you are asking one question at a time, avoid use of the word "and" in your question.

4. Avoid using "not" in your questions if you are having respondents answer "yes" or "no" to a question. Use of "not" can lead to double negatives and cause confusion.

5. If you use multiple choice questions, be sure your choices are mutually exclusive and encompass the total range of answers. Respondents should not be confused about whether two or more alternatives appear to mean the same thing. Respondents also should not have a clearly preferred answer that is not among the alternative choices of an answer to the question.

Order of Questions

1. Be careful not to include so many questions that potential respondents are dissuaded from responding.

2. Attempt to get respondents motivated to complete the questionnaire. Start with fact-based questions and then go on to opinion-based questions, for example, ask people for demographic information about themselves and then go on to questions about their opinions and perspectives. This gets respondents engaged in the questionnaire and warmed up before more challenging and reflective questions about their opinions. (Consider if they can complete the questionnaire anonymously; if so, indicate this on the form where you ask for their name.)

3. Attempt to get respondents' commentary in addition to their ratings. For example, if the questionnaire asks respondents to choose an answer by circling an answer or providing a rating, ask them to provide commentary that explains their choices.

4. Include a question to get respondents' impressions of the questionnaire itself. For example, ask them if the questionnaire was straightforward to complete ("yes" or "no"), and if not, ask them to provide suggestions about how to improve the questionnaire.

5. Pilot or test your questionnaire on a small group of clients or fellow staff. Ask them if the form and questions seemed straightforward. Carefully review the answers on the questionnaires. Does the information answer the evaluation questions or provide what you want to know about the program or its specific services? What else would you like to know?

6. Finalize the questionnaire. Finalize the questionnaire according to results of the pilot. Put a date on the form so you can keep track of all future versions.

Related Library Links

Communications (Face-to-Face)

Business Writer's Free Library

Group Skills

Interpersonal Skills

Organizational Communications

Research Methods (planning research, various methods, analyzing results, giving reports, etc.)

ON-LINE DISCUSSION GROUPS, NEWSLETTERS, ETC.

There are a large number of on-line discussion groups, newsletters (e-zines), and so forth in the overall areas of management, business, and organization development. Participants, subscribers, and so forth can get answers to their questions and learn a lot just by posing the questions to the groups, sharing insights about their experiences, and so forth. Join some groups and sign up for some newsletters.

References to major e-groups, newsletters, etc.

Used by The Management Assistance
Program for Nonprofits
2233 University Avenue West, Suite 360
St. Paul, Minnesota 55114
(651) 647-1216
With permission from Carter McNamara, Ph.D., Copyright 1999

Appendix 3

Definitions of Commonly Used Statistics

*D**escriptive statistics*: Statistics whose function it is to describe or indicate several characteristics common to the entire sample. Descriptive statistics summarize data on a single variable (e.g., mean, median, mode, and standard deviation)

1. Measures of central tendency

Mean: The mean is a summary of a set of numbers in terms of centrality; it is what we commonly think of as the arithmetic average. In graphic terms, it is the point in a distribution around which the sum of deviations (from the mean point) is zero. It is calculated by adding up all the scores and dividing by the number of scores. It is usually designated by an X with a bar over it ($\bar{X}$) or the capital letter M.

Median: The median is the midpoint in a distribution of scores. This is a measure of central tendency that is equidistant from low to high; the median is the point at which the same number of scores lay on one side of that point as the other.

Mode: The mode is a measure of central tendency that is the most frequently occurring score in the distribution.

2. Measures of variability

Range: The range is a measure of variability that indicates the total extension of the data, for example, the numbers range from 1 to 10. It gives the idea of the outer limits of the distribution and is unstable with extreme scores.

Standard deviation: The standard deviation is the measure of variability that is the sum of the deviations from the mean squared. It is a useful statistic for interpreting the meaning of a score and for use in more sophisticated statistical analyses. The standard deviation and mean are often reported together in research tables because the standard deviation is an indication of how adequate the mean is as a summary statistic for a set of data.

Variance: The variance is the standard deviation squared and is a statistic used in more sophisticated analyses.

Correlational statistics: Statistics whose function it is to describe the strength and direction of a relationship between two or more variables.

Simple correlation coefficient: The simple correlation coefficient describes the strength and direction of a relationship between two variables. It is designated by the lowercase letter *r*.

Coefficient of determination: This statistic is the correlation coefficient squared. It depicts the amount of variance that is accounted for by the explanatory variable in the response variable.

Multiple regression: If the researcher has several independent (predictor) variables, multiple regression can be used to indicate the amount of variance that all of the predictor variables explain.

Inferential statistics: Statistics used to determine whether sample scores differ significantly from each other or from population values. Inferential statistics are used to compare differences between groups.

1. *Parametric statistics:* Statistical techniques used for group comparison when the characteristic of interest (e.g., achievement) is normally distributed in the population, randomization was used in sample selection (see Chapter 10) and/or assignment (see Chapter 3), and the interval or ratio level of measurement is used (e.g., many test scores).

t test: Inferential statistical tests are used when you have two groups to compare. If the groups are independent (i.e., different people are in each group), the *t* test for independent samples is used. If two sets of scores are available for the same people (or matched groups), the *t* test for correlated samples is used.

ANOVA: The analysis of variance is used when you have more than two groups to compare or when you have more than one independent variable.

Table 1   Scales of Measurement

Scale of Measurement	Definition	Example
Nominal	Categorical data	Color: red, green, blue Label: male, female
Ordinal	Ranked data organized according to increasing or decreasing presence of a characteristic	Tallest to shortest Sweetest to sourest Heaviest to lightest
Interval	Equal intervals but zero is arbitrary	Temperature
Ratio	Equal intervals and zero is defined as meaning the absence of the characteristic	Weight, age, IQ, many personality and educational tests

ANCOVA: The analysis of covariance is similar to the ANOVA except that it allows you to control for the influence of an independent variable (often some background characteristic) that may vary between your groups before the treatment is introduced.

MANOVA: The multivariate analysis of variance is used in the same circumstances as ANOVA except that you have more than one dependent variable.

2. *Nonparametric statistics:* Statistical techniques used when the assumption of normality cannot be met, with small sample sizes, and with ordinal (rank) or nominal (categorical) data.

Chi-square: Used with nominal level data to test the statistical independence of two variables.

Wilcoxon matched pairs signed-ranks test: Used with two related samples and ordinal level data.

The Mann-Whitney U test: Used with two independent samples and ordinal level data.

The Friedman two-way analysis of variance: Used with more than two related samples and ordinal level data.

The Kruskal-Wallis one-way analysis of variance: Used with more than two independent samples and ordinal level data.

a. Ordinal and nominal data can be used in multiple regression equations through a process called "dummying-up" a variable. Refer to one of the statistical texts cited in Chapter 10 for more details on this procedure.

Table 2   Choice of a Statistical Procedure

Research question: Descriptive	
For interval or ratio data:	Mean, median or mode, and variance
For ordinal data:	Median
For nominal data:	Mode, Frequency
Research question: Relationship	
For two variables:	
For interval or ratio data:	Pearson product-moment coefficient of correlation
For ordinal data:	Spearman rank order coefficient of correlation or Kendall rank correlation
For interval and nominal or ordinal data:	Point biserial
For interval and artificial dichotomy on an ordinal scale (dichotomy is artificial because there is an underlying continuous distribution):	Biserial
For nominal data:	Contingency coefficient
For more than two variables:	
For interval or ratio data:	Multiple regression analysis
For ordinal data:[1]	Kendall partial rank correlation
For nominal data:	Discriminant analysis
Research question: Group differences	
For two variables:	
For related samples:	
For interval or ratio data:	t test for correlated samples
For ordinal data:	Wilcoxon matched-pairs signed-ranks test
For nominal data:	McNemar test for the significance of changes
For independent samples:	
For interval or ratio data:	t test for independent samples
For ordinal data:	Mann-Whitney U test or Kolmogorov-Smirnov two-sample test
For nominal data:	Chi-square test
For more than two variables:	
For related samples:	

(Continued)

Table 2 (Continued)

For interval or ratio data:	Repeated measures analysis of variance (ANOVA)
For ordinal data:	Friedman two-way analysis of variance
For nominal data:	Cochran Q test
For independent samples:	
For interval or ratio data:	Analysis of variance
For ordinal data:	Kruskal-Wallis one-way analysis of variance
For nominal data:	Chi-square test for k independent samples
Research question: Prediction of group membership	
For all data:	Discriminant function
Research question: Structure of variables	
For interval or ratio data:	Factor analysis

1. Ordinal and nominal data can be used in multiple regression equations through a process called "dummying-up" a variable. Refer to one of the statistical texts cited at the beginning of Chapter 10 for more details on this procedure.

b. All *t* tests and variations on ANOVA require that the data satisfy the assumptions for parametric statistical procedures.
c. Discriminant functions can be one-way, hierarchical, or factorial depending on the number of independent and dependent variables.

Appendix 4

Funding Sources in Special Education

*D*isability Resources (www.DisabilityResources.org) is a nonprofit organization that monitors, reviews, and reports on these resources. On its Web site, it has many links to funding agencies for researchers in special education. These include general government resources, as well as government resources from disability-related agencies. It has a list of foundations and other private grant sources, as well as funds that are sometimes available through professional associations (such as APA) and a Web resource devoted to nonprofits— http://www.nonprofits.org/npofaq/.

Government Resources - General

Two resources are available for special education funding from the federal government in general. These include:

1. *Catalog of Federal Domestic Assistance (CFDA)*, http://www.cfda.gov/ The CFDA is a comprehensive listing of all federal government programs that give out grants, contracts, or other forms of assistance. It is a searchable database.

2. The Federal Register on-line via GPO Access, http://www.access.gpo.gov/su_docs/aces/aces140.html The Federal Register announces applications for federal grant programs. This source can be searched several ways: (1) Search the Federal Register online at the above URL; (2) use the "browse" link to check the Table of Contents of

current or past issues; (3) a feature at the site called Notices of Funding Availability (NOFAs) can be used to create a custom listing of funding announcements; or (4) The Grantsmanship Center, http://www.access.gpo.gov/su_docs/aces/aces140.html, posts items from the Federal Register every day. Go to its site and click on Federal Register.

Government Resources – Disability-Related Agencies

1. The U.S. Department of Health and Human Services (DHHS) sponsors a number of funding opportunities: (1) The Agency for Health Care Policy and Research (AHCPR), http://www.ahcpr.gov/fund/, has links to information about AHCPR funding opportunities related to improving the quality of health care, reduction of costs, and broadening access to essential services; (2) The Center for Disease Control and Prevention's (CDC), http://www.cdc.gov/funding.htm, funding page focuses on protecting and promoting the health and safety of Americans; (3) The Health Resources and Service Administration (HRSA), http://www.hrsa.gov/grants.htm, provides funding opportunities through the Bureau of Primary Health Care, Bureau of Health Professions, Bureau of Maternal and Child Health, and HIV/AIDS Bureau; (4) The National Institute of Child Health and Human Development (NICHHD), http://www.nichd.nih.gov/funding/funding-opps.htm, offers funding for child health and human development projects; (5) The National Institutes of Health (NIH), http://grants.nih.gov/grants/index.cfm, provides information about grants and contracts from NIH; and (6) The National Institute on Deafness and Other Communication Disorders (NIDCD), http://www.nidcd.nih.gov/index.asp, provides information about NIDCD's grant and contract opportunities.

2. The U.S. Department of Education, http://www.ed.gov/offices/OCFO/gcsindex.html, maintains a Web site with information on grants through this department. The USDE's Office of Special Education and Rehabilitative Services (OSERS), Office of Special Education Programs (OSEP), http://www.ed.gov/offices/OSERS/OSEP/Funding/Funding.html, lists current grant opportunities in special education.

Foundations and Other Private Grant Resources

Note: There are thousands of foundations and private grant resources. The following Web sites are those recommended by DisabilityResources.org for identifying and locating pertinent foundations and private grant resources.

1. FindIt.org, http://www.uri.edu/frp/frplink12.html, is a Web site maintained at the University of Rhode Island that contains helpful information for nonprofit organizations seeking funds from foundations.

2. The Foundation Center, http://fdncenter.org/, contains many links for grantsmakers and grantseekers, including a foundation finder service. Fees are charged for some of their services.

3. LINCS, http://www.nifl.gov/cgi-bin/lincs/search/gsearch/dbsearch. cgi?action=Show%20Results, contains a list of many resources for grants, many of which are of interest to people doing special education research.

Miscellaneous

1. The American Psychological Association (APA), http://www. apa.org/, produces a funding bulletin that provides information about funding available from both federal agencies and private foundations.

2. The Internet Nonprofit Center, http://www.nonprofits.org/ npofaq/, provides many resources related to funding opportunities and hints on how to raise funds for nonprofits.

3. The DisabilityResources.org Web site also provides links to funding that is state specific.

This information was adapted from DisabilityResources.org. Retrieved January 21, 2003, from http://disabilityresources.org/GRANTS.html

Appendix 5

Basic Elements of Successful Proposals

1. Cover Letter

    Typed on your organization's letterhead, the cover letter should briefly state the need for the proposed program, concisely presenting the underlying need and connecting the program intent to the mission and goals of the receiving organization. If the proposal is solicited (in response to a request for proposals [RFP]), be certain to state the name of the solicitation and your qualifications for responding.

2. Cover Sheet

    The cover sheet is an abstract or executive summary of the proposal and summarizes the need for the study, the anticipated results, and a summary of the strategies that will be used to achieve these results. The summary might also include the applicant history and contact information, as well as the total cost of the program and the amount requested. Providing a visual of the project through a logic model is recommended, but the summary should be no longer than two pages.

3. Narrative
    a. Problem Statement

    Also known as the needs statement, this section should specifically state the situation that your program addresses – the gap you plan to close. The section should present evidence that the problem exists and the impact of the problem — why it is important.

A description of the target population and the catchment area that will be affected should be included.

b. Program Goals and Objectives

Present the goals and objectives in measurable terms. The goals are your strategic results, the overall outcome of your project. There should be three elements of the measurable goal – baseline, target end point, and timeline for accomplishing. There should be at least one objective with the same elements for each goal, and the reader should understand why the objective must be achieved if the goal is to be realized.

c. Methodology

Describe the specific actions that will be undertaken to achieve each objective. The actions should communicate who will do what, in partnership with whom, to whom, and in what time frame. The activities should inform the reader about how you are going to deploy your resources to achieve your objectives. This is the first image the reader will have about your budget justification. Reference the activities to your objectives and be certain to appropriately sequence them to let the reader know that you understand the underlying logical connections between and among activities and outcomes. A logic model is a good tool to present a visualization of these relationships, but they should be backed up by third-party research as evidence of the logic.

d. Evaluation

This section should include the methods that you will use to continuously measure the program's performance. The measures should include at least four foci: Outcomes (short-term, intermediate, and strategic), implementation, participant feedback, and contextual influences. You are convincing the reader that you plan to manage for results, using evaluation information to identify what is working and not working in the project, and make mid-course corrections where necessary to improve chances for success. An essential message to convey is that the project includes an efficient feedback loop from the evaluation to the management team to enable the utility of the evaluation information. Finally, include a mechanism to evaluate the evaluation – continuously assessing its utility to intended audiences.

4. Management Plan

a. Time Frame

This section presents a summary of the tasks according to the implementation schedule. A Gantt chart is useful for describing this relationship. The Gantt chart displays the goals, objectives, and activities, by time started and estimated completion data. Some authors like to add the person responsible and monitoring checkpoints.

   b. Personnel

This section presents the qualifications of key personnel. It is essential that you link these to proposed project activities and outcomes – why is this person of value to the program. The description of qualification should cite previous experiences that can be related to the intent of this project. Sometimes it is useful to provide a Person Loading chart (particularly if it was not done previously). The Person Loading chart shows the activities in which each person is engaged at what level of effort (hours, days, or % FTE). We recommend that you include an advisory board that is composed of experts as well as participant representatives.

5. Budget
   a. Personnel costs with fringe benefit information, noting level of commitment (hours, days, or % FTE).
   b. Travel and per diem costs including administrative (e.g., convening the advisory board) and program travel (e.g., going to research sites).
   c. Fixed contracts for consultants, rental space, and so forth.
   d. Other costs including telephone, copying, printing, equipment, postage, and supplies.
   e. Indirect costs that will cover the costs of supporting the operation of your project within the institution (usually negotiated prior to writing the proposal).
   f. Total cost of the project.
   g. Other data to be included might be in-kind contributions. For example, your institution may contribute space and administrative support as well as a percentage of staff time. Some RFPs require a certain level of match.
   h. Budget justification section – some RFPs will require the author to write a specific rationale for why a particular budget item is required. If so, be certain to tie the justification to the activities and objectives of the project.

6. Appendices – depending on the requirements of the funding source, the appendices might include:
   a. Letters of support
   b. Resumes of key personnel
   c. Samples of materials to be used in the program
   d. Samples of evaluation instruments

TIPS FOR WRITING SUCCESSFUL PROPOSALS

Non-Profit Guides: Grant Writing Tools for Non-Profits, retrieved from http://www.npguides.org/guide/introduction.htm

1. Prove that you have a significant need or problem in your proposal.

2. Deliver an answer to the need or solution to the problem, based on experience, ability, logic, and imagination throughout your proposal.

3. Reflect planning, research, and vision throughout your proposal.

4. Research grantmakers, including funding purposes and priorities, and applicant eligibility.

5. Determine whether the grantmaker's goals and objectives match your grantseeking purposes.

6. Target your proposal to grantmakers appropriate to your field and project but do not limit your funding request to one source.

7. Contact the grantmaker before you write your proposal to be sure you clearly understand the grantmaker's guidelines.

8. Present your proposal in the appropriate and complete format and include all required attachments.

9. State clearly and concisely your organization's needs and objectives. Write well; use proper grammar and correct spelling. Prepare an interesting, unique proposal.

10. Always cover the following important criteria: project purpose, feasibility, community need, funds needed, applicant accountability, and competence.

11. Answer these questions: Who are you? How do you qualify? What do you want? What problem will you address and how? Who will benefit and how? What specific objectives will you accomplish and how? How will you measure your results? How does your funding request comply with the grantmaker's purpose, goals, and objectives?

12. Demonstrate project logic and outcome, impact of funds, and community support.

13. Always follow the exact specifications of the grantmakers in their applications, Requests for Proposals (RFPs), and guidelines.

14. Contact the grantmaker about the status, evaluation, and outcome of your proposal, after it is submitted. Request feedback about your proposal's strengths and weaknesses.

References

Abelson, R. P. (1995). *Statistics as principled argument*. Hillsdale, NJ: L. Erlbaum Associates.

Achenbach, T. M. (1991). *Manual for the revised child behavior profile and child behavior checklist*. Burlington, VT: Author.

Achenbach, T. M., & Edelbrock, C. S. (1983). *Manual for the child behavior profile and child behavior checklist*. Burlington, VT: Achenbach.

Achenbach, T. M., & Edelbrock, C. S. (1987). Empirically based assessment of the behavioral/emotional problems of 2- and 3-year-old children. *Journal of Abnormal Child Psychology, 15*, 629-650.

Allen, T. E. (1992). Subgroup differences in educational placement for deaf and hard of hearing students in the United States. *American Annals of the Deaf, 137*(5), 381-388.

American Association on Mental Retardation. (2002). *Mental retardation: Definition, classification, and systems of support* (10th ed.). Washington, DC: Author.

American Educational Research Association, American Psychological Association, & National Council on Measurement in Education. (1999). *Standards for educational and psychological testing*. Washington, DC: AERA.

American Evaluation Association. (1995). Guiding principles for evaluators. In W. R. Shadish, D. L. Newman, M. A. Scheirer, & C. Wye (Eds.), *Guiding principles for evaluators, new directions for program evaluation* (Vol. 66, pp. 19-26). San Francisco: Jossey-Bass Publishers.

American Psychiatric Association. (1994). *Diagnostic and statistical manual of mental disorders* (4th ed.). Washington, DC: Author.

American Psychological Association. (2001). *Thesaurus of psychological index terms* (9th ed.). Washington, DC: Author.

American Psychological Association. (2002). Ethical principles of psychologists and code of conduct. *American Psychologist, 57*(12), 1060-1073.

Anzul, M., Evans, J. F., King, R., & Tellier-Robinson, D. (2001). Moving beyond a deficit perspective with qualitative research methods. *Exceptional Children, 67*(2), 235-249.

Asch, A., & Fine, M. (1992). Beyond pedestals: Revisiting the lives of women with disabilities. In M. Fine (Ed.), *Disruptive voices: The possibilities of feminist research* (pp. 139-172). Ann Arbor: University of Michigan Press.

Asher, S. R., Singleton, L. S., Tinsley, B. R., & Hymel, S. (1979). A reliable sociometric measure for preschool children. *Developmental Psychology, 15*, 443-444.

Autism Society of America. (1995). *Asperger's Syndrome information package.* Bethesda, MD: Author.

Banks, J. (2000). The social construction of difference and the quest for educational equality. In R. S. Bradt, *Education in a new era* (pp. 21-45). Alexandria, VA: Association for Supervision and Curriculum Development.

Banks, J. A. (1995). Multicultural education: Historical development, dimensions, and practice. In J. A. Banks & C. A. McGee-Banks (Eds.), *Handbook of research on multicultural education* (pp. 3-24). New York: Macmillan.

Barkley, R. A. (Ed.). (1998). *Attention deficit hyperactivity disorder: A handbook for diagnosis and treatment.* New York: Guilford.

Barlow, D. H., & Hersen, M. (1984). *Single-case experimental designs: Strategies for studying behavior change.* New York: Pergamon.

Barr, W. B. (2000). Epilepsy. In A. Kazdin (Ed.), *Encyclopedia of psychology.* Washington, DC: American Psychological Association.

Bear, G. G., Clever, A., & Proctor, W. A. (1991). Self-perceptions of nonhandicapped children and children with learning disabilities in integrated classes. *Journal of Special Education, 24*(4), 409-426.

Bennett, R. E. (1983). A multi-method approach to assessment in special education. *Diagnostique, 8,* 88-97.

Bennett, R. E., & Ragosta, M. (1988). Handicapped people. In W. W. Willingham, M. Ragosta, R. E. Bennett, H. Braun, D. A. Rock, & D. A. Powers (Eds.), *Testing handicapped people* (pp. 17-36). Boston: Allyn & Bacon.

Bickman, L. (1987). The functions of program theory. In L. Bickman (Ed.), *Using program theory in evaluation. New directions for program evaluation* (Vol. 33, pp. 5-18). San Francisco: Jossey-Bass.

Biklen, D., Ferguson, D. L., & Ford, A. (Eds.). (1989). *Schooling and disabilities* (National Society for the Study of Education yearbook series, Vol. 88). Chicago: University of Chicago Press.

Bogdan, R. C., & Biklen, S. K. (1998). *Qualitative research for education* (3rd ed.). Boston: Allyn & Bacon.

Bogdan, R. C., & Biklen, S. K. (2003). *Qualitative research for education* (4th ed.). Boston: Allyn & Bacon.

Bottge, B. A. (1999). Effects of contextualized math instruction on problem solving of average and below-average achieving students. *Journal of Special Education, 33*(2), 81-98.

Bowe, F. G. (1991). Access to tele-communications: The views of blind and visually impaired adults. *Journal of Visual Impairment and Blindness, 85*(8), 328-331.

Boykin, A. W. (2000). The talent development model of schooling: Placing students at promise for academic success. *Journal of Education for Students Placed at Risk, 5*(1&2), 3-25.

Boyle, T. (1995). Diagnosing autism and other pervasive development disorders. In *Autism: Basic information* (3rd ed., pp. 6-7). Ewing, NJ: The New Jersey Center for Outreach & Services for the Autism Community, Inc. (COSAC).

Bracht, G. H., & Glass, G. V. (1968). The external validity of experiments. *American Educational Research Journal, 5*(4), 437-474.

Brown, J. H., D'Emidio-Caston, M., & Benard, B. (2001). *Resilience education.* Thousand Oaks, CA: Corwin Press.

Brown, W. H., Favazza, P. C., & Odom, S. L. (1995). *Code for Active Student Participation and Engagement Revised (CASPER II): A training manual for observers.* Unpublished observer training manual, Vanderbilt University, Early Childhood Research Institute on Inclusion, Nashville, Tennessee.

Bruininks, R. H., & Thurlow, M. L. (1988). *Evaluating post-school transition of secondary students with moderate to severe handicaps (final report).* Minneapolis: University of Minnesota, University Affiliated Program.

Buchanan, N. K., & Feldhusen, J. F. (Eds.). (1991). *Conducting research and evaluation in gifted education.* New York: Teachers College Press.

Bullis, M., & Anderson, G. (1986). Single-subject research methodology: An underutilized tool in the field of deafness. *American Annals of the Deaf, 132*(5), 344-348.

Buysse, V. (1993). Friendships of preschoolers with disabilities in community settings. *Journal of Early Intervention, 17,* 380-395.

Calderon, R., & Greenberg, M. T. (1999). Stress and coping in hearing mothers of children with hearing loss. *American Annals of the Deaf, 144*(1), 7-18.

Campbell, D. T., & Stanley, J. C. (1963). Experimental and quasi-experimental designs for research on teaching. In N. L. Gage (Ed.), *Handbook of research on teaching* (pp. 171-246). Chicago: Rand McNally.

Campbell, P. B. (1988). *Rethinking research: Challenges for new and not so new researchers.* Groton, CT: Author.

Carver, R. P. (1992, April). *The case against statistical significance testing, revisited.* Paper presented at the annual meeting of the American Educational Research Association, San Francisco.

Charmaz, K. (2000). Grounded theory: Objectivist and constructivist methods. In N. K. Denzin & Y. S. Lincoln (Eds.), *Handbook of qualitative research* (2nd ed.) (pp. 509-535). Thousand Oaks, CA: Sage.

Chelimsky, E. (1998). The role of experience in formulating theories of evaluation practice. *American Journal of Evaluation, 19*(1), 35-56.

Clough, P., & Barton, L. (Eds.). (1998). *Articulating with difficulty: Research voices in inclusive education.* London: Sage.

Cole, K. N., Mills, P. E., Dale, P. S., & Jenkins, J. R. (1991). Effects of preschool integration for children with disabilities. *Exceptional Children, 58*(1), 36-46.

Cook, C., Heath, F., & Thompson, R. (2000). A meta-analysis of response rates in Web or Internet-based surveys. *Educational and Psychological Measurement, 60,* 821-836.

Cook, J. A., & Fonow, M. M. (1990). Knowledge and women's interests: Issues of epistemology and methodology in feminist sociological research. In J. M. Nielsen (Ed.), *Feminist research methods: Exemplary readings in the social sciences* (pp. 69-93). Boulder, CO: Westview.

Cook, T. D., & Campbell, D. T. (1979). *Quasi-experimentation: Design and analysis issues for field settings.* Chicago: Rand McNally.

Cooper, H., & Hedges, L. V. (Eds.). (1994). *The handbook of research synthesis.* New York: Russell Sage.

Cooper, H. M. (1989). *Integrating research.* Newbury Park, CA: Sage.

Cooper, R. (2000). Preparing students of the new millennium. *Journal of Negro Education, 68*(1), 1-3.

Council for Exceptional Children. (1997). *Code of ethics and standards for professional practice.* Retrieved April 13, 2003, from http://www.cec.sped.org/ps/code.html

Cresswell, J., Guttman, M., & Plano-Clark, W. (2002). Advanced mixed methods research design. In A. Tashakkori & C. Teddlie (Eds.), *Handbook of mixed methods in social and behavioral research* (pp. 619-637). Thousand Oaks, CA: Sage.

Cresswell, J. W. (2003). *Research design* (2nd ed.). Thousand Oaks, CA: Sage.

Cronis, T. G., & Ellis, D. N. (2000). Issues facing special education in the new millennium. *Education, 120*(4), 639-648.

Crowley, E. P. (1993). A qualitative analysis of mainstreamed behaviorally disordered aggressive adolescents' perceptions of helpful and unhelpful teacher attitudes and behaviors. *Exceptionality, 4*(3), 131-151.

Daugherty, D. W. (2001). *Overidentification: A framing paper for the National Summit on the Shared Implementation of IDEA.* Arlington, VA: IDEA Partnerships. Retrieved from www.ideainfo.org/summit

Davidson, L., Stayner, D. A., Lambert, S., Smith, P., & Sledge, W. H. (2001). Phenomenological and participatory research on schizophrenia. In D. L. Tolman & M. Brydon-Miller (Eds.), *From subjects to subjectivities: A handbook of interpretive and participatory methods* (pp. 163-179). New York: New York University Press.

Davies, D. (1996). Partnerships for student success. *New Schools, New Communities, 12*(3), 14-21.

Davis, C., & Ferguson, D. L. (1992). Trying something completely different: Report of a collaborative research venture. In P. M. Ferguson, D. L. Ferguson, & S. J. Taylor (Eds.), *Interpreting disability: A qualitative reader* (pp. 124-144). New York: Teachers College Press.

Delk, L., & Weidekamp, L. (2001). *Shared Reading Project: Evaluating implementation processes and family outcomes.* Washington, DC: Gallaudet University.

Denzin, N. K., & Lincoln, Y. S. (Eds.). (2000). *Handbook of qualitative research* (2nd ed.). Thousand Oaks, CA: Sage.

DeStefano, L., & Wagner, M. (1991). *Outcome assessment in special education: Lessons learned.* Menlo Park, CA: SRI International.

Dillman, D. A., Tortora, R. D., Conrad, J., & Bowker, D. (2001). *Principles for constructing Web surveys.* Working paper. Retrieved April 13, 2003, from http://survey.sesrc.wsu.edu/dillman/papers.htm

Dillman, D. L. (2000). *Mail and Internet surveys: The tailored design method* (2nd ed.). New York: Wiley.

Doren, B., & Benz, M. (2001). Gender equity issues in the vocational and transition services and employment outcomes experienced by young women with disabilities. In H. Rousso & M. Wehmeyer (Eds.), *Double jeopardy: Addressing gender equity in special education.* Albany, NY: SUNY Press.

Durrell, D., & Catterson, J. (1980). *Durrell analysis of reading difficulty.* San Antonio, TX: Psychological Corp.

Edgar, E. (1988). *Markers of effectiveness at the secondary level in special education.* Proceedings of the research in education of the handicapped project director's meeting. Washington, DC: Office of Special Education Programs.

Edgar, E., Patton, J. M., & Day-Vines, N. (2002). Democratic dispositions and cultural competency. *Remedial and Special Education, 23*(4), 251-241.

Edyburn, D. L. (2000). 2000 in review: A synthesis of special education technology literature. *Journal of Special Education Technology, 16*(2), 5-25.

Elliott, S. W., Kratochwill, T. R., & Gilbertson, A. (1998). *The assessment accommodation checklist.* Monterey, CA: CTB/McGraw Hill.

Englert, C. S., Mariage, R. V., Garmon, M. A., & Tarrant, K. L. (1998). Accelerating reading progress in early literacy project classrooms: Three exploratory studies. *Remedial & Special Education, 19*(3), 142-159.

Erickson, F., & Gutierrez, K. (2002). Culture, rigor, and science in educational research. *Educational Researcher, 31*(8), 21-24.

Evans, J. F. (1995). Conversation at home. *American Annals of the Deaf, 140*(4), 324-332.

Evans, J. F. (1998). Changing the lens. *American Annals of the Deaf, 143*(3), 246-254.

Favazza, P. C., Phillipsen, L., & Kumar, P. (2000). Measuring and promoting acceptance of young children with disabilities. *Exceptional Children, 66*(4), 491-508.

Ferguson, P. M. (1992). The puzzle of inclusion: A case study of autistic students in the life of one high school. In P. M. Ferguson, D. L. Ferguson, & S. J. Taylor (Eds.), *Interpreting disability: A qualitative reader* (pp. 145-173). New York: Teachers College Press.

Ferri, B. A., Keefe, C. H., & Gregg, N. (2001). Teachers with learning disabilities: A view from both sides of the desk. *Journal of Learning Disabilities, 34*(1), 22-32.

Fetterman, D. M. (2001). *Foundations of empowerment evaluation.* Thousand Oaks, CA: Sage.

Fetterman, D. M., Kaftarian, S. J., & Wandersman, A. (Eds.). (1996). *Empowerment evaluation: Knowledge and tools for self-assessment and accountability.* Thousand Oaks, CA: Sage.

Feuer, M. J., Towne, L., & Shavelson, R. J. (2002). Scientific culture and educational research. *Educational Researcher, 31*(8), 4-14.

Fine, M., & Asch, A. (1988). Disability beyond stigma: Social interaction, discrimination, and activism. *Journal of Social Issues, 44*(1), 3-21.

Fowler, F. J., Jr. (1993). *Survey research methods* (2nd ed.). Newbury Park, CA: Sage.

Freeman, R. D., Goetz, E., Richards, D. P., & Groenveld, M. (1991). Defiers of negative prediction: A 14-year follow-up study of legally blind children. *Journal of Visual Impairment and Blindness, 85*(9), 365-370.

Friedman, R. C., & Shore, B. M. (Eds.). (2000). *Talents unfolding: Cognition and development.* Washington, DC: American Psychological Association.

Fuchs, D., Fuchs, L. S., & Fernstrom, P. (1992, April). *A conservative approach to special education reform: Mainstreaming through transenvironmental programming and curriculum-based measurement.* Paper presented at the annual meeting of the American Educational Research Association, San Francisco.

Fuchs, D., Fuchs, L. S., & Thompson, A. (2002). Exploring the importance of reading programs for kindergartners with disabilities in mainstream classrooms. *Exceptional Children, 68*(3), 295-310.

Fuchs, L. S., & Deno, S. L. (1991). Paradigmatic distinctions between instructionally relevant measurement models. *Exceptional Children, 57*(6), 488-500.

Fuchs, L. S., & Fuchs, D. (1999a). Fair and unfair testing accommodations. *School Administrator, 56*(10), 24-27.

Fuchs, L. S., & Fuchs, D. (1999b). Monitoring student progress toward the development of reading competence: A review of three forms of classroom-based assessment. *School Psychology Review, 28*(4), 659-671.

Gage, N. L., & Berliner, D. C. (1991). *Educational psychology.* Boston: Houghton Mifflin.

Gall, M. D., Gall, J. P., & Borg, W. R. (2003). *Educational research: An introduction.* New York: Allyn & Bacon.

Gallagher, J. (1979). Rights of the next generation. *Exceptional Children, 46*(2), 98-105.

Gallagher, J. J. (1990). New patterns in special education. *Educational Researcher, 19*(5), 34-36.

Gallaudet Research Institute (2001). *Regional and national summary report of data from the 1999-2000 Annual Survey of Deaf and Hard of Hearing Children & Youth.* Washington, DC: Gallaudet University, GRI.

Garfinkle, A. N., & Schwartz, I. S. (2002). Peer imitation: increasing social interactions in children with autism and other developmental disabilities in inclusive preschool classrooms. *Topics in Early Childhood Education, 22*(1), 26-38.

Garland-Thomson, R. (2001). *Re-shaping, re-thinking, re-defining: Feminist disability studies.* Washington, DC: Center for Women Policy Studies.

Gaylord-Ross, R. (Ed.). (1990-1992). *Issues and research in special education* (Vols. 1-2). New York: Teachers College Press.

Gee, K., Graham, N., Goetz, L., Oshima, T., & Yoshioka, K. (1991). Teaching students to request the continuation of routine activities by using time delay and decreasing physical assistance in the context of chain interruption. *Journal of the Association for Persons with Severe Handicaps, 16*(3), 154-167.

Gelzheiser, L. M., & Meyers, J. (1992, April). *Pull-in and pull-out programs: A comparative case study.* Paper presented at the annual meeting of the American Education Research Association, San Francisco.

Gersten, R., & Baker, S. (2001). Teaching expressive writing to students with learning disabilities: A meta-analysis. *The Elementary School Journal, 101,* 251-272.

Gersten, R., Baker, S., & Lloyd, J. W. (2000). Designing high-quality research in special education: Group experimental design. *Journal of Special Education, 34*(1), 2-19.

Gersten, R., Vaughn, S., Deshler, D., & Schiller, E. (1997). What we know about using research findings: Implications for improving special education practice. *Journal of Learning Disabilities, 30,* 466-476.

Gill, C. (1999). Invisible ubiquity: The surprising relevance of disability issues in evaluation. *American Journal of Evaluation, 29*(2), 279-287.

Glaser, B. G., & Strauss, A. L. (1967) The discovery of grounded theory: Strategies for qualitative research. Chicago: Aldine.

Glass, G. V., McGraw, G., & Smith, M. (1981). *Meta-analysis in social research.* Beverly Hills, CA: Sage.

Goldberg, A. L., & Pedulla, J. J. (2002). Performance differences according to test mode and computer familiarity on a practice Graduate Record Exam. *Educational & Psychological Measurement, 62*(6), 1053-1067.

Goodley, D. (1998). "Stories about writing stories": Reappraising the notion of the "special" informant with learning difficulties in life story research. In P. Clough & L. Barton (Eds.), *Articulating with difficulty: Research voices in inclusive education* (pp. 113-127). Thousand Oaks, CA: Sage.

Greene, J., & Caracelli, V. (2002). Making paradigmatic sense of mixed-method practice. In A. Tashakkori & C. Teddlie (Eds.), *Handbook of mixed methods in social and behavioral research* (pp. 91-110). Thousand Oaks, CA: Sage.

Greene, J., & Caracelli, V. J. (1997). *Advances in mixed-method evaluation: The challenges and benefits of integrating diverse paradigms* (New Directions for Evaluation, No. 74). San Francisco: Jossey-Bass.

Greenwood, C. R., Carta, J. J., Kaups, D., Terry, B., & Delquadri, J. (1994). Development and validation of standard classroom observation systems for preschoolers: Ecobehavioral Assessment Systems Software (EBASS). *Exceptional Children, 61*(2), 197-210.

Guba, E. G., & Lincoln, Y. S. (1989). *Fourth generation evaluation.* Newbury Park, CA: Sage.

Guskin, S. (1984). Problems and promises of meta-analysis in special education. *Journal of Special Education, 18*(1), 73-80.

Hagen, C., Malkmus, D., Durham, P., & Bowman, K. (1979). Levels of cognitive functioning. In *Rehabilitation of the head injured adult: Comprehensive physical management* (pp. 87-89). Downey, CA: Professional Staff Association of Rancho Los Amigos Hospital.

Hall, C. W., Peterson, A. D., Webster, R. E., Bolen, L. M., & Brown, M. B. (1999). Perception of nonverbal social cues by regular education, ADHD, and ADHD/LD students. *Psychology in the Schools, 36*(6), 505-514.

Hallahan, D. P., & Kaufmann, J. M. (2000). *Exceptional learners* (8th ed.). Boston: Allyn & Bacon.

Hanley, J. H. (1999). Beyond the tip of the iceberg: Five stages toward cultural competence: Reading today's youth. *The Community Circle of Caring Journal, 3*(2), 9-12.

Harding, S. (Ed.). (1987). *Feminism and methodology.* Bloomington: Indiana University Press.

Harris, S. L., Handleman, J. S., Gordon, R., Kristoff, B., & Fuentes, F. (1991). Changes in cognitive and language functioning of preschool children with autism. *Journal of Autism and Developmental Disorders, 21*(3), 281-290.

Hasselbring, T. S., & Williams, C. H. (2000). Use of computer technology to help students with special needs. *Future Children, 20*(2), 102-122.

Hedrick, T. E., Bickman, L., & Rog, D. J. (1993). *Applied research design.* Newbury Park, CA: Sage.

Heiman, G. W. (2001). *Understanding research methods and statistics: An integrated introduction for psychology* (2nd ed.). Boston: Houghton Mifflin.

Henry, G. T. (1990). *Practical sampling.* Newbury Park, CA: Sage.

Higgins, P. C. (1992). Working at mainstreaming. In P. M. Ferguson, D. L. Ferguson, & S. J. Taylor (Eds.), *Interpreting disability: A qualitative reader* (pp. 103-123). New York: Teachers College Press.

Hogan, T. P. (1975). *Survey of school attitudes.* New York: Harcourt Brace Jovanovich.

House, E. R., & Howe, K. R. (1999). *Values in evaluation and social research.* Thousand Oaks, CA: Sage.

Houston, J. E. (Ed.). (2001). *Thesaurus of ERIC descriptors* (14th ed.). Phoenix: Oryx Press.

Howe, K. R., & Miramontes, O. B. (1991). A framework for ethical deliberation in special education. *Journal of Special Education, 25*(1), 7-25.

Howe, M. J. A. (1999). *The psychology of high abilities.* New York: New York University Press.

Joint Committee on Standards for Educational Evaluation. (1994). *The program evaluation standards* (2nd ed.). Thousand Oaks, CA: Sage.

Karchmer, M. A., Milone, M. N., & Wolk, S. (1979). Educational significance of hearing loss at three levels of severity. *American Annals of the Deaf, 124*(4), 97-109.

Kavale, K. (1984). Potential advantages of meta-analysis techniques for researchers in special education. *Journal of Special Education, 18*(1), 61-72.

Kavale, K. A., & Forness, S. R. (1998). The politics of learning disabilities. *Learning Disability Quarterly, 21*(4), 245-273.

Keller, C. (1993, April). *Paula: A girl with Down's syndrome integrated in a sixth-grade classroom.* Paper presented at the 1993 annual meeting of the American Educational Research Association, Atlanta, GA.

Keller, C., Karp, J., & Carlson, H. L. (1993, April). *The community and school contexts for the integrations of students with disabilities in general education.* Paper presented at the 1993 annual meeting of the American Educational Research Association, Atlanta, GA.

Kerlinger, F. N. (1973). *Foundations of behavioral research.* New York: Holt, Rinehart & Winston.

Kirkhart, K. (1995). Seeking multicultural validity: A postcard from the road. *Evaluation Practice, 16*(1), 1-12.

Kittleson, M. (1997). Determining effective follow-up of e-mail surveys. *American Journal of Health Behavior, 21*, 193-196.

Klin, A. (1991). Young autistic children's listening preferences in regard to speech: A possible characterization of the symptom of social withdrawal. *Journal of Autism and Developmental Disorders, 21*(1), 29-42.

Kolb, S. M., & Hanley-Maxwell, C. (2003). Critical social skills for adolescents with high incidence disabilities: Parental perspectives. *Exceptional Children, 69*(2), 163-179.

Koppenhaver, D. A., & Yoder, D. A. (1992). Literacy issues in persons with impairments. In R. Gaylord Ross (Ed.), *Issues and research in special education* (Vol. 2). New York: Teachers College Press.

Krauss, M. W., Upshur, C. C. Shonkoff, J. P. & Hauser–Cram, P. (1993). The impact of parent groups on mothers of infants with disabilities. Journal of early intervention, 17(1), 8-20.

Kubiszyn, T., & Borich, G. (2003). *Educational testing and measurement: Classroom applications and practice* (7th ed.). New York: Wiley/Jossey-Bass.

Laing, J., & Farmer, M. (1984). *Use of the ACT assessment by examinees with disabilities* (Research Report No. 84). Iowa City, IA: American College Testing Program.

Langenbach, M., Vaughn, C., & Aagaard, L. (1994). *An introduction to educational research.* Needham Heights, MA: Allyn & Bacon.

Lemkuil, A., Ysseldyke, J., Ginsburg-Block, H., & Spicuzza, R. (in press). *Effects of implementing a learning information system on mathematics achievement as a function of intervention integrity.* Minneapolis: University of Minnesota, National Center on Educational Outcomes.

Levin, B., Hibbard, K., & Rock, T. (2002). Using problem-based learning as a tool for learning to teach students with special needs. *Teacher Education & Special Education, 25*(3), 278-290.

Levitan, S. A. (1992). *Evaluation of federal social programs: An uncertain impact.* Washington, DC: George Washington University Center for Social Policy Studies.

Levy, B.A., & Lysunchuk, L. (1997). Beginning word recognition: Benefits of training by segmentation and whole word methods. Scientific Studies of Reading, 1, 359-387.

Lewis, A. C., & Henderson, A. T. (1997). *Families crucial to school reform.* Washington, DC: Center for Law and Education. (ERIC Document Reproduction No. ED 418480)

Li, S., Marquart, J. M., & Zercher, C. (2000). Conceptual issues and analytic strategies in mixed-method studies of preschool inclusion. *Journal of Early Intervention, 23*(2), 116-132.

Lincoln, Y. S., & Guba, E. G. (1985). *Naturalistic inquiry.* Beverly Hills, CA: Sage.

Lipsey, M. W. (1990). *Design sensitivity*. Newbury Park, CA: Sage.

Lipsky, D., & Gartner, A. (Eds.). (1989). *Beyond separate education: Quality for all*. Baltimore: Brookes.

Loeding, B., & Crittenden, J. (1994). The development of SHIPS: An interactive videodisc assessment for youth who use sign language. *Exceptional Children, 61*(2), 148-158.

Losen, D. J., & Orfield, G. (Eds.). (2002). *Racial inequity in special education*. Boston: Harvard Education Press.

MacMillan, D. L., Widaman, K. F., Balow, I. H., Hemsley, R. E., & Little, T. D. (1992). Difference in adolescent school attitudes as a function of academic level, ethnicity, and gender. *Learning Disabilities Quarterly, 15*(1), 39-50.

Marder, C., & Cox, R. (1990). More than a label: Characteristics of youth with disabilities. In M. Wagner, L. Newman, & D. L. Shaver (Eds.), *Young people with disabilities: How are they doing? A comprehensive report from Wave I of the National Longitudinal Transition Study of Special Education*. Menlo Park, CA: SRI International.

Marinellie, S. A., & Johnson, C. J. (2002). Definitional skill in school-age children with specific language impairment. *Journal of Communication Disorders, 35*(3), 241-259.

Marschark, M. (1997). *Raising and educating a deaf child: A comprehensive guide to the choices, controversies, and decisions faced by parents and educators*. New York: Oxford University Press.

Maruyama, G., & Deno, S. (1992). *Research in educational settings*. Newbury Park, CA: Sage.

McGrew, K. S., Thurlow, M. L., & Spiegel, A. N. (1993). An investigation of the exclusion of students with disabilities in national data collection programs. *Educational Evaluation and Policy Analysis, 15*(3), 339-352.

McIntosh, R., Vaughn, S., Hager, D., & Okhee, L. (1993). Observations of students with learning disabilities in general education classrooms. *Exceptional Children, 60*(3), 249-261.

McLaughlin, J. A., & Jordan, G. B. (1999). Logic models: A tool for telling your program's performance story. *Evaluation and Program Planning, 22*(1), 65-72.

McNamara, C. (1998). *Basics of developing questionnaires, the management assistance program for nonprofits*. Retrieved from www.mapfornonprofits.org

Meadow, K. (1980). *Deafness and child development*. Berkeley: University of California Press.

Meadow, K. P. (1967). *The effects of early manual communication and family climate on the deaf child's development*. Doctoral dissertation, University of California Berkeley.

Meadow-Orlans, K., Mertens, D. M., & Sass-Lehrer, M. (2003). *Parents and their deaf children; the early years*. Washington, DC: Gallaudet Press.

Merriam, S. B. (1998). Qualitative research and case study applications in education. San Francisco, CA: Jossey-Bass.

Mertens, D. M. (1989). Social experiences of hearing impaired high school youth. *American Annals of the Deaf, 134*(1), 15-19.

Mertens, D. M. (1990a). Practical evidence of the feasibility of the utilization-focused approach to evaluation. *Studies in Educational Evaluation, 16*, 181-194.

Mertens, D. M. (1990b). A conceptual model of school placement and outcomes for the hearing impaired student. In D. Moores & K. Meadow (Eds.), *Research in educational and developmental aspects of deafness* (pp. 25-72). Washington, DC: Gallaudet University Press.

Mertens, D. M. (1991a). Instructional factors related to hearing impaired adolescents' interest in science. *Science Education, 75*(4), 429-441.

Mertens, D. M. (1991b). Implications from the cognitive paradigm for teacher effectiveness research in deaf education. In D. S. Martin (Ed.), *Advances in cognition, education, and deafness* (pp. 342-347). Washington, DC: Gallaudet University Press.

Mertens, D. M. (1992). *Evaluation of the planning process for the project for inclusion of students in neighborhood schools: The rural evaluation report.* Baltimore: Maryland State Department of Education.

Mertens, D. M. (1993, November). *Empowerment through participatory evaluation in an international context.* Paper presented at the 1993 annual meeting of the American Evaluation Association, Dallas, TX.

Mertens, D. M. (1998). *Research methods in education and psychology: Integrating diversity with quantitative and qualitative methods.* Thousand Oaks, CA: Sage.

Mertens, D. M. (2000). Researching disability and diversity: Merging paradigms. In *The new paradigm on disability: Research issues and approaches* (pp. 99-100). Washington, DC: U.S. Department of Education, National Institute on Disability and Rehabilitative Research, Office of Special Education and Rehabilitative Services.

Mertens, D. M. (2002). Mixed methods and the politics of human research: The transformational and emancipatory perspective. In A. Tashakkori & C. Teddlie (Eds.), *Handbook of mixed methods in social and behavioral research* (pp. 135-164). Thousand Oaks, CA: Sage.

Mertens, D. M. (2003a). The inclusive view of evaluation: Visions for the new millennium. In S. I. Donaldson & M. Scriven (Eds.), *Evaluation social programs and problems: Visions for the new millennium* (pp. 91-108). Mahwah, NJ: Lawrence Erlbaum.

Mertens, D. M. (2003b). Inclusivity and transformation: Evaluation in 2010. *American Journal of Evaluation, 22*(3), 367-374.

Mertens, D. M., Delk, L., & Weidekamp, L. (2004). Early intervention program evaluation for children who are deaf or hard of hearing and their families. In B. Bodner-Johnson & M. Sass-Lehrer (Eds.), *Early education for deaf and hard of hearing infants and toddlers and their families.* Baltimore: Brookes.

Mertens, D. M., Harper, J., Haigh, J., & Hayden, D. (1992, March). *Reclassification of exceptional students in Maryland.* Invited presentation at the 1992 Sixth Annual Conference on the Management of Federal/State Data Systems, Washington, DC.

Messick, S. (1989). Meaning and values in test validation. *Educational Researcher, 18*(2), 5-11.

Messick, S. (1995). Validity of psychological assessment. *American Psychologist, 50*(9), 741-749.

Miles, M. B., & Huberman, A. M. (1994). *Qualitative data analysis.* Beverly Hills, CA: Sage.

Miller, M. D., Brownell, M. T., & Smith, S. W. (1999). Factors that predict teachers staying in, leaving, or transferring from the special education classroom. *Exceptional Children, 65*(2), 201-218.

Minter, M. E., Hobson, R. P., & Pring, L. (1991). Recognition of vocally expressed emotion by congenitally blind children. *Journal of Visual Impairment and Blindness, 85*(10), 411-415.

Moeschler, J., Gibbs, E., & Graham, J., Jr. (1990). *A summary of medical and psychoeducation aspects of Rett's Syndrome.* Lebanon, NH: Clinical Genetics and Child Development Center.

Moores, D. F. (1987). *Educating the deaf.* Boston: Houghton Mifflin.

Morrison, G. M., & D'Incau, B. (2000). Developmental and service strategies of students with disabilities recommended for expulsion from school. *Exceptional Children, 66*(2), 257-272.

Morse, J. (2002). Principles of mixed- and multi-method research design. In A. Tashakkori & C. Teddlie (Eds.), *Handbook of mixed methods in social and behavioral research* (pp. 189-208). Thousand Oaks, CA: Sage.

Morse, J. M. (1995). The significance of saturation. *Qualitative Health Research, 5,* 147-149.

Morse, M. T. (1994). Just what is qualitative research? One practitioner's experience. *Journal of Visual Impairment & Blindness, 88*(1), 43-52.

Mounty, J. L., & Anderson, B. T. (1993). *Assessment.* Paper presented at the 1993 annual meeting of the American Educational Research Association, Atlanta, GA.

Murphy, K. R., & Davidshofer, C. O. (1998). *Psychological testing: Principles and applications.* Englewood Cliffs, NJ: Prentice Hall.

Myers, D., & Schirm, A. (1999). *The impacts of Upward Bound: Final report for phase I of the national evaluation* (Contract No. LC-92001001, MOR Reference No. 8046-515). Washington, DC: U.S. Department of Education, Planning and Evaluation Services.

NASDSE. (1988). *NAEP testing for state comparisons: Issues related to the inclusion of handicapped students.* Washington, DC: National Association of State Directors of Special Education.

National Association of State Boards of Education. (1992). *Winners all: A call for inclusive schools.* Alexandria, VA: Author.

National Information Center for Children and Youth with Disabilities. (2003). *Autism and pervasive developmental disorder.* Washington, DC: Author.

National Science Foundation. (1997). *User-friendly handbook for mixed-methods evaluations.* Retrieved from http://www.ehr.nsf.gov/EHR/REC/pubs/NSF97-53/start.htm

Newborg, J., Stock, J. R., Wnek, L., Guidubaldi, J., & Svinicki, J. (1988). *Battelle Developmental Inventory.* Allen, TX: DLM.

Newman, I., Ridenour, C. S., Newman, C., & DeMarco, G. M. (2002). A typology of research purposes and its relationship to mixed methods. In A. Tashakkori & C. Teddlie (Eds.), *Handbook of mixed methods in social and behavioral research* (pp. 167-188). Thousand Oaks, CA: Sage.

Nielsen, J. M. (Ed.). (1990). *Feminist research methods: Exemplary readings in the social sciences.* Boulder, CO: Westview.

No Child Left Behind Act of 2001. Public Law 107-110. (2001). Retrieved April 13, 2003, from http://www.ed.gov/legislation/ESEA02/107-110.pdf

North Carolina Department of Public Instruction. (1993). *Procedures governing programs and services for children with special needs.* Raleigh, NC: Author.

Odom, S. L. (1988). Research in early childhood special education: Methodologies and paradigms. In S. L. Odom & M. B. Karnes (Eds.), *Early intervention for infants and children with handicaps* (pp. 1-22). Baltimore: Brookes.

O'Donnell, L. M., & Livingston, R. L. (1991). Active exploration of the environment by young children with low vision: A review of the literature. *Journal of Visual Impairment and Blindness, 85*(7), 287-291.

Okie, S. (2000). Health official debate ethics of placebo use. (2000, November 24). *The Washington Post*, p. A3.

Oliver, M. (1992). Changing the social relations of research production? *Disability, Handicap, & Society, 7*(2), 101-114.

Onwuegbuzie, A., & Teddlie, C. (2002). A framework for analyzing data in mixed methods research. In A. Tashakkori & C. Teddlie (Eds.), *Handbook of mixed methods in social and behavioral research* (pp. 351-384). Thousand Oaks, CA: Sage.

Patton, M. Q. (1997). *Utilization-focused evaluation: The new century text* (3rd ed.). Newbury Park, CA: Sage.

Patton, M. Q. (2002). *Qualitative research & evaluation methods.* Thousand Oaks, CA: Sage.

Paul, P. (2001). *Language and deafness* (3rd ed.). San Diego, CA: Singular Thomson Learning.

Paul, P. V., & Quigley, S. P. (1990). *Education and deafness.* New York: Longman.

Peck, C. A., & Furman, G. C. (1992). Qualitative research in special education: An evaluative review. In R. Gaylord-Ross (Ed.), *Issues and research in special education* (Vol. 2, pp. 1-42). New York: Teachers College Press.

Pellegrino, J. W., Chudowsky, N., & Glaser, R. (Eds.). (2001). *Knowing what students know: The science and design of educational assessment.* Washington, DC: National Academy Press.

Phillips, S. E. (1994). High-stakes testing accommodations: Validity versus disabled rights. *Applied Measurement in Education, 7,* 93-120.

Pitoniak, M. J., & Royer, J. M. (2001). Testing accommodations for examinees with disabilities: A review of psychometric, legal, and social policy issues. *Review of Educational Research 71*(1), 53-104.

Pollard, G., & Oakland, T. (1985). Variables associated with the educational development of residential deaf children. *Special Services in the Schools, 1*(4), 67-82.

Pugach, M. C. (2001). The stories we choose to tell: Fulfilling the promise of qualitative research. *Exceptional Children, 67*(4), 439-453.

Reid, D., & Hresko, W. (1981). *A cognitive approach to learning disabilities.* New York: McGraw-Hill.

Reiff, H. B., Gerber, P. J., & Ginsberg, R. (1993). Definitions of learning disabilities from adults with learning disabilities: The insider's perspective. *Learning Disabilities Quarterly, 16*(3), 114-125.

Reinharz, S. (1992). *Feminist methods in social research.* New York: Oxford University Press.

Roethlisberger, F. J., & Dickson, W. J. (1939). *Management and the worker.* Cambridge, MA: Harvard University Press.

Rossi, P. H., Freeman, H. E., & Lipsey, M. W. (1999). *Evaluation: A systematic approach* (6th ed.). San Francisco: Sage.

Rousso, H. (2001). *Strong proud sisters: Girls and young women with disabilities.* Washington, DC: Center for Women Policy Studies.

Russell, N. K. (1993). Educational considerations in traumatic brain injury: The role of the speech-language pathologist. *Language, Speech, and Hearing Services in Schools, 24,* 67-75.

Salkind, N. J. (2000). *Statistics for people who think they hate statistics.* Thousand Oaks, CA: Sage.

Salpeter, J. (2000). Accountability: Meeting the challenge with technology. *Technology & Learning, 22*(6), 20-30.

Salvia, J., & Ysseldyke, J. (2001). *Assessment in special and remedial education* (8th ed.). Boston: Houghton-Mifflin.

Sarason, I. G., Johnson, J. H., & Siegel, J. M. (1978). Assessing the impact of life changes: Development of life experience survey. *Journal of Consulting and Clinical Psychology, 45,* 932-946.

Scheurich, J. J. (2002). The destructive desire for a depoliticized ethnographic methodology: Response to Harry F. Wolcott. In Y. Zou & E. T. Trueba (Eds.), *Ethnography and the Schools* (pp. 49-54). Lanham, MD: Rowman & Littlefield Publishers, Inc.

Schildroth, A. (1989). *Educational placement of hearing impaired students.* Paper presented at Gallaudet Research Institute Symposium, Washington, DC.

Schunk, D. H., & Rice, J. M. (1992). Influence of reading-comprehension strategy information on children's achievement outcomes. *Learning Disability Quarterly, 15*(1) 51-64.

Schwandt, T. (2000). Three epistemological stances for qualitative inquiry: Interpretivism, hermeneutics, and social constructionism. (pp. 187-214). In N. K. Denzin, & Y. S. Lincoln, (Eds.), Handbook of qualitative research. 2nd ed. Thousand Oaks, CA: Sage.

Scriven, M. (1991). *Evaluation thesaurus* (4th ed.). Newbury Park, CA: Sage.

Scruggs, T. E., & Mastropieri, M. A. (1998). Summarizing single-subject research. *Behavior Modification, 22*(3), 221-242.

Seelman, K. (1999). Testimony to the Commission on Advancement of Women and Minorities in Science, Engineering, and Technology. Washington, DC: National Institute on Disability and Rehabilitation Research.

Seelman, K. D. (2000). *The new paradigm on disability: Research issues and approaches.* Washington, DC: National Institute for Disability and Rehabilitative Research.

Seligman, M. E. P., & Csikszentmihalyi, M. (2000). Positive psychology: An introduction. *American Psychologist, 55*(1), 5-14.

Shakeshaft, C., Campbell, P., & Karp, K. (1992). Sexism and racism in educational research. In M. C. Alkin (Ed.), *Encyclopedia of educational research* (6th ed., Vol. 4, pp. 1210-1216). New York: Macmillan.

Shapiro, E., & Lentz, F. E. (1991). Vocational-technical programs: Follow-up of students with learning disabilities. *Exceptional Children, 58*(1), 47-59.

Shavelson, R. (2002). Evidence-based education policies: Transforming educational research and practice. *Educational Researcher, 31*(7), 15-21.

Shaver, J. P. (1992, April). *What statistical significance testing is, and what it is not.* Paper presented at the annual meeting of the American Educational Research Association, San Francisco.

Sieber, J. E. (1992). *Planning ethically responsible research.* Newbury Park, CA: Sage.

Siegel, L. (2001). The educational and communication needs of deaf and hard of hearing children: A statement of principle regarding fundamental systemic educational changes. *American Annals of the Deaf, 145*(2), 64-77.

Slavin, R. E. (2002). Evidence-based education policies: Transforming educational practice and research. *Educational Researcher, 31*(7), 15-22.

Slosson, R. L. (1963). *Slosson oral reading test.* East Aurora, NY: Slosson Educational Publications.

Smith, W. (1993). Survey research on African Americans. In J. Stanfield & R. Dennis (Eds.), *Race and ethnicity in research methods* (pp. 217-229). Thousand Oaks, CA: Sage.

Snyder, P., & Lawson, S. (1992, April). *Evaluating statistical significance using corrected and uncorrected magnitude of effect size estimates.* Paper presented at the annual meeting of the American Educational Research Association, San Francisco.

Solomon, D. J. (2001). *Conducting Web-based surveys.* (ERIC Document Reproduction Service No. ED458291.)

Solomon, P. G. (2002). *The assessment bridge: Positive ways to link tests to learning, standards, and curriculum improvement.* Thousand Oaks, CA: Corwin Press.

Spradley, J. P. (1980). *Participant observation.* New York: Holt, Rinehart & Winston.

Stainback, S., & Stainback, W. (1988). *Understanding and conducting qualitative research.* Dubuque, IA: Kendall/Hunt.

Stake, R. E. (2000). Case studies. In N. K. Denzin & Y. S. Lincoln (Eds.), *Handbook of qualitative research* (2nd ed., pp. 435-454). Thousand Oaks, CA: Sage.

Stanfield, J. H. (1993a). Epistemological considerations. In J. H. Stanfield & R. M. Dennis (Eds.), *Race and ethnicity in research methods* (pp. 16-36). Newbury Park, CA: Sage.

Stanfield, J. H. (1993b). Methodological reflections. In J. H. Stanfield & R. M. Dennis (Eds.), *Race and ethnicity in research methods* (pp. 3-15). Newbury Park, CA: Sage.

Stanfield, J. H., II. (1999). Slipping through the front door: Relevant social scientific evaluation in the people-of-color century. *American Journal of Evaluation, 20,* 415-432.

Stark, R., & Tallal, P. (1981). Selection of children with specific language deficits. *Journal of Speech and Hearing Disorders, 46,* 114-122.

Sternberg, R. J., & Grigorenko, E. L. (2002). *Dynamic testing: The nature and measurement of learning potential.* Cambridge, England: Cambridge University Press.

Stix, Andi. (1997). *Creating rubrics through negotiable contracting and assessment.* Washington, DC: U.S. Department of Education. (ERIC Document Reproduction Service No. ED411274)

Storey, K., & Horner, R. H. (1991). An evaluative review of social validation research involving persons with handicaps. *Journal of Special Education, 25*(3), 352-401.

Strauss, A. L., & Corbin, J. (1998). Basics of qualitative research: Techniques and procedures for developing grounded theory (2nd ed.). Thousand Oaks, CA: Sage.

Stufflebeam, D. L. (2001). *New directions for evaluation, Evaluation models,* No. 89. San Francisco: Jossey-Bass.

Sugai, G., & Horner, R. (2001). *School climate and discipline: Going to scale.* A framing paper for the National Summit on the Shared Implementation of IDEA. Arlington, VA: IDEA Partnerships. Retrieved from http://www.ideainfo.org/summit

Suran, B. G., & Rizzo, J. V. (1983). *Special children: An integrative approach.* Glenview, IL: Scott, Foresman.

Swadner, B. B., & Lubeck, S. (Eds.). (1995). *Children and families "at promise": Deconstructing the discourse on risk.* Albany, NY: State University of New York Press.

Swain, J., & French, S. (1998). A voice in what? Researching the lives and experiences of visually disabled people. In P. Clough & L. Barton (Eds.), *Articulating with difficulty: Research voices in inclusive education* (pp. 40-53). London: Sage.

Swanson, H. L. (2001). Research on intervention for adolescents with learning disabilities: A meta-analysis of outcomes related to higher-order processing. *Elementary School Journal, 101*(3), 331-348.

Swanson, H. L., & Hoskyn, M. (1998). Experimental intervention research on students with learning disabilities: A meta-analysis of treatment outcomes. *Review of Educational Research, 68,* 277-321.

Switzky, H. N., & Heal, W. L. (1990). Research in speech education methods. In R. Gaylord-Ross (Ed.), *Issues and research in special education* (Vol. I, pp. 1-81). New York: Teachers College Press.

Szarkowski, A. (2002). *Positive aspects of parenting a deaf child.* Unpublished doctoral dissertation, Gallaudet University, Washington, DC.

Tashakkori, A., & Teddlie, C. (1998). *Mixed methodology.* Thousand Oaks, CA: Sage.

Tashakkori, A., & Teddlie, C. (Eds.). (2002). *Handbook of mixed methods in social and behavioral research.* Thousand Oaks, CA: Sage.

Tawney, J. W., & Gast, D. L. (1984). *Single subject research in special education.* Columbus, OH: Charles E. Merrill.

Teddlie, C., & Tashakkori, A. (2002). Major issues and controversies in the use of mixed methods in the social and behavioral sciences. In A. Tashakkori & C. Teddlie (Eds.), *Handbook of mixed methods in social and behavioral research* (pp. 3-50). Thousand Oaks, CA: Sage.

Tellier-Robinson, D. (2000). Involvement of Portuguese-speaking parents in the education of their special-needs children. *Bilingual Research Journal, 24*(3), 309-323.

Tesch, R. (1990). *Qualitative research: Analysis types & software tools.* New York: Falmer.

Thompson, B. (1988, November). *Common methodology mistakes in dissertations: Improving dissertation quality.* Paper presented at the annual meeting of the Mid-South Educational Research Association, Louisville, KY. (ERIC Document Reproduction Service No. ED301595)

Thompson, B. (1992, April). *The use of statistical significance tests in research: Source criticisms and alternatives.* Paper presented at the annual meeting of the American Educational Research Association, San Francisco.

Thompson, S., Blount, A., & Thurlow, M. (2002). *A summary of research on the effects of test accommodations: 1999-2001* (Technical Report 34). Minneapolis: University of Minnesota, National Center on Educational Outcomes. Retrieved April 13, 2003, from http://education.umn.edu/NCEO/Online Pubs/Technical34.htm

Thompson, S., & Thurlow, M. L. (2001). *2001 State special education outcomes: A report on state activities at the beginning of a new decade.* Minneapolis: University of Minnesota, National Center on Educational Outcomes.

Thompson, S. J., Quenemoen, R. F., Thurlow, M. L., & Ysseldyke, J. E. (2001). *Alternate assessments for students with disabilities.* Thousand Oaks, CA: Corwin Press.

Thurlow, M. L., House, A., Boys, C., Scott, D., & Ysseldyke, J. (2000). *State participation and accommodations policies for students with disabilities: 1999 update* (Synthesis Report 33). Minneapolis: University of Minnesota, National Center on Educational Outcomes.

Thurlow, M. L., Ysseldyke, J. E., & Silverstein, B. (1993). *Testing accommodations for students with disabilities.* Minneapolis: University of Minnesota, National Center on Educational Outcomes.

Tillman, M. H. (1973). Intelligence scales for the blind: A review with implications for research. *Journal of School Psychology, 11*(1), 80-87.

Towne, R. L., & Entwisle, L. M. (1993). Metaphoric comprehension in adolescents with traumatic brain injury and in adolescents with language learning disability. *Language, Speech, and Hearing Services in School, 24,* 100-107.

Trochim, W. (2001). *The research methods knowledge base* (2nd ed.). Cincinnati, OH: Atomic Dog Publishers.

Trochim, W. M. (1999). *The research methods knowledge base.* Retrieved from http:// trochim.human.cornell.edu/kb

U.S. Department of Education. (1989). *"To assure the free appropriate public education for all handicapped children": Eleventh annual report to Congress on the implementation of the Education of the Handicapped Act.* Washington, DC: U.S. Government Printing Office.

U.S. Department of Education. (2001a). *To assure the free appropriate public education of all children with disabilities. Twenty-third report to Congress on the implementation of the Individuals with Disabilities Education Act.* Washington, DC: Author.

U.S. Department of Education. (2001b). *OSEP data dictionary.* Washington, DC: Office of Special Education Programs.

U.S. General Accounting Office. (2000). *GAO policy and guidance materials.* Retrieved from http://www.gao.gov/policy/guidance.htm

Van Cleve, J. V., & Crouch, B. A. (1989). *A place of their own.* Washington, DC: Gallaudet University Press.

Van Maanen, J. (1988). *Tales of the field: On writing ethnography.* Chicago: University of Chicago Press.

Vaughn, S., Gersten, R., & Chard, D. J. (2000). The underlying message in LD intervention research: Findings from research syntheses. *Exceptional Children, 67*(1), 99-114.

Vaughn, S., Kinger, J., & Hughes, M. (2000). Sustainability of research-based practices. *Exceptional Children, 66*(2), 163-171.

W. K. Kellogg Foundation. (1998). *Evaluation handbook.* Retrieved from http:// www.wkkf.org/Pubs/Tools/Evaluation/Pub770.pdf

Wagner, M. (1992, April). *Being female—A secondary disability? Gender differences in the transition experiences of young people with disabilities.* Paper presented at the annual meeting of the American Educational Research Association, San Francisco.

Wagner, M. (2003). *The National Longitudinal Transition Study-2 (NLTS2).* Retrieved January 20, 2003, from http://www.sri.com/nlts2/

Wang, M. C., Reynolds, M. C., & Walberg, H. J. (Eds.). (1990). *Special education research and practice.* Oxford, England: Pergamon.

Wehmeyer, M. L., Palmer, S. B., Agran, M., Mithauz, D. E., & Martin, J. E. (2000). Promoting casual agency: The self-determined learning model of instruction. *Exceptional Children, 66*(4), 439-453.

Weitzman, E. A. (2000). Using computers in qualitative research. In N. Denzin & Y. Lincoln (Eds.), *Handbook of qualitative research* (2nd ed., pp. 803-820). Thousand Oaks, CA: Sage.

Wholey, J. S., Hatry, H. P., & Newcomer, K. E. (1994). *Handbook of practical program evaluation.* San Francisco: Jossey-Bass.

Williams, C., Kantor, R., & Pinnell, G. S. (1992, April). *The language and literacy worlds of profoundly deaf preschool children: Informing developmental theory.* Paper presented at the 1992 annual meeting of the American Educational Research Association, San Francisco.

Willingham, W. W., Ragosta, M., Bennett, R. E., Braun, H., Rock, D. A., & Powers, D. A. (Eds.). (1988). *Testing handicapped people.* Boston: Allyn & Bacon.

Wilson, C. L., & Sindelar, P. T. (1991). Direct interaction in math word problems: Students with disabilities. *Exceptional Children, 57*(6), 512-519.

Winterling, V. (1990). The effects of constant time delay, practice in writing or spelling, and reinforcement on sight word recognition in a small group. *Journal of Special Education, 24*(1), 101-116.

Wodward, J., & Reith, H. (1997). A historical review of technology research in special education. *Review of Educational Research, 67*(4), 503-536.

Wolcott, H. F. (2001). *Writing up qualitative research.* Thousand Oaks, CA: Sage.

World Health Organization (2002). *International Classification of Diseases* (10th ed.). Geneva, Switzerland: Author. Retrieved October 7, 2002, from http://www.who.int/pbd/pbl/data.htm#definitions

Worthen, B. R., Sanders, J. R., & Fitzpatrick, J. L. (1997). *Program evaluation: Alternative approaches and practical guidelines.* New York, NY: Longman.

Yin, R. (1998). *Case study research.* Newbury Park, CA: Sage.

Yin, R. K. (1993). *Applications of case study research.* Newbury Park, CA: Sage.

Ysseldyke, J. (2000). Commentary: Deja vu all over again: What will it take to solve big instructional problems? *School Psychology Review, 29*(4), 595-597.

Ysseldyke, J. (2001). Reflections on a research career: Generalizations from 25 years of research on assessment and instructional decision making. *Exceptional Children, 67*(3), 295-309.

Ysseldyke, J., & Bielinski, J. (2002). Effect of different methods of reporting and reclassification on trends in test scores for students with disabilities. *Exceptional Children, 68*(2), 189-200.

Ysseldyke, J. E., & Algozzine, B. (1990). *Introduction to special education* (2nd ed.). Boston: Houghton Mifflin.

Ysseldyke, J. E., Thurlow, M. L., Bruininks, R. H., Gilman, C. J., Deno, S. L., McGrew, K. S., & Shriner, J. G. (1993). *Educational outcomes and indicators for individuals at the post-school level.* Minneapolis, MN: National Center on Educational Outcomes.

ZERO TO THREE: National Center for Infants, Toddlers, and Families. (1994). *Diagnostic classification of mental health and developmental disorders of infancy and early childhood.* Washington, DC: Author.

Index

**CORWIN
PRESS**

The Corwin Press logo—a raven striding across an open book—represents the happy union of courage and learning. We are a professional-level publisher of books and journals for K-12 educators, and we are committed to creating and providing resources that embody these qualities. Corwin's motto is "Success for All Learners."